Louis Hyman

BORROW

Louis Hyman attended Columbia University, where he received a BA in history and mathematics. A former Fulbright scholar and a consultant at McKinsey & Co., he received his PhD in American history in 2007 from Harvard University. He is currently an assistant professor in Cornell University's School of Industrial and Labor Relations, where he teaches history.

Also by Louis Hyman

Debtor Nation: The History of America in Red Ink

BORROW

BORROW

THE AMERICAN WAY
OF DEBT

Louis Hyman

VINTAGE BOOKS

A DIVISION OF RANDOM HOUSE, INC.

NEW YORK

Library of Congress Cataloging-in-Publication Data
Hyman, Louis, 1977–
Borrow : the American way of debt / Louis Hyman.
p.   cm.
Includes bibliographical references and index.
ISBN 978-0-307-74168-4 (trade pbk. : alk. paper)
1. Consumer credit—United States—History.   2. Debt—United States—
History.   3. Loans, Personal—United States—History.   4. United States—
Economic conditions.   5. United States—Economic policy.   I. Title.
HG3756.U54H95 2012
332.7'43—dc23
2011041427

For Patty

CONTENTS

BORROW

INTRODUCTION
EVERYTHING OLD
IS NEW AGAIN

"Dick" and "Jane" Smith met shortly after they had both moved to the city, coming upon each other in the park on a sunny Sunday afternoon. Romantic sparks flew, declarations of love were exchanged, rings and vows followed—and then they began their search for a home of their own, where they would start their new life together.

Dick hadn't gone to college, but he had recently found work in a new industry whose products were sweeping the country. The company's IPO a few years back had been one of the most successful in history and he was going to help manufacture the killer product that, as one of his executives had said in his firm's annual report, had "given us all something worth working for." Dick and Jane, like the rest of the country, were caught up in the heady optimism of what newspaper pundits said was a New Era.

Flush with love and short on cash, the Smiths went to their local bank to find out if they could get a mortgage. The home that they wanted was expensive, like all houses those days, but the Smiths knew that houses were a good investment. Prices had gone through the roof in the past few years, and real estate was always a sure thing. "You can't make more land!" Jane remembered her father always saying.

At the bank, the Smiths met with a well-dressed mortgage officer. Looking over the application, the mortgage officer asked them far fewer questions than they had expected: how long had Dick had his job, how long had they lived at their current address, how much did he make? After a few calculations, the mortgage officer somberly informed them that an "amortized" mortgage—one in which they repaid against both interest *and* principal every month—would not get them the house they wanted. Dick's income was just not enough to cover it.

But the Smiths didn't have to worry. The bank offered another, better option that most smart people were using those days: an interest-only "balloon" mortgage. With a balloon mortgage, Dick and Jane could buy the house immediately, sleeping soundly with the knowledge that their household income had nowhere to go but up, right alongside real estate values. When the time to pay off the principal finally came a few years down the road, they could simply refinance with a new loan that was just as affordable as the first. Why slowly pay down the principal when they would probably just sell it for more in a few years, anyhow? Like the mortgage officer had said, it was the smart thing to do.

In fact, they would have to refinance since the loan was for only four years, but that wouldn't be a problem at all. The mortgage officer explained, in confident tones, that refinancing would never again be a problem because banks had started issuing mortgage-backed securities to finance their customers. Investors were always looking for a good deal, and real estate was a sure thing.

Four years! Dick would almost certainly move up in his burgeoning high-tech industry in that time. Jane already envisioned a bigger space, the envy of her sisters. The couple looked at each other knowingly, trusting in the guidance of the mortgage officer, and signed the papers he offered them.

Dick and Jane thought they couldn't go wrong. They were in the middle of one of the greatest housing booms in U.S. history, with home values seeming to double every time they turned around. Developers couldn't build houses fast enough. Smart buyers would act fast, they thought, before home prices rose even more. There was no risk, only reward.

Dick and Jane moved into their house, and Dick went to work. Within the year, orders began to slow down. He didn't lose his job, but his overtime was cut. Then it hit. At first the big stock market crash didn't affect him, but it soon spilled over into the real world. Everywhere confidence in the economy slid. The newspaper stopped using "New Era" except in derision. Then, just as he had to refinance his house, everything fell apart.

House values began to plummet; balloon mortgages became impossible to refinance; foreclosures in their neighborhood became, seemingly overnight, more common than rare. Like the stock speculators who had borrowed on the margin, millions of Americans just like Dick and Jane were living on the edge of their household incomes so that they could "own" their homes. They would be fine, though—wouldn't they?—because their mortgage fit their budget. All too late, Dick and Jane realized that they were speculating just like those hucksters on Wall Street.

Dick walked into the savings and loan only to find that his mortgage officer had been sacked. His replacement, considerably less friendly than his predecessor, told him in no uncertain terms that he had to come up with the principal or he would be foreclosed on. Dick sputtered. He had done what the man in the suit had told him. How had this happened? Before turning his back and returning to his work, the new guy at the bank told Dick that investors no longer wanted to buy real estate bonds. The well was dry. Without mortgage funds to lend, the bank had to collect.

When the bank repossessed their dream house, Dick and Jane didn't have even the most basic of personal luxuries—no iPod, no tablet, not even a hand-me-down smartphone. Desperate as they were, they literally couldn't even give those things up in one last fruitless effort to save their home. After all, none of them would be invented until the next century.

It was 1932.

Dick had gotten his manufacturing job at General Motors in Flint, Michigan, only a few years earlier. Like Jane, Dick was part of a broad population shift from the country to the city in the early part of the century that tipped the census, for the first time, in favor of urban America. After moving to the city, Dick and Jane did what so many of their generation did: they borrowed.

As investors fled the mortgage markets, the U.S. housing industry fell apart—not initially from unemployment but from a credit crisis. By 1933, the national foreclosure rate had reached 1,000 homes a day. After four years of withdrawals that withered even the sturdiest of mortgage funds, in 1933 the U.S. housing industry was effectively dead, having shrunk to just one-tenth what it had been only a few years before. A third of all American families who qualified for "relief" at the height of the Great Depression landed there by losing a construction job. Dick didn't work in construction, but his business, building automobiles, was hit just as hard.

The 1920s were similar to today in terms not only of young love and mortgage debt but of all forms of debt. In fact, it was the spread of automobile debt that had given Dick his job in the first place. Automobile finance emerged after World War I as one of the hottest industries, spreading its methods in just a few years to nearly all other household durables. Vacuum cleaners, washing machines, and oil burners could all be had on the installment plan. The U.S. savings rate dropped precipitously, and nearly all of what would have been saved went into paying off installment credit.

In the 1920s, Americans, both borrowers and lenders, discovered new ways to finance consumer credit, and of course that was only the beginning. Debt was everywhere, and its ubiquity was made possible by changes in finance, manufacturing, and law that had occurred after the First World War. High interest on consumer loans had long been illegal in the United States, but around World War I, progressive reformers, seeking to drive out loan sharks, pushed states across the country to raise the legal interest rate. Now able to lend money legally at rates that could be profitable, a new consumer finance industry sprang up overnight. The changes coincided with a new generation of cars and electrical appliances that were both expensive and mass-produced. Installment credit allowed manufacturers to sell these new wonders at high volume, and consumers could afford them because of the easy monthly payments. What ultimately made all this lending possible was that lenders could now, for the first time, resell their debt.

Networks of finance stood behind each consumer purchase. When Dick bought his first car, the dealer had him sign some papers. Dick agreed to pay for the car over twenty-four months and pay some additional fees, but that was it. He never knew where the money behind the credit came from, and if he wondered at all, he probably thought that it came from the dealer. But the dealer took that agreement and sold it, the next day, to General Motors Acceptance Corporation (GMAC). The dealer didn't have the capital to finance all his customers, but GMAC did. GMAC could issue bonds in the market or use its own profits to finance its dealers. As networks developed for all forms of debt—mortgages, cars, retail—credit became cheaper and easier to use. Retailers and financiers used credit to drive their sales and profits. Some networks, such as car financing, emerged from the private sector, while others, such as mortgages, emerged from the federal government. Wherever they came from, the new networks of debt made this consumer utopia possible. When those networks failed, as with

The Skinny Man and the Fat Man reveal a world where lending is not profitable—the opposite of today.

the resale of mortgage bonds during the Great Depression, credit could just as quickly turn dystopian.

This picture could have hung in any small late-nineteenth-century shop—maybe a grocery, maybe a hardware store—any who didn't want to give more credit to its customers. Though cash loans were illegal, legal credit in the nineteenth century was retail credit—but its logic was nearly the mirror image of today. Today credit lending is profitable, however, in the nineteenth century it was anything but. The well-fed, prosperous man sold only for cash, while the emaciated, nervous man with the mice sold on credit.

The picture's message was clear: we don't want to lend. Yet its logic, like ours today, was grounded in a very particular set of historical circumstances. Borrowing is more than numbers, it is a set of relationships between people and institutions. More than any graph, this picture, if we can understand it, clarifies the differences between then and now—and how debt has changed.

Shopping every few days for food—generally the largest portion of an 1890 budget—customers could quickly build up a tab. On payday, wives were supposed to stop by and settle the bill. Yet many did not. Grocers charged higher prices for credit purchases, but there was no interest, which would have violated usury laws. So if someone paid every week or didn't pay for months, it was the same price—and the same profit or lack thereof. Shopkeepers could quickly lose money on credit sales because the money they lent was their own.

Customer credit came out of the grocer's own pocket not a bank's coffers. As you can see in the picture, the credit lender's vault is empty while his basket is filled with IOUs. Americans didn't have credit cards. No bank would lend the skinny guy money to finance his customers. No third party would buy the debt and try to collect what was owed. Loans were not commodities bought and sold as they are today. In our economy, financiers figure out ways to get us to borrow and then resell the debt to investors. Debt is produced like any other commodity—shoes, steel, computers—for the market. Buyers of our debt—whether mortgages, credit cards, or car loans—evaluate it like any other investment, weighing the return against the risk. Today's debt is easy to resell. In the 1890s, consumer debt was business error. That is to say, bankers and entrepreneurs didn't think debt was a good investment. It was not a good use of their scarce capital. Consumer debt was a way to lose money. If we can understand how this grocer turned into our retail life today, we can understand how small loans became big business. We can understand how creditors became fat.

Who would invest in debt? The history of how corner grocers, and all other retailers, began to resell their debt is a complex one, spanning the twentieth century from the first automobiles to our present financial crisis. Though borrowing might be as ancient as currency itself, markets for consumer debt are as modern as a bobbed haircut. In the 1920s, a few changes in business and law came together to move personal debt from the margin of capitalism to its center, taking a position alongside commercial and national debt. Usury laws had limited interest rates for centuries, but progressive reformers, seeking to provide a profitable alternative to the loan shark, pushed for higher legal rates. As states raised usury limits and institutions began to buy personal debt from retailers, debt escaped the personal and became a commodity to be bought and sold. Once debt could be sold, it could be invested in. Personal debt became a place for investors to put money, connecting it with the most basic operations of capitalism.

Though your parents told you that in the good old days nobody borrowed, this commodified debt enabled the growth of the twentieth-century economy. In the Roaring Twenties, Americans used this resellable debt to buy their first automobiles, and, having learned the trick, retailers began to promote installment credit to sell all their other manufactured goods as well. The first insight that allowed the modern personal debt system to arise was deceptively simple: though personal loans were never invested in productive assets, the person borrowing might himself be productive. Personal loans, when they became legal around 1920, relied on income instead of assets for repayment. This insight reflected the changing way in which Americans lived and worked. Whereas farmers might seamlessly blend their borrowings for land, crop seeds, and hats for church, urban industrial workers had firmer boundaries between home and work. Modern workers might not own assets, but by golly, they got paid every two weeks like clockwork. The ubiquity of the steady stream of wage income, so natural to us today, had begun only in the mid–nineteenth century, but it took some time, and some legal changes, for the new way of borrowing to emerge. Turning that future income into present consumption was what consumer credit was all about, but implementing it was anything but simple.

Though the Great Depression ended the party of the 1920s, credit found a new privileged position as New Deal policy makers used federally insured mortgages to restart the economy. Out of that calamity, American politicians, industrialists, and financiers reorganized the economy, restraining lending here and promoting lending there to create a postwar United States that economists describe as "the golden age of capitalism." The upswing in consumption that defined the Roaring Twenties paused only briefly during the Great

Depression to take off with gusto after World War II. This postwar consumption continued to be financed by debt, by taking up income before it was earned. Though postwar consumers told their children and grandchildren that they had never borrowed a dime in their lives, debt was the lifeblood of postwar suburbia. Living in FHA-financed homes, driving in GMAC-financed cars, postwar consumers gleefully shopped on charge cards at the Bloomingdale's branch store that just opened at the new shopping center. In the postwar period, Americans borrowed as much as they could, living it up in the plush suburbs and paying those debts with good-paying jobs. The scarcity caused by depression and war ended when Americans could borrow again.

Though most postwar observers of credit marveled at its ability to turn a promise of future payment into a concrete purchase today, critics (of a different vein than Ford from years prior) remained. Installment credits fit neatly into postwar budgets but, through their interest payments, still sapped the wealth of the American family. William Whyte, before he wrote his best seller *The Organization Man,* denounced the "budgetism" of the young middle class in the pages of *Fortune* magazine, not, as you might expect, for the lack of keeping a budget but for their obsessive zeal in fitting the monthly budget to the monthly income.[1] Budgets, for Whyte, were the "opiate of the middle class," dulling them to the dangers of overspending. Whyte, who had come of age during the Depression, warned the young couples of the 1950s that such faith in the steadiness of the future was foolish. Incomes falter and markets fail. The danger of budgets, ultimately, is believing they will tame not only you but the world around you. For the postwar generation, however, Whyte's warnings proved wrong. The meaning of debt, you see, depends as much on the larger economic context as on the debt itself.

Economic volatility, it seemed, had been mastered by Keynesian economics. Budgeters of the 1950s lucked out. Incomes grew and jobs were rarely lost. Instead of ruining workers, borrowing helped them. Home values rose steadily, and as today, all the interest on those mortgages could be deducted from one's taxable income. Unlike today, not just mortgage interest but all consumer interest could be deducted as well. Minks and cars were just as deductible as a mortgage. The postwar suburb was a debtor's paradise. An earlier era's anxieties about borrowing were forgotten in the warm glow of the television.

As debt changed, so did we. As consumers, Americans enjoyed a surging prosperity fueled by rising wages and easy credit, but in the process the foundation of our economy changed. Dollars invested in debt displaced dollars invested in factories. Debtors began to rely on credit rather than income to maintain a rising standard of living. In doing so, Americans became ever more dependent on the vagaries of financial markets, ultimately leading to the events of the past few years.

The postwar splendor came undone, suddenly, in the early 1970s. As inflation rose and jobs disappeared, stagflation savaged the complacent world that many Americans had assumed would last forever. The 1950s nostalgia embodied by *Happy Days* extended to more than milk shakes, as oil prices went through the roof. Credit assumed a new role in this more volatile age, making up the difference between what we wanted and what we had. The dawning age of credit cards and securitization would contain different lessons from the 1920s and 1950s but would be just as difficult to ignore.

Understanding the history of debt gives us a sense of both debt's possibilities and its dangers. Rather than being an always evil bogeyman, credit has the capacity to enrich our lives and make our dreams come true. Misused and misunderstood, though, credit can just as easily become the stuff of nightmares. In the past ninety years, Americans have both slept soundly and been made sleepless because of their debt, but to plan where we need to go now, we must understand debt's all-too-concrete realities today now that we are awake.

The story of debt is equally the story of borrowers and lenders. Most of us, however, simply borrow from whoever will give us money, and let them sort out where they, in turn, will borrow their money. Though this is fine for buying a car, if we want to understand the story behind credit, we have to grapple with the source of all that money and how the decision to invest in debt shapes our economy and guides our lives.

Borrow tells the story of how Americans came to rely on expected future income rather than money in hand. It is a narrative that begins with that great American industrial enterprise—the automobile—and carries through to the financial crisis of today. Showing the hidden world of finance behind everyday consumption, *Borrow* will give you a historical perspective on what is new and what is not about today's economic turmoil. Understanding the changing role of debt requires more than economic jargon, it requires a human face or, even more important, a human mind. Lending and borrowing had been stigmatized and even criminalized for hundreds of years in the West, yet in only a few generations became completely normal. How did Americans come to be so comfortable with borrowing? How did they draw distinctions between "good" and "bad" debt—as we might have, until recently, drawn between mortgages and credit cards? *Borrow* will help explain the ways that finance and feelings intersected to produce new ways of living. Freed of the moral categories through which we normally encounter debt, *Borrow* will reveal the origin of Dick and Jane's credit and how it changed their lives.

Borrow is, in many ways, a uniquely American tale—but one with a global finale.

CHAPTER ONE

WHEN PERSONAL DEBT WAS REALLY BUSINESS DEBT (2000 B.C.– A.D. 1920)

Academic histories of debt in America usually start in Italy, their introductory paragraphs awkwardly positioning the fourteenth-century Medici bankers as Citibankers in tunics. Popular histories, such as those scattered in newspaper articles, CEO speeches, or lenders' pamphlets, go even further into the past, like this account from one of the largest U.S. credit card companies: "Credit dates back as far as man's known existence. Clay tablets belonging to the year 2000 B.C. tell of credit transactions, and records indicate that ancient Romans bought homes and other durable goods on installment plans—just as men do today."[1] Though it's true that people have always borrowed, the way in which we borrow in the United States today is unprecedented. Never before has personal debt been so central to how an economy works. Never before has borrowing in order to consume been such big business.

Big business, on the other hand, has always borrowed. Historians frequently date the beginning of the modern capitalist (as opposed to the medieval) era to when states and businesses began to incur large debts. Trade, war, and Christianity turned the disjointed polities of a peninsula into the continent of Europe. Beginning with long-distance IOUs for the Crusades in the medieval period, negotiable bills of exchange enabled long-distance trade. This trade slowly reignited the European economy, laying the foundation of modern capitalism. The Crusades against Islam all too quickly became wars within Christendom itself. Wars cost money. Starting in fifteenth-century Italy, European governments began to issue debt to pay for those wars, borrowing vast sums from their own subjects. The Bank of England, founded in 1694, enabled Britain to both fund its wars and create an easy way for the British to invest their money. These liquid, deep debt markets only encouraged other forms of nongovernmental borrowing, and national central banks underpinned European commercial banking. Merchants and industrialists could eventually borrow from commercial banks to invest in their capitalist endeavors. In the United States, central banks had a more checkered history. Though a national bank was founded in 1791, its first incarnation lasted only forty years, as Jacksonian populism triumphed over federalism. In the United States, commercial banking, absent a central bank, developed in a more piecemeal fashion at the state level. Commercial banking was no less successful in America than in Europe, however, and as in Europe banks enabled the sustained growth of the Industrial Revolution in the nineteenth century.

Though financiers, merchants, and industrialists could borrow without difficulty from banks—if they had a good reputation and a good business model—ordinary people could not. There was no personal lending from banks until the 1920s. Legal borrowing, since the Crusades, had always been for profitable investment or for government purposes (which, depending on how you look at it, may or may not be profitable). Personal debt of an everyday nature was not part of this system. Merchants borrowed to buy inventory to trade overseas. Industrialists borrowed to build rails. States borrowed to make war on one another. But you and I could not borrow two nickels for consumption, which, by its definition, cost rather than created money. Profits came from investing in production and trade, not consumption.

Legal borrowing, like business loans, relied on the idea of the productive investment. Investors and bankers gave money to ship captains and factory owners because they used that money to make more money. That is how investors and bankers knew they would get paid back. The whole enterprise of banking turned on this idea of assets producing profits. Loans to deadbeat brothers or aging widows might help the borrowers out of a jam but would not produce profits. It was just bad business—or so the conventional wisdom went.

Bankruptcy laws, today nearly always used for personal debt, were created to help small-business men take risks. Before bankruptcy laws, debts never went away, and before the mid–nineteenth century, a debtor could be thrown in jail. The infamous debtors' prisons were filled mostly with failed businessmen, not degenerate samplers of pleasure.[2] Debt in the fifty years before and after the American Revolution served two wildly divergent purposes. As you might expect, loans could be for business, but equally common was debt as a substitute for currency. In most areas of the country, particularly rural areas, cash was scarce. Store owners needed to sell on account if they were to have customers. Every year the period when the crop came in saw a minor financial crisis, as cash flowed spasmodically through the economy to settle the yearlong accounts.

Small-time debtors could sometimes not meet their obligations, but even more than today, the failure to repay a loan was a moral failure—indeed, such a moral failure that it could send you to jail. Today, lending is an impersonal act. Every lender knows that there is a chance the debt will not be repaid and can either refuse the loan or increase the interest rate. In the eighteenth century, debt, especially on account, was a moral act of charity that happened to enable trade. Borrowing without repayment was seen as a moral failure akin to fraud. Duplicitous customers duped store owners. Despite the grip of debtors' prisons on our popular imagination, such prisons were rare in the United States. Save for a few debtors' prisons modeled on British examples, such as the Prune Street prison in Philadelphia or the New Gaol in New York City, most debtors would find themselves bedding down with murderers, rapists, and other reprobates—or, more accurately, sleeping in hallways and on stone floors with other criminals.

In the early nineteenth century, that clear moral vision of debt began to become murkier. As nineteenth-century students of economy read their Adam Smith and David Ricardo, a new rationalism took hold. Lenders ought to have known that some borrowers would default. Every loan was a business decision, not a personal trust. Risk, as every lender who cut off a credit line knew, had to be weighed. This new perspective did not supplant the moral view of debt, but it did temper it. For the economy to grow and for innovation to occur, risks have to be taken. For every business that succeeds, many more necessarily fail. We would not want to live in a society in which reasonable risk could not be taken, because that would be a society without growth. In 1800, the first U.S. bankruptcy law exemplified this perspective, as it absolved only large business debts. Practically as well, imprisonment hampered repayment, as the imprisoned could not work. Only loans to the wealthy, who owned assets worth selling, could be repaid if they were imprisoned. By 1833, federal law eliminated imprisonment for debt. Most states abolished their imprisonment laws around the same time, in the 1830s and 1840s.

Even though imprisonment was abolished, bankruptcy as an opportunity to wipe the slate clean persisted for only a moment. The Bankruptcy Act of 1800 was repealed a few years later. Another version came in 1841 and again was rolled back. Our modern bankruptcy laws date back only to 1898. Like the act of 1800, this law was intended to encourage risk taking in business investment and was never intended to shelter consumers.

The merchants and industrialists who used these bankruptcy acts, however, were the elite of the U.S. economy. Though the manufactured goods of cities were ubiquitous, the United States in the nineteenth century remained an agricultural, rural country. Not until 1920 would the census reckon that most Americans lived in cities, and that term, defined as places with more than five thousand inhabitants, was used quite loosely. In this agricultural world, American borrowing was farm borrowing.

In the mid–nineteenth century, farmers in the West lived and died by credit. The harvest came but once a year, but they needed goods—farm equipment, clothing, groceries—year-round. Independent farmers may have owned their land, but they still depended on the manufactured goods of eastern textile mills and ironworks. The connection between the farmers and factories was the general goods merchant of the nearest town. In Davenport, Iowa, that connection was John Burrows. Cash poor and crop rich, farmers could offer Burrows little but wheat, eggs, and hogs. Burrows wanted to be a grocer, but he ended up as a wheat market. Selling on credit to the farmers, at harvesttime Burrows took their farm goods in trade, selling them in far-flung locales north and south on the Mississippi. Burrows "felt that this country had to be settled up, and to accomplish this, some one must buy the farmers' surplus, or it would remain a wilderness."[3]

For a time Burrows was the only game in town and could charge high prices for his services. Few merchants possessed the capital to finance such a business. Running a business for farmers on credit meant that payment could come as little as once a year. After the harvest in the North, moreover, there was little time left to ship crops before snow blocked the land and ice locked the rivers. Burrows would always have to store a portion of his goods until spring. Every debt that went unrepaid until autumn and every bale that went unsold till spring was Burrows's money sitting idle. To run such a business required large amounts of capital. At the same time, a would-be merchant would need Burrows's skill and connections at selling in New Orleans and buying from Philadelphia. This merchant would also need to be able to convince these merchants to trust him—never an easy task. Burrows enjoyed his prosperity as the biggest big shot of Davenport for twenty years, until the railroad arrived and changed everything.

With the railroad, in this case the Chicago and Rock Island Railroad, the barriers to competition that kept Burrows wealthy ended. With the coming of the railroad, Chicago was no longer a distant name but a quick trip of only eight hours. Rivers could freeze but railcars still ran. No longer did merchants need enough capital to finance inventory and customers for a year. Shipments could arrive from Chicago the next day. Hogs didn't need to be stabled all winter; they could be shipped as quickly as they were bought. The merchants now didn't need to know wholesalers in New York, Philadelphia, and Boston, just in Chicago. The barriers of capital, skill, and relationships that kept competition out fell. New merchants opened everywhere in Davenport, "bewilder[ing]" Burrows. Losing money steadily, he finally closed his business in 1860, becoming one of the farmers he had previously gouged. By the end of the nineteenth century, at least where there were railroads, the credit of northern and western farmers, who owned their own land, fell in cost. Credit prices still existed but competition drove them steadily down.

Credit flowed more freely not only at stores but on the land as well. The opening of the West to rail also opened it to mortgages. Whereas before the Civil War western lands had generally been free and clear, by the late nineteenth century independent farmers relied on mortgages. Even with the railroad, mortgage credit was cheaper than store credit, enabling farmers to invest in and expand their cultivation. The newer lands took greater advantage of eastern credit. In the Dakotas, even before statehood, 75 percent of farms were mortgaged, but farmers turned that investment into a rapid expansion of production. From just 1880 to 1885, Dakota wheat production increased from 3 million to 40 million bushels—or the equivalent of the combined production of Illinois and Indiana, both of which had been farmed for decades. At the same time, "mortgage indebtedness," as the Michigan commissioner on labor wrote in 1888, "operates as a mammoth sponge, constantly and unceasingly absorbing the labor of others."[4] Hard work by western farmers became hard cash only for eastern bankers, fostering a widespread resentment of mortgages.

As long as production grew, however, the mortgages made sense for farmer and banker alike. Easy eastern money bid up land values, anticipating continued future growth in wheat production. After all, God wasn't making any more land. In fact, eastern investors demanded such a quantity of western mortgages that companies sent solicitors west, traveling from farm to farm, offering money to hard-strapped farmers, who happily took it. Some improved their lands, investing in new drainage tiles that did, in many parts of the West, double and triple production by artificially drying overly wet soil. Many other farmers took a different course, having grown weary of the hard life, and with their local knowledge and eastern capital speculated in land or even stocks. Mortgages sometimes exceeded the value of the land, as the demand for mortgages in which to invest so exceeded supply. Nonetheless, mortgage repayments went smoothly once crop production rose, as did crop prices, because American wheat could be sold in the growing eastern cities and around the world.

In the East, western farm mortgages became fashionable investments. Just as an earlier generation invested in western railroad bonds, eastern investors of the 1880s poured money into western mortgages. Insurance companies as well as individuals bought into the western mortgage boom. To satisfy all the investors, New York financiers began to repackage western mortgages into that quintessentially eastern investment vehicle: the bond. "Bond houses" bought mortgages from brokers, called "mortgage bankers," and in turn issued bonds. Investors' capital paid for the mortgages, and the bond houses issued payments to the bondholders as if they owned a railroad corporation's debt. As much as possible, these mortgage bonds were modeled on the language and payments of railroad bonds. Slowly, beginning after 1900, the mortgage bankers began to bring their western financial schemes to the eastern cities, offering mortgage bonds to back commercial and residential real estate. Their national organization, the Farm Mortgage Bankers Association of America, spread the mortgage bond across the United States.

In the South, King Cotton continued to rule as it had before the Civil War, but instead of slavery, sharecropping now organized cotton production. Sharecropping is remembered as a particularly grueling economic arrangement, but what is less well known is the incredible credit system that underpinned it and cotton-producing slavery before it. In sharecropping, a farmer contracted with a plantation owner for a section of land. In exchange, the landowner had the right to a share of the crop. Because of southern crop lien laws, the first claim on the crop went to the landowner. This legal right meant that the farmer had to repay the landowner before any other creditor. With the vagaries of crop production, much less crop prices, lending to farmers was a very risky business—unless you were the plantation owner, who had the first right to the crop. But where could a planter get enough money to finance not only crop production but also the personal lives of his tenants and croppers?[5]

Even by 1860, the entire cotton South had only about a hundred banks—less than the total number of banks in Massachusetts alone! Southern agriculture was financed through coastal middlemen called factors. At the beginning of each season, the planter would write to his factor, in a place such as Savannah or New Orleans, to request cash as well as crop seed, goods, and all the miscellany that a remote cotton planter would need to get through the year. Cash could be used at nearby merchants, such as a Montgomery store that advertised "Wholesale and Retail Dealers in Dry Goods, Clothing, Groceries, Hardware, Boots, Shoes, Hats, Caps, Bonnets, Cutlery, Flowers, Combs, etc., etc., etc.,"[6] The factor would look at the request and in turn request a loan from a banker in New York. The banker would in turn borrow from a banker in Great Britain. Capital could flow halfway around the world, from Europe to north Georgia. After the Civil War, this system survived largely intact, despite the end of slavery. Only the last step changed. Instead of providing for his slaves, the plantation owner simply loaned money to his sharecroppers through his farm's "commissary."

Farmers, especially small independent farmers, could also borrow at the local country store, but prices were high no matter where you went. If the local merchant couldn't get first right to the crop, prices had to be higher to cover that risk. If you couldn't get credit at the local store, the planter could charge monopoly prices. Either way, the farmer paid too much. But accounts had to be in credit. Harvesttime was a moment when all the year's debts were settled. Before that, cash was scarce. Borrowers needed access to credit to get through the seasons, and storekeepers had to give it to have a viable business. Only those too disreputable or untrustworthy could not get an account at the store. It is from this that we get our colorful terms for an untrustworthy person—"no-account" and "good-for-nothing" as in "no-account, good-for-nothing, lazy cuss." Shopkeepers accepted repayment either in cash (which was rare) or cotton (which was expected). Store owners thus sold factory goods to farmers and farm goods to factories, forming a key link in the distribution chain, moving cotton as well as credit through the southern economy. The Montgomery store that traded all those bonnets and cutlery for cotton did well as an intermediary. Opening in 1845, when the first of three brothers came from Europe, H. Lehman and Company changed its name to Lehman Brothers when the second and third brothers arrived in 1850 to take their part in the family business, and soon thereafter opened a branch in Manhattan, following the cotton money from Montgomery to New York.

As in the North, railroads changed the movement of goods. Between 1860 and 1880, overland cotton transportation increased from 2.3 percent to 19 percent of all cotton. Seventy-two percent of cotton for northern manufacturing went overland. But because of the control of southern land by the few, unlike in the North, the balance of power in credit changed little. Debt kept tenant farmers and sharecroppers in thrall to monopolistic country stores where each year's crop never quite made enough to free them from last year's debt. Without paying their debts, sharecroppers found that their freedom to move, to pursue loved ones or new opportunities, was a legal fiction compared to debt's reality. Debt peonage in which a lifetime was spent in debt to a landowner—all too real even into the twentieth century—trapped many sharecroppers, especially African Americans, in gruelingly oppressive lives.[7]

The same credit that made farming possible in the cotton South and the wheat North also enabled personal consumption. Private and business purchasing were jumbled. The money borrowed for farmers' wives' hats in Georgia ultimately came from a British bank. Agriculture, along with railroads, was the big U.S. business. In the cities, however, the intermingling of work and home no longer occurred as it did on the farm, particularly for those who worked for someone else, as Americans increasingly did over the last half of the nineteenth century. For those split into consumer and worker, personal lending became more necessary. In the cities, moreover, the reselling and refinancing of everyday borrowing that made all those country stores possible did not happen. No cotton grew in Manhattan, but of course Lehman Brothers knew that when they moved there, and started to become, by 1900, more of an investment bank than a cotton and dry goods merchant. Bank capital never wended its way to financing tenement workers' wives' hats in quite the same way as in Alabama.

As farmers' children moved to the cities around the end of the century, they brought their ideas of what debt meant: it was dangerous, illicit, and immoral. Their thinking was born of an agricultural world. Whether mortgaged to a bank or in debt to a store, the farmer borrower felt somewhat less than free. The promise of hard work for a good life was unmet as long as there were bills to pay—and those bills seemed never to end. One way out, at least for farmers' sons and daughters, was moving to the city.

The industrial world offered them, and the people who lent them money, opportunities for credit that could not exist on the farm. Legal personal debt, then, has a more recent vintage than either commercial or national debt. Though personal, commercial, and national debt are all called "debt," personal debt is really something apart from those other forms of borrowing. Whereas commercial and national debt have always been a part of the central flow of capital in Western economies, personal debt has been consigned to its margins. For business and religious reasons, during most of Western history, though loans existed, charging interest on them—usury—was a sin, forbidden to most members of society. Our country was born into a world already capitalist, and the authority of our federal government, in one sense, emerged from the need for somebody to deal with the debts incurred during the Revolution. For everyday people, however, usury laws remained, and an untenably low interest rate ceiling restricted the flow of legal cash loans to a trickle. This debt—installment credit, ethnic lending circles, and loan sharks—existed outside the main flows of capital, yet for the borrowers involved—whether from rural Illinois or rural Sicily—access to credit made their lives in the city possible.

Americans came to the cities not only from our hinterland but from across the sea as well. The late nineteenth and early twentieth centuries were the heyday of European immigration.[8] New arrivals came by the millions until 1924, when the Johnson-Reed Act, reflecting nativist anxiety about all those oddly speaking foreigners, cut off immigration across the Atlantic. Like those from American farms, they were predominantly rural in origin, and they, like native-born Americans, encountered a new commercial world. Rural folks, whether from the American Midwest or the European shtetl, began great journeys to the American city. And for both, arrival there meant incurring debt.

Immigrants' credit, except for retail, occurred in a shadow economy disconnected from the large movements of capital. The legality of the borrowing varied, but the price was always the same: high. Credit access was also uncertain and highly personal. What somebody thought about you mattered as much as, or more than, your finances. Credit scores wouldn't exist until decades in the future, and in the turn-of-the-century city, character and collateral mattered most. For recent immigrants, lending always began in the neighborhood and was always personal. The only way to get money was to know somebody. Whether the loan was legal or illegal, personal connections were the foundation of urban lending.

Though cash loans were hard to come by, credit could and did take other forms. The most common form of borrowing was from retailers. As in the country, urban grocers lent money to shoppers, charging higher "credit prices" but not interest as such. Even so, the common wisdom of the nineteenth century, when the thin, anxious merchant fretted about his loans, was that credit was the surest road to retail penury. Scribbles in a leather-bound ledger were not enforceable in any court. In a time before credit agencies, debtors could easily skip out. Yet the corner grocery, desperate for customers and willing to extend credit until the next paycheck, helped the newly arrived to bridge the weeks. Credit prices might have been higher than cash prices but were rarely high enough to cover the skips and deadbeats. The only science in retail lending was the certainty of loss.

For recent immigrants, cash loans could come from ethnic lending circles, such as Jewish *axias* (from the Yiddish word for "shares"), which offered many new Americans a source of money for home down payments or to start new businesses, similar to the West Indian *susus* or Korean *kyes* today. Like microfinance banks, these lending circles relied on the trust born of close-knit groups to make individuals responsible for their debts. Lending ranged in formality from a few friends pooling money for another to buy a sewing machine to full-fledged banks—but without the banking regulations. *Axias* and other lending circles did not make a profit, just as frequently losing money as enabling dreams, as unemployment could hit a group of people all at once. The common ethnic and occupational background that underpinned a group also made them vulnerable to a downturn in a particular industry or even a company. More disappointed were the credulous members whose treasurers fled with the group's savings, as Max Teicher, treasurer of one Lower East Side *axia*, did in 1928. When he disappeared from the circle's headquarters at 179 Suffolk Street with $40,000, Teicher left the two hundred members, all Jewish immigrants, with only $8.74. Outside banking regulations, members had little recourse but social pressure. Teicher and the $40,000 were never found.[9]

Repossession was always public in the city. Debt collectors take a piano and other goods bought on the installment plan. Repossessed goods were then resold.

For those whose needs were more immediate or more private, loan sharks provided another source of money. Not all borrowers wanted their neighborhoods to know that they needed money or that they wanted it for less honorable pursuits than to start a new business. Unlike retail and lending circles, loan sharking was immensely profitable. In one month loan sharks could charge a year's worth of legal interest. With usurious rates like these, loan sharks' revenues could overcome the riskiness of lending to urban workers. Borrowing from a loan shark was rarely a debtor's first choice. Loan sharks, as lenders of last resort, more frequently than not refinanced more conventional loans for borrowers who had exhausted other sources of credit.

For many urban borrowers, the road to the loan shark began at the furniture store. Installment credit—that is, borrowing in monthly payments secured against the goods bought—flourished long before cash lending was legal. In the nineteenth century, pianos, furniture, and other consumer durables could all be bought on the time payment plan. Like the corner grocer, retailers self-financed these loans. For honest merchants, the credit helped them sell more goods. But, limited to relatively low rates of interest, furniture houses typically priced 10 or 20 percent higher than the goods would have cost in a credit-free store. Even for a successful merchant, the loans were repaid, but the interest itself was not profitable. Installment credit enabled merchants to sell their expensive wares and consumers to buy them. Credit buying was the norm. A Federal Trade Commission survey done in the early 1920s found that of 556 dealers surveyed, only 78 set prices based on a cash sale and only 13 sold only for cash.[10] Colloquially, credit furniture stores, which sold low-to midgrade goods on installment, were called Borax Houses. The origins of "Borax" are uncertain. Some writers claimed it came from the Yiddish word *borgs* for credit, but others said that, like the cleaner Borax, the places cleaned you out.[11]

This system had some serious dangers for both borrower and lender. Lenders faced enormous expenses if a borrower stopped paying. Repossession was expensive. City marshals would have to be compensated for their time in overseeing the repossession, workmen hired to remove the goods, and of course a horse and wagon rented to carry them back to the store. If the goods were damaged, they could not be resold. For the unscrupulous Borax House, however, repossession represented an opportunity for profit. Selling overpriced furniture to customers who could probably not afford the payments, the store could collect the down payment and a few installments and then repossess the goods. The furniture, with a little spit and shine, could then be resold to the next sucker. In a world where the cost of goods was high (i.e., before IKEA could mass-produce beds in Asia), such a system was profitable.

The case of a deckhand named John S. in the late 1920s was all too typical. For a borrower like John, the financial costs of repossession could be staggering. Living with his wife and four children, he worked on a ferryboat in New York City. With his small savings, he had bought a house with an interest-only mortgage.[12] He had outfitted the house through the installment plan with furniture and a radio. He had borrowed to make a comfortable life for his family, and on his salary, could afford the payments. For five months everything went well; then John fell on an "icy sidewalk" and severely sprained his wrist. He was out of work for two months, and the family quickly went through its savings. Finally John went back to work, and after two weeks went to get his paycheck, which he found, to his surprise, had been totally garnished by the Borax House. Wage garnishment was commonplace, and there were no laws limiting how much of a paycheck lenders could take. John owed $240, which meant that every paycheck for the next six weeks would go to the furniture store. Without savings, he had counted on his wages to pay his current

bills and the interest on his mortgage. Because of the garnishment, he could lose his house and be unable to eat. He could
afford his debts but could not afford to be out of work. John
appealed to the pro bono Legal Aid Society, which was luckily able to work out a deal between John S. and his creditors,
but John's good fortune was rare. The Legal Aid Society noted
in its annual report that his was one of the few cases able to
be adjusted that year. More common was garnishment followed by repossession. Repossession meant that debtors lost
not only their bed, couch, and table but also all the installments that they had paid thus far. Installment debtors had
no equity. Missing payments meant losing everything. Installment credit created a crisis that only quick cash could solve.
The loan shark could easily step in at this moment, offering a
solution that would not involve garnishment or repossession.

Most loan sharks operated in a quasi-legal limbo. After all,
it was legal to lend money, just not at the rates that they did.
Edward Erd, a turn-of-the-century Chicago loan shark, for
instance, advertised in the *Chicago Tribune* every afternoon for
twenty-five years and even had his borrowers fill out elaborate
yet bogus contracts. Lending money was not illegal, just the
rates that Erd and other loan sharks charged. For example,
when a Chicago carpenter, Oscar Norman, borrowed $30
from Erd, he meticulously paid $65 in interest, $1.50 a month
(54 percent a year) for four years, never managing to pay off
the principal. After Norman tried to stop paying—having
paid back more than double the original loan—Erd threatened him with a "bum notice," claiming the right to repossess
his belongings, as if Norman had bought furniture on the
installment plan. Frightened by the legalistic language, Norman nearly let Erd take all his alleged repossessions.[13] Only
through intervention of a crusading anti–loan shark lawyer,

enlisted by Norman's wife, was the account settled. Yet the tactics of the fake contract and the threats continued, if not in Norman's case, then in the cases of other borrowers from loan sharks.

The old-time banker always loaned money with the beneficent air of a charity worker.

Before the 1920s, personal borrowing offered more shame than profit.

Borrowing remained shameful for some and disreputable for many. Americans of the 1920s may have witnessed a titanic change in the practices surrounding debt, but still there remained remnants of an older rural moral order. John Raskob, the creator of the General Motors Acceptance Corporation (GMAC), who did as much as any individual to inaugurate this new era of borrowing, reflected in 1927 on the credit practices of his youth: "I was raised in a community where a mortgage on your home was considered a disgrace. If a home was mortgaged, the children didn't know about it, usually for fear they'd tell the other children about it and let loose the family skeleton."[14] The person who lent the mortgage money was a "tight skinflint who charged extremely high rates of interest and made the house buyer feel that he was lending him the money more as a favor than as a sound business transaction." "The old-time banker," as a banker's picture was subtitled in a 1926 issue of *Collier's*, "loaned money with the beneficent air of a charity worker." Lending was personal no matter what its context, and the need to borrow remained personally shameful. Edward Erd, who could smugly defend his methods to the *Chicago Tribune* that carried his advertisements, learned, in the end, the true meaning of debt. He never denied that he had preyed on borrowers, but did not the "improvident" spender deserve such treatment? In Erd's view "people who borrow are fools" and even he "wouldn't employ a man or woman who found it necessary to do business with the shark." But until his interview, Erd's name had never been in the *Tribune,* he said, except for advertising his business in the classifieds. Afterward, however, he was known for what he was: a loan shark. The shame of being exposed quickly brought on a nervous condition. A month after the piece describing his tactics ran in the *Tribune,* he was found dead by his wife in his apartment, killed by his own hand with a revolver. The social significance of debt, despite Erd's insistence on blaming the borrower, applied to him as well. Whether lending or borrowing, debt remained a shameful affair.

Nonprofit alternatives to loan sharks, called remedial loan societies, had been attempted for years, but with little success, partially because of how they were organized and partially because they exacerbated the shame of borrowing. In 1893, for instance, the Provident Loan Society of New York City was founded to provide small loans, within the limits of usury law, to New York's workers. Though other similar organizations, such as the Workingmen's Loan Association of Boston, predated it, none matched the success and growth of the Provident Loan Society.[15] Interest on loans was a third to a half of the rates charged by pawnbrokers.[16] Rates could be so low—12 percent per year—because the Provident Loan Society, largely funded by generous New York philanthropists, required no profit. By 1909, there were at least fourteen such organizations across the United States.[17]

Reformist lenders believed that there was as much need to reform workers' financial habits as to provide them with emergency access to borrowing. Understandably, debtors were loath to go to the remedial lenders, fearing a patronizing lecture on how they ought to live. Archie Chadbourne, a Colorado trucker writing about his financial circumstances, complained that such a loan had an interest rate of 12 percent and had to be renewed every three months. Instead of evading many store owners, there would be only one lender with a firm schedule of repayment. More grating than the interest cost, Chadbourne claimed, would have been having "to swallow all [the loan officer's] advice just like [he] enjoyed it." The oversight by someone to whom the debtor was paying interest was the most galling part. Chadbourne described a trip to the loan office as less a business action than a social supplication: "I gave the manager my pedigree, my budget plans, and itemized what I would do with the money, and crawled about the office furniture on my hands and knees while he puffed at a lazy pipe."[18] Consolidating debts with a charity lender was possible, but doing so would cost the debtor both money and self-respect. Loan sharks, whatever their drawbacks, never lectured borrowers on their moral failures.

The realities of capital ultimately constrained reform lenders more than their moral vision. Limited to only a 6 percent annual return by their charters, investors contributed money as a form of charity rather than an investment. Remedial loan societies were not entrepreneurial opportunities. By 1925, they totaled only forty nationwide and never exceeded that number.[19] Two years later, their number had dropped to only twenty-eight.[20] Though rhetorically important, they never really affected the rates or number of loan sharks. Without profits to reinvest, such nonprofit lenders could never grow to meet the ever-surging demand for loans. Like retailers, they self-financed their loans, and, like retailers', their loans were not profitable. To end loan sharking, a legal—and profitable—alternative would have to be found.

The 1910s and 1920s were ripe with change in the ways Americans borrowed. New impersonal economic pressures began to force borrowing to become less personal. Borrowing began to seem more like an economic choice than a depraved situation. As hard as it was to collect from borrowers, even more restrictive was retailers' inability to resell their debt. Every debt has a chance of repayment and a certain value, but until the 1920s it was not possible for ordinary retailers to resell their customers' debts to investors who had money to spare. Capitalism depends on investment to function; self-financed business simply isn't possible in a developed economy. Though retailers today can borrow against the debts owed by the customers or even resell that debt to a third party, back then no corner grocer could resell the debt in his ledger, making that debt expensive for the retailer and in turn for the customer. Without resale, consumer credit could not expand.

In the 1920s, reformers succeeded in removing usury restrictions in many states so that legitimate businesses could lend cash to working people. With higher legal rates, small-loan businesses could profitably displace loan sharks. Reginald Smith, a lawyer with the colorfully named Legal Reform Bureau to Eliminate the Loan Shark Evil, complimented the "well-intentioned" people who supported usury laws to "prevent the poor man from paying excessive rates of interest," but, he said, the limits on interest rates made life worse.[21] In this brief to the Massachusetts legislature, Smith was part of a vast small-loan reform movement. By the early 1920s, working people could borrow cash in most states and use that cash for whatever they needed. By 1930, the nonprofit think tank the Twentieth Century Fund estimated that the average American family borrowed from a small-loan company every other year.[22] Yet, just as with loans taken from loan sharks, 40 percent of them refinanced existing loans. Debt rolled over year after year, earning interest.

Yet the outrage and reform surrounding small loans and usury had little impact on what would be the greatest source of debt in the 1920s: the installment plan. Unlike usury laws, which regulated cash loans, installment plans were for goods and usury laws didn't apply.[23] The moral need to protect the desperate and poor did not apply to consumers in want of luxury goods such as vacuum cleaners, gramophones, and—most important—cars. In the 1920s, the retailers that lent their own money would find new sources of capital. The scarce capital that limited grocery stores and furniture houses would be found. The car—that quintessential installment purchase—would usher in a new era of debt through its creation of the finance company. Anonymous investment in anonymous borrowing was something that had never happened before. Thousands of years of personal lending intuitions ended when a borrower's numbers mattered more than his name. This resale of debt, liberating consumers and retailers from the restricted world of self-financed personal debt, began when selling an automobile required lending would-be drivers money. The restrictions on usury paled before the restrictions on capital and, freed from that constraint, the modern credit system arose as borrowers and lenders learned how to lend to workers who had only their incomes and how to resell that debt. The resale of debt would end the world in which the Skinny Man and Fat Man poster made sense.

CHAPTER TWO

EVERYBODY PAID CASH
FOR THE MODEL T
(1908–1929)

The second most expensive purchase most of us ever make is a car, and when Americans think of cars, we think of Henry Ford. Though fewer of us today drive Fords than Hondas, Henry Ford's name is forever linked to the automobile. Yet the auto loan, which makes buying cars possible, has nothing to do with Henry Ford, despite being invented at just about the same time as his car company, Ford Motor Company. Indeed, Henry Ford fought tooth and nail not to sell his cars through installment credit and in the process nearly destroyed his company. Where did auto loans come from, if not from the father of the car? And why did he resist helping his customers buy his cars?

Before 1919, nearly all cars, including the Model T, were sold for cash. As one General Motors executive remarked, the car had "given us all something worth working for."[1] It was the ultimate luxury good, giving purpose to the savings of millions of Americans. The best-selling car in the United States and the world was the Model T from Henry Ford, whose innovative production techniques transformed the car from a hobbyist curio into a mass-market love affair.

Before Henry Ford, the automobile languished as a hobbyist's gadget, a rich man's plaything. Usually the Germans Karl Benz and Gottlieb Daimler are credited with its invention in 1885, and by the 1890s many varieties of car proliferated in Europe. In the United States alone there were around 2,500 automobile companies. But none of these start-ups managed to transform cars into a mass-consumption item. Hand-tooled and built one by one, they were expensive oddities. A few guys got together and made cars piece by piece. The parts were never interchangeable. Each one required a great deal of skill to produce, and the prices of the cars were unbelievable.

In the United States the story was largely the same as in Europe. In the 1890s, there were already about thirty companies building cars. By 1909, the low-volume, high-price model of automobile production was standard for the nearly three hundred American automobile companies. All except for one: Ford Motor Company.

The introduction of the Model T in 1908 changed U.S. industry forever. But the Model T was not the first car Ford worked on. The company had started in 1903. What happened in those first five years? Models A, B, C, F, K, N, R, and S all came and went as Ford struggled to find the right car for the American market. He aimed for a car that would suit not only a high-end novelty audience but a mass market as well. He wrote in 1906 that "the greatest need today is a light low-priced car with an up-to-date engine of ample horsepower, and built of the very best material."[2] Ford sold the initial Model Ts for $850 but by 1924 dropped the price to only $290, which is amazing considering the rising inflation of the period. Quality was key, but so was price. How to reconcile the two?

Working alongside a small group of other mechanics, Henry Ford built the first Model T simply. The engine could be cast in one piece, out of a relatively inexpensive but light vanadium-steel alloy. The process of production of the Model T, as well as the product itself, was novel. The young mechanics Ford arrayed about him drew on the organizational techniques of many different industries, from meatpacking to gun manufacturing, to invent a new way of building cars. The oddly spaced heaps of parts that defined garage manufacturing were replaced with gravity slides and orderly arrangements of machines and mechanics. Like the mortgage bond, the assembly line had come from the West. William Klann, the head of the engine department, remembered later that the idea for the assembly line had occurred to him as he toured a Chicago slaughterhouse's "disassembly line," where pigs and cows hung from overhead hooks as workers sliced: "If they can kill pigs and cows that way, we can build cars that way and build motors that way."[3]

Ford quickly adapted the methods to a much larger factory at Highland Park in Detroit, which opened for production on January 1, 1910. A four-story building, 865 feet long and 75 feet wide, the factory would produce only the Model T. Four models—the runabout, the touring car, the town car, and the delivery car—would all be based on the same interchangeable chassis. The car was brought to the worker, not the worker to the car. A complete Model T emerged from the factory every forty seconds. By merging production techniques from a variety of industries, as well as pushing the limits of machining,

Ford dropped the production time of a Model T from twelve and half hours in 1908 to less than thirty minutes by 1914. The car stayed the same while the machines used to produce the cars constantly improved. In 1915, Ford Motor Company celebrated its millionth sale.

Though Henry Ford loved building cars, he hated business, especially finance. A mechanic by training, he started his company in 1903 with a capital of $28,000 from twelve partners. By 1920, it was worth over a billion dollars. After the initial investment, no more investments were received. No stocks were sold. No money was borrowed. By 1919, Ford had bought out all his original partners and the company was completely private. With profits of $750 million by 1920, Ford Motor Company, owned entirely by Henry Ford, had no need for outside investment. The company, for better or for worse, reflected the unique vision of its founder, and he ran it without the interference of Wall Street.

Henry Ford's vision reflected the populist politics of his youth, which celebrated those who produced over the "parasites," such as railroad executives and financiers, who took money for doing nothing. Populism, the largest political movement of the late nineteenth century, emerged from the unequal relationship of eastern capital and western farmers, particularly the dependence of western farmers on eastern-controlled railroads and mortgages. From the end of the Civil War until around 1900, the U.S. economy was deflationary. A dollar today was worth more—not less—tomorrow. Mortgages thus became ever more expensive to pay back over time. Populists described bankers as unscrupulous, "hyena-faced Shylocks" who represented the "Money Power."[4] The Money Power was, as the 1892 Populist platform described it, "a vast conspiracy against mankind . . . if not met and overthrown at once it forebodes terrible social convulsions, the destruction of civilization, or the establishment of an absolute despotism." Ford thought himself—with his privately held, stockholder-less corporation—apart from this vast conspiracy of capitalists.

Ford always thought of himself as a mechanic first and a businessman last. While "business men believed that you could do anything by 'financing' it," Ford "determined absolutely that [he] never would . . . join a company in which finance came before the work or in which bankers or financiers had a part."[5] Ford, more than anything else, was a builder of cars. He liked to know how they worked. He liked to improve them. Selling cars was great, but that was secondary to building a quality machine. Once you had a great machine, he would say, the only thing left to decide was its price, and a lower price for the same quality was all that mattered.

Following World War I, however, the meaning of the car changed. "Pleasure cars," as a GM executive put it, became "economical transportation."[6] For manufacturers to keep growing in the 1920s as they had through the 1910s, the market would have to expand to include those who could not save up for their cars. Despite the clear incentive to provide consumer financing, however, manufacturers only accidentally developed ways for consumers to borrow.

Selling goods—not just making them cheaply—quickly became the chief challenge of the automotive industry and of American industry more generally. If the main problem of the nineteenth century was how to produce enough, the problem of the twentieth century would be how to sell enough. The "producerism" of Ford's youth began to give way to the "consumerism" of the new century. Whereas Ford romanticized a mechanic's ability to build a car from a pile of bolts and chains, his own workers gave up their control in the work-place for more control in the marketplace. Though it could be kind of fun to assemble a car from scratch, it was the worst kind of hell to tighten the same nut nine hours a day. Ford himself wrote that "repetitive labor—the doing of one thing over and over again and always in the same way—is a terrifying prospect to a certain kind of mind. It is terrifying to me. I could not possibly do the same thing day in and day out, but other minds, perhaps I might say to the majority of minds, repetitive operations hold no terrors. In fact, to some types of mind thought is absolutely appalling."[7]

Yet even for the majority, the work was intolerable. In the early 1910s, Ford had to rehire his entire workforce three or four times a year because everyone quit. The "five-dollar-day," started in 1914, when Ford paid his workers $5 a day—twice the market wage—virtually eliminated absenteeism and kept the assembly line running. The higher wage also enabled a new generation of American workers to privilege their consumer identity over their producer identity.[8] Wages mattered more than workplace control as long as the work was steady and well paid. But in this context of high wages and high productivity, selling all the goods could no longer be taken for granted. Consumer finance would thus assume a new importance. Economic historians have called this new high-wage system, where workers could buy the goods that they make, "Fordism" because the five-dollar-day is so closely associated with its inauguration. Yet, rather than the first Fordist, Henry Ford should be thought of as the last mechanic. He was like Moses on the verge of the Promised Land: he could take the Hebrews there from out of Egypt but could not himself enter. He was a prisoner of his populist origins, unable to accept the importance of finance.

His upstart rival General Motors would teach Ford about that and in the process nearly bankrupt him. Unlike Ford Motor Company, GM was founded by a man, William Durant, who knew little about how to build a car and couldn't care less. In 1885, young William Durant was a twenty-four-year-old insurance salesman in Flint, Michigan. Buying a patent for a new kind of two-wheeled cart, he had gone into business with a local hardware salesman. Since they were both salesmen, they subcontracted the actual building of the carts to local carriage builders. Flint, at that point, was one of the largest centers for carriage building in the country. With so many builders around, it made more sense to contract the work out than to build a factory themselves. Without a factory, Durant could concentrate on selling, which was what he did best.[9]

And sell he did. He set up distributors. He peddled in the city. He sold in the country. All across the nation, Durant and his partner sold their two-wheeled carts. Then Durant took this model of subcontracting developed for carriages, ditched his hapless partner, and set about building a car company.

Whereas Ford grew his company through innovation, Durant bought out competitors, preferably when they went bankrupt and could be had on the cheap. While doing so, however, he maintained small cash reserves. Unlike Ford, who financed everything internally by saving, Durant spent his capital on acquisitions and borrowed to the hilt. Durant was a wild optimist who thought demand would always outpace growth. He produced as many parts and bodies as he could, anticipating rising demand. Such a strategy works well in an expanding market, but in 1910 there was a sudden drop in demand that even Durant, the supersalesman, could not overcome. He lost control of his company to a group of

East Coast bankers from Boston and New York, who pushed Durant out and reorganized the company.

Though Ford remained in the hands of the original mechanics who built cars, by 1920 GM, through a series of corporate intrigues, had passed into the control of the Du Pont Corporation, famed for its ability to organize finance as well as production. So on the one hand there was Ford Motor Company, headed by one man, who believed in nothing but production, and on the other hand there was a vast corporation, drawing on the organizational resources of many different men and predicated entirely on profit.

For the auto industry to continue the breakneck growth of the 1910s, new ways to sell cars would have to be found. Though Henry Ford saw finance as antithetical to production, General Motors saw salvation in finance. Then, as now, most Americans bought their cars in the summer. Yet for factories to be run profitably, they had to be run 24/7, even in the winter. Who would pay for the storage of all the excess production? Once production began to seriously outpace seasonal demand, GM hit upon a clever idea.

GM would finance dealers' purchases of cars from the factory. Then the automaker wouldn't have to deal with the excess inventory, and dealers would have stock on hand for any potential customers. If you think the dealers got the raw end of the deal, you would be right. They had to pay for cars that could not be sold until the summer, while GM got the interest on the financing, plus the profitable operation of the factory. But a dealer had little choice in the matter, since GM could easily stop selling its cars and simply find another dealership that was willing to play ball.

One of Du Pont's vice presidents, a finance expert named John Raskob, set up a new subsidiary corporation to handle this new financing plan, General Motors Acceptance Corporation (GMAC). Though originally created to handle wholesale dealership financing, GMAC eventually realized that consumers had financing problems of their own. Though dealers were loath to go into debt to deal with GM's excess inventory problem, consumers clamored to borrow. In the first few years of the 1920s, small finance companies across the country recognized the opportunity and began to offer consumers the option to borrow against their rising wages. Recognizing the possibilities to be found in lending to consumers, GMAC expanded beyond just lending to dealers.

This reorientation to consumers was hard for a large manufacturer such as GM. It was accustomed to caring only about production; sales were the dealerships' problem. Thus, it was not until 1924 that GM used "sales to consumers" as its "fundamental index" for measuring success instead of just sales to dealers.[10] Still, by 1924, GMAC provided about 5 percent of the total annual profit for GM and its subsidiary companies. Whereas the General Motors Annual Report for 1919 describes the primary purpose of GMAC as "to assist dealers in financing their purchase of General Motors' products," by 1927, the GMAC annual report describes "provid[ing] credit to the consumer of goods as its most important function."[11] Though we might think of GM's shift to financing as a relatively recent phenomenon, its long road from a manufacturing company to a finance company began nearly at its outset. By 1927, GMAC's annual gross revenues totaled more than $40 million, and its assets totaled more than $300 million.

In 1926, GMAC connected high finance with consumer finance for the first time. To maintain its growth, GMAC issued its first 6 percent bond in February 1926. The investment bank J.P. Morgan sold the bonds, raising $50 million in cash.[12] Begun only seven years earlier, GMAC had assets of $275 million, or 30 percent of General Motors proper.[13] The successful 1926 bond issue was followed in 1927 by another $50 million sale, giving GMAC the capital it needed to grow.[14] Ford, in contrast, relied on its own profits—called retained earnings—to fund its growth. In 1926, it dispersed 62 percent of profits to stockholders and reinvested an ample $64 million in its operations. Automobile companies, in particular, did not tend to rely on loans. Car companies tended to fund only 2.3 percent of their capital from bond issues, compared to 9 percent in other industries. Yet even among that relatively debt-free industry, Ford stood out, with only 0.02 percent—$145,000—of its capital backed by bonds.[15]

Finance enabled GMAC to expand, which in turn allowed GM to expand. Raskob imagined consumer credit as an alternative to socialism, since credit might make possible "the dream haven of plenty for everybody and fair shake for all, which the socialists have pointed out to mankind. But our route will be by the capitalist road of upbuilding rather than by the socialistic road of tearing down."[16] Financing also made money: by the late 1920s, auto sales faltered, but the number of cars financed by GMAC grew from 646,000 in 1926 to 824,190 in 1927. In 1927, GMAC financed slightly over one million GM cars.

Henry Ford, meanwhile, fought back against putting Americans in debt. As GM became the leading American car company in 1927, Ford groused, "I sometimes wonder if we have not lost our buying sense and fallen entirely under the spell of salesmanship. The American of a generation ago was a shrewd buyer. He knew values in the terms of utility and dollars. But nowadays the American people seem to listen and be sold; that is, they do not buy. They are sold, things are pushed on them. We have dotted lines for this, that and the other thing—all of them taking up income before it is earned."[17] He realized that credit drove sales but he did not want a part of it. He took a principled stance. He stood for old-fashioned ways. Despite his principles, he continued to lose market share.

In all things, Ford, like the homesteading pioneer of a generation earlier, pushed for self-sufficiency. The triumph of this urge was his magnum opus: the River Rouge plant. Begun in 1918, it was situated in the country seven miles from Dearborn, allowing Ford to imagine layouts at a scale never possible in a city. While in Detroit, limited space had forced Ford to rely on elevators; at River Rouge he could lay out every building in one story. Production could be flatter and thus more efficient. It could also be self-sufficient. Ford had fumed at the shortages of World War I. Unlike GM, which continued to outsource whenever possible, as Durant had done from the very beginning, Ford pushed toward full vertical integration. The River Rouge Plant could take in raw ore and uncut lumber, and then, thirty-three hours later, turn out a new car. Nothing could compete with the mechanical apotheosis of the River Rouge plant. River Rouge lowered automobile production costs to the absolute minimum. Ford didn't need anyone else. He had attained what was in his mind the ideal product and the ideal way to make that product. But that was not enough. By 1927, when River Rouge was fully functional, employing 100,000 workers and sprawling over 1,100 acres, Ford Motor Company nearly went under.

Nobody wants to be seen in yesterday's ride, and by the mid-1920s, no matter how low the price on the Model T dropped, people did not want to buy it. By the end of the

1920s, GM had become the dominant auto manufacturer in America and Ford struggled to keep up as it rapidly lost profits and market share. By that point the Model T was nearly twenty years old, and its low-price design had never changed. It had no roof. It had no shock absorbers, no electric starter, no battery-powered ignition. It came in any color you liked, as long as that color was black. Americans were now willing to pay more to get a car with a color—and a roof. And they were willing to borrow to do so. Within ten years of World War I, installment sales of automobiles rose to 60 percent of total car sales—from zero. Ford resisted consumer choice and consumer finance at every turn.

With his success beginning to sour, Ford's hostility to finance stretched into a hostility to financiers, which to Ford meant Jews. For Ford, all the troubles he was having in his company were caused by the financiers (such as the decidedly not-Jewish du Ponts who ran GM) who were part of the "invisible government," by which he meant the secret conspiracy of Jewish bankers that truly ran the world. His belief was inspired by a fabricated book he encountered sometime around when he bought the local newspaper *The Dearborn Independent* in 1920. Fabricated by tsars to justify Russian pogroms, *The Protocols of the Elders of Zion* claimed to be an authentic manual on how Jews were to use international finance and Communist revolution—that is, capitalism and communism at once—to overthrow the Christian world. In *Ford Ideals,* Ford wrote that "this concealed international control of the world flourishes because people do not believe that it exists. They don't see how it can exist." *The Dearborn Independent,* which was anything but independent due to Ford's intrusions, was Ford's way to get the word out. His obsession with Jews became public with an article entitled "The International Jew: The

World's Problem," in which he outlined the troubles caused by Jews in all aspects of life around the world. But it did not stop with one article. Every week, Ford published articles in the *Independent*: how Jews corrupted politics; how Jews had caused World War I. The newspaper became a mouthpiece for his anti-Semitic-inflected critiques of finance.

Now, I don't discuss this because I want to slander the reputation of Henry Ford. Such xenophobic and anti-Semitic thinking was all too common at the time. After all, it was in 1921 and 1924 that Congress passed immigration acts to stop the continued immigration of Jews, as well as all other kinds of eastern and southern Europeans, who were believed to be unassimilable and destructive to the American way of life. His anti-Semitism might have been only a historical curiosity except that his monomania blinded him to the shifting currents of business. He believed that the money supply, controlled by the Money Power, was the source of all U.S. woes. And who controlled the money supply, in his view? Jewish international financiers. He was not going to put his company or his customers in hock to the Jews.

Ford never took outside investors because of his antipathy to finance and his belief in self-reliance. He didn't want any money from any New York financier—read Jewish financier—affiliated with his company. And in the 1920s, when American consumers were first beginning to enjoy the benefits of installment credit, Ford's resistance to consumer finance almost undid the company.

Instead of consumer finance, Ford offered a "Ford weekly purchasing plan" through his dealerships, starting in 1923. In this scheme, a possible buyer would start a savings plan at the dealership, which would be credited with interest only if, in the end, the consumer used the savings to buy a

Ford. Advertisements reassured depositors that they would receive "interest...computed at our regular savings rate."[18] Such a savings plan accorded with Ford's moral vision of American consumption and did not send money back east to bankers—Jewish or gentile. But Americans did not want a new savings account, they wanted a new car! Though the program's failure is not that surprising, the fact that thousands of people deposited their money at a Ford dealership is. Ford did not understand that a high-quality, affordable product was no longer enough. He had to sell, and consumers wanted credit.

Ford's anti-Semitism sprang from mechanic ideals, I believe, rather than a deep-seated hatred of Jews. At one point in 1922, he remarked to his biographer that he was concerned that there was "too much anti-Semitic feeling. I can feel it around here. If we were to keep this up, something might happen to the Jews. I do not want any harm to come to them."[19] Many Ford employees, after all, were Jewish. No doubt he had many Jewish acquaintances. Though he was a great mechanic, he was often not a clear thinker.

There was an anecdote in the 1920s that conveyed Ford's odd mixture of industrialist and populist: Two Wall Street "personages" were discussing Henry Ford. " 'Ford talks like a Socialist,' said one. 'Yes, but he acts like one of us,' replied the other softly, 'and he gets away with it.' "[20]

Finance—the real issue—and Jews became muddied in his mind. Within a few years, Ford told the editor of his paper, "Put all your thought and time to studying and writing about this money question. The Jews are responsible for the present money standard and we want them on our side to get rid of it." And with a quick word from Mr. Ford, the anti-Jewish screeds stopped. Ford published a retraction of his years of propaganda: "The so-called Protocols . . . I learn to be gross forgeries." He also expressed regret for his years of "contending that the Jews have been engaged in a conspiracy to control the capital and industries of the world."[21] It was not Jews but Jewish financiers that ultimately distressed Ford. This financial world that produced nothing and yet reaped profits was the real enemy. Newspapers across the country supported Ford's change of heart. The *Atlanta Constitution* was typical in its editorial opinion that "although manly and courageous, the retraction is no more than Mr. Ford should have made. The pity is it was not made long ago." More conciliatory was the statement by Samuel Stern, a lawyer and former president of the Washington Bar Association who thought that Ford's "efforts should be and, I think, will be received by my people in the true Christian spirit so well exemplified by the Jew."

The rugged independence of the mechanic, which Henry Ford valued most (while, ironically, doing more than any other man to destroy it), had been sapped from the American people through borrowing and salesmanship. Ford, in a kind of principled stance, realized that sales and credit were driving consumption, but he did not want any part of it. Despite his principles, he was losing market share. While GM grew, Ford Motor Company collapsed. Ford's market share plummeted from over half of all cars sold in 1921 to less than a fifth by the end of the decade. The company's profits, once stellar, were negative by 1927, showing a net loss of $30 million. In contrast, GM earned $262 million on $1.3 billion in sales in 1927. While Ford dominated the 1910s as a low-cost car was needed for a growing market, GM dominated from the 1920s to the 1980s, as its superior corporate strategy dominated the stumbling Ford. Fordism was really GM-ism.

By 1928, forced into it by unyielding market pressures,

Ford reluctantly started a subsidiary credit company called the Universal Credit Corporation. Buyers could put down 10 percent and finance for up to year. But by that point, Ford had missed most of the 1920s, as GM expanded sales through its better products and financing. Indeed, Henry Ford, though forced into offering consumer credit, could not abide it and sold off the subsidiary a few years later, in 1933, to CIT. Meanwhile, GM expanded its reliance on consumer finance, consolidating GMAC into the profit and loss statements of GM in 1929. Demonstrating how important consumer finance was to its business model, when, in 1929, GM bought the German car manufacturer, Adam Opel, it immediately founded a new entity, Opel Finanzierung, to be the GMAC of Germany.[22] So as GM enjoyed the fat profits of consumer finance through the Depression and indeed through today, Ford retreated. Henry Ford sold off the financing arm, which could have provided his company with additional profits, thus hampering the growth of Ford as both a finance company and a manufacturing company.[23]

Henry Ford produced the first car for the masses, but by the late 1920s, the masses no longer existed. Consumer markets had begun to segment, fragmenting along different lines of income. GM offered cars at every price point and the financing that made those points possible. Americans started to be paid enough to exercise choice, no longer chained to whatever was cheapest. Masses became consumers. In the process, the car for the masses, produced for the cheapest possible price, lost out. Hardscrabble independence was nowhere near as comfortable as a car.

As wages rose, so too did expectations. By 1929, workers expected a car. They wanted a radio. They wanted a standard of life much higher than their parents had had in 1900. A survey in 1929 found that the average Detroit-area Ford worker earned $1,712. But what was considered "necessary" by 1929 called for an income of $1,728—$16 short. And Ford workers, as well as any of the semiskilled workers in growing industries such as automobiles, electrical goods, and other mass-production industries, were relatively well paid. Progressives worried that "dollar-down serfdom" would "deliver the workman to his employer swathed in the tightly binding bandages of payment due dates," preventing strikes.[24] Consumption on credit was the sure road to lower wages. Only by borrowing from the future could that $16 difference be made up, though, and in the 1920s, Americans chose comfortable serfdom.

By the late 1920s, nearly all goods could be had on the installment plan. Cars and radios could be bought on time, and so too could vacuum cleaners, phonographs, washing machines, cabinets, clothes, and nearly anything else. Conservatives worried that all this borrowing—implicitly a lack of saving—reflected a failure of the American character. Republican senator James Couzens of Michigan, an early investor in Ford Motor Company and lifelong friend of Henry Ford, was an outspoken critic of installment credit. The "growing evil" of installment credit, he said, "results in weakening of character and neglect of the more substantial things of life."[25] Budgeting to spend instead of budgeting to save, Couzens thought, undermined the purpose of budgets. Echoing today's denunciations, he could "say from [his] personal knowledge that the education of children, their physical well-being generally, even the care of their teeth are being neglected to enable families to purchase on instalments many luxuries [sic]." "If this is sound," he said, "then let the orgy proceed."

It did. Retailers and manufacturers, ignoring politics in favor of profits, learned to lend, creating finance companies not just for automobiles but for everything, linking consumers' desire with banks' capital. One of the main justifications for all this lending was, of course, the character of the people who borrowed. Early-twentieth-century "Credit men" evaluated borrowers by what they called the four Cs: "character, capacity, capital, [and] collateral," of which character, it was claimed, was the basic rock foundation of the four big Cs.[26] If borrowing required character and the act of borrowing itself eroded character, then all those credit men were in quite a fix. Luckily it was not just character but the other Cs that mattered as well. More important than character was the stability of income. Even the *Saturday Evening Post* could explain, in 1928, that a car loan "cannot be sold with safety to a man with even a large income if he has no stability and no character."[27] While character, depending on what one thinks, is within our control, stability often is not. Couzens's "warning against the continuance of practices which everyone who has had any experience at all knows to be unsound, unwise, and dangerous" went happily ignored as long as the economy chugged stably along. Those who grumbled, like the economist C. Reinhold Noyes writing in the *Yale Review*, about "financing prosperity on tomorrow's income" and the inevitability of the business cycle were unheeded.[28] Noyes held "the motor industry to be the storm centre of the next period of depression, and it will be entirely to blame" for infusing installment credit so thoroughly into the economy. The Depression, which he correctly predicted in 1927 to be "two or three years" away, would be "automatic and inevitable" as it was the result of "retribution for economic sin."[29] The "various bubbles" of cars and houses would burst and drag down the economy.

Noyes, like all bellyachers, was blissfully ignored. The celebrated economic pundits pronounced the late 1920s as a New Era forever free of recession. Expansion, made possible by the electrical age and enabled through credit, would continue forever. Another Yale economist, Irving Fisher—much more famous than Noyes for his optimism—pronounced in 1929 that stocks, in this new economy, would never fall again.

And then, three days later the world—including Yale—watched slack-jawed as the stock market crashed.

CHAPTER THREE

FANNIE MAE CAN
SAVE AMERICA
(1924–1939)

If owing money to a bank on a car threatened the yeoman ideal that Henry Ford held so dear, imagine how he felt about home mortgages. The "homestead" was at the center of the nineteenth century's independent ideals, yet in the twentieth century it was simply truncated to "home." A farm was more than a place to sleep and keep things; it was a place of production. Modern employees, in either a factory or an office, produced nothing at home and always had a boss. Farmers worked at home. Unless they had a mortgage, they didn't have to answer to anybody. If they had a mortgage, it was something to be ashamed of. A writer in *House & Garden* in 1931 "remember[ed] as a small boy being called upon to deliver the interest money for [his] grandmother."[1] The relationship was personal and terrifying. Knees knocking and hands trembling, he rapped on the door of the old man, whose "rough, whiskered face peered out" to collect his interest. Since his youth on the farm, "sentiment and usage" had changed.

Yet the feeling of independence in owning one's own home persisted. Another writer, in *The National Republic,* could casually write in 1932 that "today, as it was with the Founding Fathers, the American home is the cornerstone of American prosperity, and one of the national bulwarks of our national liberties."[2] The ready availability of mortgages had catapulted U.S. home-ownership rates to the highest levels in the world—but that ownership came at a price. The dangers of Americans' obsession with home ownership are nothing new. In the 1920s, a very similar set of financial services, such as the balloon mortgage and the mortgage-backed security, helped lead to the collapse of the housing market in the Great Depression. Every nightmare, however, begins with a dream.

If I told you that two young people fell in love, got married, and bought a house, you would not be surprised. If I told you that the house was bought with a balloon mortgage only a few years long and financed through mortgage-backed securities, you would probably shake your head but wouldn't be surprised. But if I told you that this was 1925 and not 2006, you would probably be shocked if you hadn't read the introduction. Though we consider mortgage-backed securities and balloon mortgages to be the recent inventions of Wall Street wizards, they have, in fact, a far longer history. In the 1920s, both kinds of financial instruments were widespread, underpinning the borrowing and lending of millions of Americans. Then, as now, the nature of these financial instruments led to tragedy as home owners across the country defaulted on their mortgages during the Great Depression. Like the stock speculators who borrowed on margin, home owners of the

1920s lived on the margin of their incomes to own their homes. How did the inherently unstable mortgage system of the 1920s become the stable thirty-year fixed-rate mortgage that we now remember to be "old-fashioned"?

A young couple, flush with love and short on cash, might have gone to a local savings and loan bank in 1924. This couple might have recently come to the city from the countryside, which in fact lingered in a depression, beginning in 1921, that would not fully abate until after World War II. In the cities, however, the United States' manufacturing economy flourished. Factories turned out all the appliances that installment credit could sell. With the husband finding a new job at the car factory, the couple could, after a year or two, apply for a mortgage. Looking over the application, the S&L's mortgage officer would examine only a few key qualities: how long had he had his job, how long had they lived at their current address, how much did he make? The wife's income and work history would count for nothing. Lenders assumed that as soon as she had a child, she would no longer work. At the end of the interview, the mortgage officer would tell them that they could get the longest possible mortgage—the ten-year mortgage—paying off the interest and the principal every month, but doing so would not get them the house that they wanted. In the housing boom of the 1920s, budgets were pushed to the limit to afford the rapidly built, shoddily constructed urban houses. An amortized mortgage was available but would reduce the price of the house the couple could buy. What the mortgage officer suggested and the couple cheerfully accepted instead was an interest-only balloon mortgage.

Balloon mortgages preyed on the optimism of 1920s home buyers, who, caught between resurgent prosperity and rising urbanization, bought into one of the great housing booms of the twentieth century. The wartime demand for city housing and city businesses drove rents as high as the skyscrapers themselves. Prices seemed as though they would rise forever. To make the monthly payments affordable, home buyers would pay only the interest on the mortgages. Every few years, the balloon mortgage would have to be refinanced. Borrowers rarely paid off the principal of the mortgage, counting on good job fortune or rising home values to make the interest-only payments worthwhile. Following the crash in 1929, that good fortune would be a long time in coming.

The collapse of the housing market was so catastrophic because the U.S. economy had come to depend on its unending growth. Along with automobiles, houses propelled the United States to a new prosperity. Writing in MIT's well-regarded but seldom read *Review of Economics and Statistics* in 1930, W. C. Clark remarked that when the "economist of the future compiles the business annals of the past decade, he will find the key to our prolonged and unprecedented prosperity in the stimulus provided by two great industries—building construction and automobile manufacturing."[3]

Looking back, it is hard to disagree with Clark's assessment, but nonetheless it seems odd. Houses and cars could not have been more dissimilar. Houses stay put; cars move. Houses were built on-site; cars came from massive factories on the other side of the country. Houses were made of wood, cars of metal. Houses were built to last; cars, despite what the salesman told you, would be around for at most a decade.

Despite these differences, economically cars and houses were perhaps uniquely similar. The United States had the highest rates of car ownership and house ownership anywhere in the world, 1 car for every 5.3 people. In France and Great Britain the ratio was more like 1 car per 44 people.

Houses and cars both consumed not just one kind of labor and one kind of materials but a nearly untold multitude. Houses needed wood and nails, but they also needed insulation, appliances, wiring, pipes, stone, and glass. By 1927, the auto industry consumed 64 percent of plate glass manufactured, 60 percent of upholstered leather, 14 percent of rolled finished steel, 22 percent of tin, 17 percent of lead, 12 percent of copper, 29 percent of nickel, and 13 percent of hardwood, as well as paints and other products. Houses needed carpenters, but they also needed architects, real estate agents, ditch diggers, masons, and general contractors. There was another way, too, in which houses and cars were similar: their reliance on consumer credit. Cars and houses were both bought on installment, and it was this crucial connection between demand and finance that brought the U.S. economy to its knees. More than most other products in the economy, buying a house or a car multiplied demand, as the dollars trickled down through the economy through all those hands and companies. When the demand for houses and cars fell, as it did in the early 1930s, the effect was multiplied throughout the economy.

After the crash of 1929, however, even Clark wondered if construction could regain its footing. His wonder should have been certainty. In 1925, 500,000 new homes were built.[4] By 1934, only 22,000 new homes were built, despite an additional 400,000 families needing shelter every year. To put it into perspective, more homes burned down in 1934 than were built.[5] Housing was at the center of the American economy, and restoring the building boom was necessary to animating it.

The construction boom of the 1920s was based on easy credit. Banks and other financial institutions made more money available for mortgages than ever before. State and federal regulators attempted to contain the lending, but in the midst of a bubble, where opportunity is everywhere, it is always difficult to be pessimistic. And lenders will find a way to lend more money. Banks lent as much as they could. In New York, for instance, state-chartered banks were allowed to lend up to 70 percent of their deposits as mortgages, which was liberal compared to the 50 percent limit imposed by the Federal Reserve on federally chartered banks. In 1925, only 13 percent had reached this limit. By 1929, two-thirds of New York banks had 65 to 70 percent of their deposits lent out. Balloon mortgages, then, were financed through local savings and loan banks, which depended, to a large extent, on the deposits of savings accounts to lend money out. Without today's CDs (which didn't exist until the late 1950s), drawing in sufficient deposits to meet demand for mortgage funds could be difficult. Running short on deposits, banks innovatively turned to bonds.

In the 1920s, savings and loan banks began to rely more upon another source for funds: the participation certificate (PC). The PC was like a bond. An investor bought it and received a monthly interest payment. At the end of a predetermined time, usually a few years, the principal of the bond could be redeemed. Unlike normal bonds, which were backed by the government or a corporation, these bonds were backed by mortgage payments, usually balloon mortgages. There was not the complicated financial machinery that exists in today's mortgage-backed security markets, but the basic idea was the same: money came into the bank from the mortgages and went out of the bank to pay the PC investors. Whether enough money was available at the bank to refinance the balloon mortgages of all those home owners depended on whether the PC investors decided to reinvest their money. In good times, when it seemed that mortgage borrowers could make their payments, PCs seemed like a reliable investment. *Time* magazine reassured readers in 1926 that "real estate bonds are by no means jeopardous investments. In fact, they should be the best of all securities, for they are backed by tangible buildings and real estate." The familiar fallacious reasoning reassured investors then, as now, of the inevitability of rising house prices. As houses went up in value, the investment became even more secure. "The scheme," as one banker writing in 1925 describing participation certificates, was "ingenious, convenient, self-sustaining, and extraordinarily safe and sound."[6] That is, until house prices fell.

Americans had learned during the war, through the wartime Liberty Bond drives, how to save by buying bonds. In 1918, like the many other bond houses advertising their broker services in *Scribner's*, Herrick & Bennett celebrated the patriotic and personal virtues of partial payment: "Thrift has helped France to hold back the Hun hordes and save freedom to the world. You can acquire the habit of thrift in no better way than by our partial payment plan. This plan will also enable you to subscribe to the Fourth Liberty Loan."[7] Buying bonds on the "part-payment" plan reinforced installment plan–like habits for millions of Americans. This new plan helped borrowers adjust to paying small amounts every month, which in turn partially enabled the mortgage boom of the 1920s.

Even more curiously, real estate bonds could be bought but could not be sold now. Real estate mortgages could be traded, and seasoned mortgage bonds—the ones that had been around a while and for which default seem unlikely—even more so. Yet few of those bonds ever saw a trading floor. From the get-go, they were toxic. Unlike houses or even mortgages, real estate bonds could be sold only to the bond houses that

Mortgage bonds, such as this one, helped to fuel the 1920s real estate boom and were one of the causes of the 1930s mortgage crisis.

had issued them (and then only if they were buying). For most investors, this lack of a secondary market didn't matter; they were unsophisticated small-time investors who believed in holding a bond to maturity. A bond was a prudent investment compared to the margin accounts of those who speculated in stocks. Though we toss stocks and bonds together in our ordinary, mad money–laden speech, "bond" has other meanings as well: fidelity, connection, trust, promise. A bond is a promise to an investor. A word can be a bond. Like honor and land, it is meant to be relied on to support you, even into your twilight years. Bonds had a moral valence that stocks lacked. Moral or not, without a secondary market, if the bond house went bankrupt, the bond was worthless.

Most buyers were not wealthy. Bond issues came in denominations as low as $100. Most buyers had never owned a corporate bond before. A salaryman or even a union man, the typical investor lived modestly and regular savings in bonds fit neatly into the monthly budget. Moreover, the investor believed in his bond house above all else. Every month the investor received a complimentary magazine from his bond house that mixed investment advice on the virtues of its bonds over the competition's with fascinating articles on medieval architecture or ancient archaeology. If nothing else, it should teach you never to trust anyone who mixes history and finance, especially when they are selling bonds.

For the small investor, the financial realities mattered less than the feeling of being part of history and part of the big game. Many real estate bonds backed commercial real estate. The Waldorf-Astoria hotel, then as now one of the most famous hotels in the world, issued real estate bonds bought by everyday Joes. At work, they could brag that they owned part of the new Waldorf-Astoria hotel. Even if the bond later defaulted, for a while, at least, the investor felt like a big shot.

Right from the outset, the real estate bond was trouble, for many of the same reasons that the mortgage business is in trouble today: the people selling the mortgages didn't put any of their own money at risk. Banks that issued mortgage bonds frequently insured them with large insurance companies—generally United States Fidelity and Guaranty Company, the National Surety Company, or Maryland Casualty Company—and used investors' capital.[8] More dubious were bonds issued outside of banks and brokered through "real estate bond houses." The bond issuers advertised aggressively and employed salesmen who received commissions on their sales volume. Volume, not reliability, drove profits. Despite the "guarantees" offered by the bond houses, usually the only guarantee was that of the bond houses' assets, which rarely constituted even a small fraction of the value of the mortgages they financed. Shoestring developers paid their architects and contractors in mortgages rather than cash, promising them a piece of the action down the line, putting none of their own money at risk. The largest companies—U.S. Mortgage & Title Guaranty Company (New York), Mortgage Guarantee Company (Baltimore), U.S. Mortgage Bond Company (Detroit), American Home Security Corporation (Chicago)—may have spread across the country, but wherever they were, the financial instruments they sold, and the companies themselves, encountered the same desperate fate in the Great Depression.[9]

The Federal Reserve was, in principle, opposed to banks issuing bonds but in practice tacitly condoned it. For instance, in July 1925, the Fed sent a scolding letter to the Lincoln Bank and Trust Company in Louisville, Kentucky, explaining that in "principle, the Federal Reserve Bank is strongly opposed to any method of banking which combines with the business of commercial banking the business of issuing debentures or selling real estate loans with the bank's guarantee."[10] Though the Federal Reserve Act of 1913 allowed banks in small towns to act as investment brokers, banks were not allowed to guarantee the interest or principal of such loans. Federal Reserve officials believed that "such business should be conducted by an institution other than one engaged in commercial banking."[11] Investment banking, which issued securities, was dangerous to blur with commercial banking, which lent money. Despite those beliefs, the Fed granted the Louisville bank an exception and allowed it to enter the securities business under a set of provisions so loose as to be meaningless. Lincoln Bank and Trust Company was to lend no more than ten times its capital. It should spin its mortgage business off into a separate company "as soon as it is able." Most tellingly, if it sold mortgages but maintained the guarantee, the mortgages could be moved off the account books entirely.

Lincoln Bank and Trust Company, like so many other banks across the country, got caught up in the real estate excitement and by 1929 had lent more than ten times its capital. The Federal Reserve Board, after consulting with the bank, decided that the earlier limits had been too stringent and the current lending levels were not "a matter of serious concern."[12] In short, the Fed protested the fusion of commercial and investment banking but did nothing to prevent it from happening, even when it had the power to do so. Trade associations also failed to contain the real estate bubble.

At the height of the excitement, in September 1925, the Farm Mortgage Bankers Association of America, at its annual convention (which that year was in Nashville, described adorably as the "dimple of the universe"), voted to become the Mortgage Bankers Association of America (MBAA).[13] Though the FMBA had been denounced as big-city bankers from the East (and that was true of the investors if not the bankers themselves), opening the members to urban lending marked the new primacy of urban lending. No longer would they just sell farm mortgages. The "great progress" in "standardizing and stabilizing the farm mortgage" meant that lenders, themselves in cities, began to take a closer look at their own concrete backyard. The bankers felt that "a national organization of city loan companies will develop and standardize the city loan business, increase the marketability of city loans and in many ways improve the service to both borrowers and investors."

Yet for all their visionary talk, the mortgage bankers were playing catch-up. Even after a brief recession in 1920–1921, urban America enjoyed President Warren Harding's "return to normalcy," while rural America languished in an enduring depression, which did not end until World War II. Mortgaging and expanding, farmers had expected food prices to rise forever, but in 1921, the price of corn fell from $1.85 per bushel to $0.41 per bushel and stayed there.[14] Grain and livestock prices—the mainstay of Great Plains agriculture—dropped similarly.[15] Presaging what was to come for the entire mortgage market in the 1930s, western farm mortgages in the 1920s hit unprecedented foreclosure levels.[16] Nationally, farm foreclosures rose. From 1913 to 1920, lenders foreclosed on 3.2 farms per thousand. From 1921 to 1925, that number tripled to 10.7. In the West the numbers were even more arresting. In 1926, North Dakota had 46.3, South Dakota 52.5, and Montana 60.8 foreclosures per thousand compared to the much lower Massachusetts 5.5, Ohio 11.2, and California 14.2. The overvalued farms collapsed in value. From 1920 to 1940, a farm acre in South Dakota lost 77 percent of its value.[17] Necessarily, then, mortgage bankers looked to the cities for new markets.

In the cities, the mortgage bond reached new heights of popularity in the mid-1920s. The MBAA estimated that in 1925, investors bought $675 million in mortgage bonds. In five years, the volume had increased more than 1,000 percent. According to the bankers, "the real estate mortgage bond is now firmly established as a standard form of safe investment, and the possibility of development in this field can hardly be exaggerated."[18]

Over the next year, editorials in the trade press pounded home the notion that including lenders who sold real estate bonds would only "develop the quality and marketability of their securities and they can prevent unreliable fly-by-night companies from continuing in the business."[19] The following year in Richmond, attendees denounced the "European corn borer" (a parasite) and "socialistic schemes" as the greatest coequal threats to the U.S. mortgage system.[20] By including urban lenders in their organization, they felt that the market would inevitably be safe, without the need for further government oversight. Confidently, the conventioneers retired to play golf at the nearby "course on the site of the battle and surrender at Yorktown." The first tee was at the "breach in the Cornwallis fortifications," while the "sixteenth fairway [was] the ground over which Alexander Hamilton made his attack." On "this spot [where] the freedom of America was established," the mortgage bankers celebrated their newly expanded membership and the stability it would bring to the U.S. mortgage system. The flow of capital to the cities followed the flow of people.

As the decade wore on, the inevitability of rising house prices seemed less and less certain. When, in 1925, Walter Stabler, who oversaw the investments of the Metropolitan Life Insurance Company along with those of prominent institutional investors, expressed suspicion of a real estate bubble in New York, an equally prominent developer denounced Stabler's comments as "more to be feared by the community in which we live than the utterances of Bolshevists."[21] Such words, the developer felt, "carr[ied] possibilities of grave disaster to the progress of our city and the nation." Pessimism about real estate was just un-American.

Despite the apparent Bolshevism of one of America's largest insurance companies, the system worked fine for a few years, as rising rents propped up profits and the buildings themselves. The first portent came in 1925, as the Florida real estate market, fueled by New York mortgage bond funds, began to burst. With the Miami Hurricane in 1926, the developments sank back into the swamps, along with investors' capital. In 1926, a financial hurricane hit New York as one of the largest bond houses—G. L. Miller & Company—collapsed after $50 million in defaults.[22] Mortgage bankers around the country wrung their hands in anxiety but consoled themselves that the system itself was sound. The Mortgage Bankers Association rolled out the ill-named "6-6-6 program" to reassure investors that with six guiding principles formulated over six months, the real estate bond market could be disciplined within a half year.[23] Even amid these crises, Americans invested approximately $1 billion in mortgage bonds in 1926. At their peak, real estate bonds funded one-quarter of all urban mortgage debt, equal in volume to the bonds of industrial corporations.

Particular examples of failure could not dampen most small investors' faith in the reason of real estate. Yet by 1927, even conservative probusiness groups such as the Rotary Club found naysayers castigating mortgage bonds in the pages of their official publications. A 1927 issue of the *The Rotarian* warned its membership that "under the old and established system of lending money on real-estate security it rarely happened that too much money was loaned . . . for the borrower and the lender were closer together than they are now." The article's author, the Harvard graduate, World

War I naval officer and investment banker Malcolm Lay Hadden, described the flow of mortgage funds as a "magic spring" of money, not unlike that famous Floridian fountain of youth that also poured forth the hope of eternal health. Florida, whether in fountains of youth or in real estate, always seems to disappoint. The crucial difference between the old mortgage system and the bond-backed system, he noted, was the the personal connection of borrowing. When lending happened at a distance—impersonally, through bond issues—the old social checks of personal obligation broke down. Without money at risk, a bond salesman's promise was as certain as eternal youth.

Without risk, intermediaries such as bond salesmen and shoddy contractors quickly erected buildings sold on bonds to take advantage of the opportunity for profit. The construction of the mid-1920s was notoriously unsound, but not as unsound as the finance underpinning it. By 1935, 80 percent of the $10 billion in real estate bonds outstanding would be in default. That the Securities Act of 1933 also discouraged real estate bonds mattered less, as one contemporary economist observed, than the "distaste already acquired by investors."

The regulation of real estate bonds was, of course, but one part of the sweeping federalization of consumer finance during the New Deal. In the aftermath of the Depression, the federal government felt that the states, which until the establishment of the Securities and Exchange Commission in 1934 regulated stocks and bonds, could not adequately oversee financial markets. "Blue-sky" laws, instituted by states in the 1910s and '20s to protect borrowers against stock frauds, worked only against those who peddled outlandish investments such as nonexistent oil wells and the rights to the eponymous blue sky. Bonds had the veneer of reality, backed up as they were by buildings and land. Real estate is, for better and worse, real. You can go to a house, tap its walls, walk around it, and even see how tall young Billy might have been on his eighth birthday. Blue-sky laws could do little to affect bad appraisals or underestimated risks. Though buildings are concrete, their values are not, and laws cannot set prices. They can only correct for bad intentions and misinformation—of which there were plenty.

The mortgage racket—old hat today—was new in 1931.

The "Mortgage Racket," as it was termed in a 1931 *Collier's* exposé by the assistant attorney general, Nugent Dodds, had "taken advantage of the traditional reputation for safety which the real estate mortgage [had] justly enjoyed."[24] That reputation was no more. Many fraudulent mortgage securities had been issued against existing securities—like the

CDO^2 and CDO^3 of today, collateralized debt obligations (CDOs) made of CDOs (squared) made of CDOs (cubed). In a boom era, when demand outstrips supply, it is all too easy to find the next sucker.

The foreclosure crisis of the Great Depression, it turned out, was more a problem of mortgage funds than unemployment. The "permanent mortgage," as the balloon mortgage was described, turned out to be fleeting.[25] After the crash, investors became bearish. Mortgage bonds, like all investments, seemed riskier. As the participation certificates came due, skittish investors stopped reinvesting and the amount of money available for mortgages dried up. Whereas throughout the 1920s home owners could expect to refinance their balloon mortgages, banks now demanded that they pay off the loan or face foreclosure. Few home owners could pay the principal on their mortgages all at once, having spent the 1920s simply paying the interest every month. Since all the lenders wanted their money at once, properties across the country were foreclosed on, further depressing the real estate market and making investment even more unwise. Rather than a smooth decline in prices, there was a collapse. As *BusinessWeek* styled it in a 1930 article, "the sins of the mortgage bonds are visited on the building field."[26]

When the crash happened, speculators desperately tried to cover their margin accounts. Suddenly, $195 million was withdrawn from American banks—the first decline in deposits in twenty years. In 1933, federally chartered banks alone held $1.2 billion in mortgage bonds and participation certificates.[27] If anything, $1.2 billion *underestimates* the loan volume before the mortgage crisis since just from 1932 to 1933, 805 banks, one-third of which offered mortgage bonds or participation certificates, left the Federal Reserve System. Banks offering such loans collapsed at twice the rate of banks that did not.[28] Locales with the highest proportion of lending—in Texas, for instance, mortgage bonds backed 53 percent of all loans—were hardest hit.[29] Luckily for banks, the bulk of that lending was insured, which, even if it doomed the insurance companies, saved the banks.

President Herbert Hoover launched a group to study the housing crisis in 1931, the White House Conference on Home Building and Home Ownership, whose ideas would provide the seedbed for many ideas we usually attribute to the New Deal. Hoover inaugurated the conference by reminding the attendees about the meaning of housing: "Those immortal ballads, Home, Sweet Home; My Old Kentucky Home; and the Little Gray Home in the West, were not written about tenements or apartments. They are the expressions of racial longing which find outlet in the living poetry and songs of our people." While the purpose of the conference was to "facilitate the ownership of homes and . . . protect the owners of homes," this larger cultural ambition could not be ignored.[30] The conference produced many ideas—including Hoover's proposal for a system of "home loan discount banks," which would become the nucleus of New Deal housing reform—but not enough action.

Foreclosures, which had been rising since the peak of the market in 1925, accelerated in 1931 and 1932. By 1933, the foreclosure rate hit one thousand homes a day. After four years of withdrawal-withered mortgage funds, the housing industry in 1933 was effectively dead, dropping to a tenth of the size it had been only a few years earlier. Without a viable housing industry, millions of skilled and unskilled construction workers filled the unemployment lists. One-third of the families on relief found their way there due to the loss of a construction job. Restoring the mortgage markets was crucial to the restoration of the economy. But to put the economy back onto a sound footing, the financial instruments that had gone so awry in the face of recession—balloon mortgages and participation certificates—would have to be done away with and a new way found to finance construction.

The collapse of the real estate bond market begged for government intervention. In New York State, where nearly half of the major bond houses were located, a mortgage commission was set up to have "control of mortgages and underlying collateral" that was liquidated by the state superintendent of insurance or the superintendent of banking. The "public," in this case 200,000 certificate holders who had invested $685 million, could not be held responsible for their situation. They had done no wrong save trusting in a supposedly sure thing. Just to be sure, however, New York State outlawed real estate bonds completely in 1936. Of course, by that point there were no longer any bond salesmen peddling them.

In desperation, Americans wrote to Eleanor Roosevelt, the first lady, nearly every day. The pleas encompassed all varieties of human need from simple justice to abstract theology ("Mrs. Roosevelt, what is spirit?"). Many letters to Mrs. Roosevelt concerned money, especially mortgages. In her monthly page in *Women's Home Companion,* she explained how the new government program, the Home Owners' Loan Corporation, could help them.[31] The Home Owners' Loan Corporation, inaugurated in 1933, arrested the collapse of the mortgage markets. Our young couple, if they found themselves unable to refinance their house, could turn to the HOLC for a new mortgage. The HOLC didn't pay off the mortgage but swapped 4 percent bonds for the mortgage in trouble, so that the home owners now owed the HOLC instead of the bank.

Applicants had a fifty-fifty chance of getting a new HOLC mortgage. Some people were just not good enough risks, and the HOLC had only a limited amount of capital. Equally possible, as Mrs. Roosevelt explained, a mortgage holder might simply refuse the HOLC bonds. Giving banks long-term government bonds in return for their toxic assets, the HOLC took the bad debt of millions of young couples off the books of the banks, refinancing one-fifth of all U.S. mortgages and injecting much-needed liquidity into the U.S. mortgage market. The free fall of housing prices stopped. The young couple could trade in their balloon mortgage for a longer fifteen-year amortized mortgage that kept monthly payments the same but guaranteed, at the end of those fifteen years, that the couple, not the bank, would own the house. Yet the HOLC, with its 20 percent foreclosure rate, could only stanch the fall of the markets. To put America's housing markets on a sound footing the whole mortgage system would have to be rebuilt.

During the Great Depression, Americans rethought their relationship to credit. The morality tale of borrowing began to change, largely through the new legitimacy of borrowing accorded by government programs. Change came slowly, however. In Josephine Lawrence's 1935 best-selling cautionary novel about consumer debt, *If I Have Four Apples,* the Hoe family, nominally in the "white-collar class," confronted the limits of borrowing in the midst of the Great Depression.[32] In her book Lawrence brought her own perspective to bear as a financial columnist for the *Newark Sunday Call,* where week in, week out, she counseled letter writers on how to best construct their budgets. The novel, in most ways, was a veiled critique of her readership, expressing both their opinions and what Lawrence saw as their mistakes.

In the fictional Mr. Hoe's opinion, a renter was nothing

but a "shiftless cuss" whose lack of self-reliance was what he thought was "filling up our institutions with paupers."[33] Yet, in his hope of being a good citizen and home owner, Mr. Hoe has mortgaged himself, like so many real Americans in the late 1920s, beyond his ability to repay. The Hoe family, burdened by mortgage debts exacerbated by Mr. Hoe's unemployment, struggles to make the payments on the numerous installment credit purchases made by Mrs. Hoe, even as Mr. Hoe increasingly locates his self-worth in his ever-more-perilous home ownership.

In desperation for advice on how to maintain her family's lifestyle, Mrs. Hoe writes to a newspaper columnist, Mrs. Bradley, who, based on Lawrence's own real-life work, publishes sample family budgets every week. The solution for the Hoes, Mrs. Bradley opines, is simply to live within their means without borrowing. For Mrs. Bradley, the arithmetic of budgets was invariant—"two and two make four"—apples despite the Hoes' wish that they make eight apples. *If I Have Four Apples* became a best seller because the problems Mr. Hoe and his family confronted as individuals besieged Americans as a whole in the 1930s and offered a way to understand the crisis in moral terms that readers could viscerally feel.

Yet the problem of "living within one's means" is never as straightforward as it might appear. If one's life is stable, then yes, a budget is very straightforward. If you know what is happening next month and even next year, planning is easy, and those who exceed their means have no one to blame but themselves. Debt and bankruptcy could easily be seen as a failure of character.

Most people do not live in such ideal circumstances. Nature can intrude in unexpected ways: for example, through pregnancy or illness. Even more unexpectedly, a job can be lost, even after years of diligent service. Economies lurch forward, and not everyone is brought along, despite how hardworking they might be. Wages might not rise as fast as inflation. Even the hardest workers might find that if and when they do get a job, it doesn't pay as much as the old one. Was this borrower irresponsible? Should we live our lives preparing for the worst? What should the balance between optimism and pessimism be? The answers to such questions depend less on the individual and more on the times in which that individual lives. In the Great Depression, it became strikingly apparent that even men who played by the rules, who did everything they were supposed to do, could still lose out.

Mr. Hoe's fictional problems were all too common real ones. His boom-era house was "flimsy," and although it could be "easily improved if he only had a few hundred dollars to spend on it," all his income went to the mortgage.[34] Because he had paid too much for his shoddily constructed house during the boom of the 1920s, Mr. Hoe could barely meet his mortgage payments as his wages fell. Desperate appeals to the Home Owners' Loan Corporation went unanswered for months and then were ultimately denied. Despite his own desire to work and to pay his bills, Mr. Hoe fell prey to forces beyond his control. He had done everything right, yet everything had turned out wrong. Though the book's narrator seems to support the budget as an economic panacea, Mr. Hoe had followed his budget. He had simply lost his job in the Great Depression. Millions of Americans, following the rules, had had the same experience, and suddenly it was no longer so clear that individuals were completely responsible for their economic lives. Structures, not spendthrifts, may have caused the Great Depression, but ideas about economic life were slower to change than circumstances.

Installment credit, like mortgages, helped consumers "follow the rules" while still getting what they wanted. Budgets promulgated by home economists in the 1920s to curb consumption and promote saving unwittingly helped promote installment credit. Planned expenditures were more virtuous than unplanned expenditures. Of course, this advice was given to help fit the many competing demands on a working-class household's dollar into a tight budget. Our Colorado trucker Archie Chadbourne earned $100 a month in 1927, of which $87.45 was already budgeted: "Groceries, $48; fuel, $7; rent, $23; lights, $2; 'phone, $2; Life insurance, $1.45; auto upkeep, $4.[35] With $12.55 to spare, his budget offered some wiggle room. But $12.55, even in 1927, went quickly. The budget didn't include furniture, clothes, doctor's bills, Christmas presents, eyeglasses, or schoolbooks. A proper middle-class 1927 budget would have included all those additional expenditures, as well as a margin for saving, but in practice, such things could not be shoehorned into a $100 budget. Installment credit allowed families like the Chadbournes to enjoy the amenities of the modern world without having to save for them in advance. Money already budgeted for installment payments was money that wasn't wasted.

While critics of installment credit lamented how much money families lost by not saving up in advance for their purchases, financial advisers emphasized that consumption, as long as it was budgeted for, was fine. Installment credit, which spread payments over many months, fit neatly into this scheme, even as the interest costs sapped wealth. Families allocated money not over a lifetime but from month to month. Overall costs mattered less than fitting expenditures and savings into the budget. Consumers could buy through installment credit without violating the moral rules of the budget. A phonograph's installment payments became the budgetary equivalent of rent or food. Bills are bills.

In the New Era economy of the late 1920s, a lack of thrift, though morally dubious, would not threaten the country. In the aftermath of the stock market crash, what had passed as merely profligate now seemed traitorous. The very centrality of installment credit to the New Era is what made it so susceptible to blame for that era's demise. Historians today do not believe that overextension of installment credit caused the Great Depression—they don't even discuss it as a viable possibility—but to those who lived through the Great Depression, installment credit's role was more certain.[36] Installment credit, in this view, was akin to the speculative credit that had fed the stock market bubble. The "artifice" of installment credit attracted much blame. In 1932, for example, a Johns Hopkins economics professor identified credit among the three main causes of the Depression: "perversion of the stock exchanges," "degradation of banking," and "reckless installment selling."[37] He argued that by hampering savings, America's installment credit "retard[ed] the growth of its productive capital" and "morally . . . it loosened the restraint upon recklessness in optional expenditures." By enabling the demand for goods that consumers could not otherwise afford—or worse, for which they could budget installment payments but refused to save—installment credit encouraged overinvestment in productive capacity, which could be made profitable only by what *The New York Times* called the "continuing and increasing doses of the [installment credit] stimulant."[38] Unearned and not quite real, this "artificial stimulus" smacked of excess. As in the stock market bubble, there was only a symbolic value, not a real one. The shocking experience of the crash emerged from the economy's very unreality. As the undersecretary of the Treasury wrote in 1932, the "sweeping decline was . . . inevitable" because "the country was living too much on credit."[39] The director of the Federal Reserve Bank of St. Louis, Max Nahm, argued that "if we could pay the debt of the world today, the depression would be over tomorrow."[40] Saving, not spending, would bring prosperity. Only after the reckoning and the restoration of a moral and economic order based on real values could recovery begin. A 1932 National Industrial Conference Board study found that the most common solution offered by business executives for ending the Depression was "a return to the early principles of individual thrift." The denunciation of borrowing held so much weight because it felt so ethically right—even if it was economically wrong.

Economists argued, backed by sound reasoning, that by committing their payments to goods already purchased, consumers could no longer buy new goods or services. The expansion of purchasing power in good times through installment credit worked only to prevent spending in bad times, hampering recovery. According to this view, paying back the $3 billion of installment debt owed in 1929 required forgoing new purchases, condemning the U.S. economy to years of languishing depression.[41] Substantial fractions of purchasing were done on the installment plan. Even if the lenders were happy because the loans were repaid, for the economists concerned with the larger picture and not the lenders' profits, it did not obviate the fact that consumer dollars repaid interest and did not buy real, tangible commodities. Without consumer demand today, the economy would not recover tomorrow.

Though critics of installment credit in the 1920s expected its lenders to go under in a serious depression and the borrowers to be punished through repossession, much to their chagrin, reality differed.[42] Surprisingly, lost jobs and tighter budgets did not lead the majority of consumers to default on their payments. For example, in 1931, the customers of the large finance company Commercial Investment Trust had repaid 95 percent of their outstanding loans within one year of the crash.[43] The next year, a finance industry analyst claimed that consumers had repaid more than 99 percent of the money loaned by finance companies in 1929.[44] Even Herbert Hoover's assistant secretary of commerce, the Harvard economist Julius Klein, announced that "the alleged weaknesses in the system had failed to materialize."[45] Klein provided the clearest rejoinder to critics of consumer credit: "the installment plan, with all its flourishing growth, has created no new economic danger. As a system, it has now been put under the most grilling of tests by a world business Depression of almost unparalleled intensity and it has demonstrated its right to survive." American consumers of the 1930s could be counted on to fulfill their obligations. But even if Americans kept their promises, they did restrain their spending, particularly when they lost their jobs. Durable goods spending fell by half and durable goods manufacturing, on which most of installment credit was based, fell to a fifth of its 1929 level by 1932.[46]

Americans across the country had unemployment stories like Mr. Hoe's that tangled austere budgets and unfortunate job losses, although their desperation, unlike his fictional account, was all too real. For policy makers confronting the economic ruin of the Great Depression, where to start rebuilding and how to do it were the greatest questions of the day. Should programs focus on the poorest, or should they try to mobilize the still extant money of the wealthy? Should the government rely on the private sector, or had capitalism failed? The correct path was uncertain, but a path had to be chosen. It was a time of experimentation.

Common sense and recent experience were dead set against using credit, in any form, to get out of the Depression. There was even less sympathy for debt relief for those like the Hoe family who mismanaged their money, prioritizing luxuries over solvency. Lawrence's mouthpiece character, Mrs. Bradley, echoes, no doubt, the feeling of many readers: "Must the tax-payers who haven't as yet been ruined, be forced to undertake the support of five people who couldn't struggle through a world that didn't include oil burners and Venetian blinds?"[47] Oil burners and Venetian blinds were the iPods and granite countertops of their day, and, as now, those who avoided eco-nomic troubles blamed the insolvent for their own poor deci-sions. Decisions prudently made during prosperity took on a new cast during a recession. Yet if sophisticated bankers could not handle the Depression, how could a housewife's budget?

Some members of President Franklin D. Roosevelt's inner circle, the New Deal Brain Trust, saw real American families' needs for better housing and financing not as a tragedy but as an opportunity. They shared Mrs. Bradley's belief that the Hoe family were "not charity cases," that the family had "a foundation on which to build," and if the promise of Amer-ica was to be a meaningful one, "they musn't be allowed to lose out."[48] Government planners answered Mrs. Bradley's, and Lawrence's, question, "Suppose the economic system *is* cock-eyed, need we scrap arithmetic? Isn't it still a practical science?" but not in the manner she would have liked. In the Hoe family, FHA planners saw a huge untapped demand for better housing as a possible solution to the Depression. A fixed wage could be turned, through the right policy, from a constraint into an opportunity. FDR and his advisers—the famous Brain Trust—would figure out ways to enable American home owners to borrow more, not less, hoping to harness that magical possibility of deferred payment—of turning four apples into eight—to restart the economy.

In 1934, the Federal Housing Administration (FHA) rolled out an audacious plan to remake, from the ground up, the entire way Americans borrowed. Unlike the other New Deal housing programs, the FHA didn't directly build anything; it simply provided a new way for capital to be invested in houses. The FHA channeled private capital back into the construction industry—without spending any taxes. Without nationalizing the housing industry, the government fashioned a new financial system to replace the inherently unstable mortgage system of the 1920s.

The leader of this transformation was James Moffett. Moffett, unlike the ivory tower–drawn Brain Trusters, had been a vice president of Standard Oil of New Jersey (the forerunner of today's ExxonMobil) and so brought a hard-nosed business sense to the FHA that was perceived to be lacking in other New Deal agencies. No stranger to Washington regulators, Moffett had helped write the National Recovery Administration's oil codes governing prices, wages, and other trade arrangements. In writing the oil code, he had even worked side by side with the prominent Brain Truster Secretary of the Interior Harold Ickes.[49]

As today, in 1933 private capital piled up in the coffers of bankers, who were too afraid to lend it. President Roosevelt and Moffett agreed that for the economy to reignite, capital needed to flow nationally. FDR believed that a national mortgage market would be a more stable and just mortgage market. Writing to Moffett, he reaffirmed to him "that the refunding of existing mortgages in long term, amortized mortgages . . . will result in a safer mortgage structure for the country."[50] But FDR's vision was not just about market stability. If Hoover had promised a chicken in every pot, then FDR took it to the next level, believing that "lowering the cost of homes to the great mass of our people [was] worthy of our best efforts."

Not all those in the Brain Trust agreed. As Moffett headed the FHA, so too did Ickes go on to administer the alternative to the FHA, the Public Works Administration (PWA). Ickes wanted billions of dollars in government funds to build public housing through the PWA, declaring:

> I've seen no evidence that the holders of private capital are ready to use it. We can't sit around indefinitely waiting for private capital to get going. . . . If private industry charges rates socially too high, why shouldn't we compete? . . . We could build very attractive houses at a low rate of interest. We've been paying 3% for money, whereas private financiers have to pay much more. Conceivably we can make an agreement with labor so that we can pay lower rates and offer year round work.[51]

As Ickes told the press his position shortly after Moffett had announced the FHA's program, Moffett could not have been more outraged. Moffett had a short fuse (his wife, Kim, would divorce him in 1937 for his "ungovernable temper") and quickly called a press conference.[52]

The plan, as announced only a few days earlier, was nothing short of a revolution in finance. No longer would home owners have to borrow on balloon notes for a few years. Instead they could borrow for fifteen or twenty years—a period of time that bankers had previously thought was an immoral length of time to keep a borrower in debt. Moral or not, long-term mortgages stabilized the housing markets and increased the quality of U.S. housing stock. The loans could be only for good housing that would last for that long a period, and the government would inspect all the houses to make sure they met approved standards. Finally, with guaranteed mortgages, the risk fell to nothing, and FDR wanted mortgage rates—as high as 12 percent—to fall as well. FHA mortgages cost a fixed 5 percent nationwide.

The most imaginative part of the FHA plan was that, unlike for the HOLC, the government would not pay for any of it. Lenders would chip into an insurance pool, organized by but not paid for by the federal government, and if there was a default on a mortgage, the lender would be paid out of the pool. Paid in low-yielding bonds, the lender would not lose the principal of the mortgage, but neither would the lender have an incentive to wildly lend to the uncreditworthy. With such a long repayment period, the monthly payments could incorporate both an interest payment and a payment on the principal. Amortizing the mortgage, as such a plan is called, eradicated the need for refinancing that had made the balloon mortgages so precarious. A long period made the mortgages independent of short-term fluctuations in the economy. Borrowers would not have to weather unemployment and refinancing at the same time. The FHA preserved private choice while accomplishing a public good. Lenders did not *have* to comply with the FHA, but if they did, their business was so much easier to conduct. Risk-free loans with guaranteed buyers provided an incredible—and noncoercive—

incentive to lend private capital. Unlike Ickes's plans, which would have competed with private industry, Moffett's fostered private industry.

Confident in his new system, Moffett summoned reporters to his office, denounced Ickes, and told them that "such a plan would wreck a 21-billion-dollar mortgage market and undermine the nation's real estate values. If the Government steps in now to finance housing projects when private capital is able and willing to do it, our whole program will be wrecked."[53] The press naturally had a field day reporting the rancor within the administration, and the White House was forced to issue a press release claiming that there had been a "misinterpretation" of the differences in policy. But those differences were real, and they were based on whether or not one believed that all that idle capital could once again be mobilized to drive the economy. The two men's tempestuous relationship reflected the difficult personality of Moffett, the stubbornness of Ickes, and their substantially different perspectives on the future of American capitalism after the failure of the mortgage markets.

The American public embraced the FHA in a way that the rest of the New Deal was viewed suspiciously. Seeing "federal mortgage," many believed that the government was lending money. For a public that had elected FDR on a platform of balanced budgets, government spending was an outrage. After some considerable public outreach, however, middle America came to embrace the new mortgage system. Magazine articles, like one in *Time*, described the difference between the "old-fashioned mortgage that was renewed in good times and foreclosed in bad" and the new FHA loans, outlining the differences in repayment period, interest rates, and amortization.[54] Moffett authorized pamphlets explaining how the building and banking industry could both profit from the FHA. Animosity toward government spending remained but support of the FHA grew. Public opinion lashed out against Ickes's PWA housing plan as nothing but a "rent dole" instead of a wage dole. His programs diverted taxes to pay for the "chiselers."[55] To directly spend tax dollars was Ickes's way, but Moffett's way, which didn't spend government dollars, was an easier sell to taxpayers.

To make the FHA successful, however, required Moffett to sell "the excellence and security of this type of investment"— as FDR described the home mortgages—to the banks and insurance companies that had just watched their sure-thing mortgages evaporate, not just the potential home owners. When the FHA remade borrowing, it also remade investing. The Federal Reserve, as well as the new agency to oversee the savings and loan banks, the Federal Home Loan Bank Board, forbade participation certificates. Banks would have to find a new source of capital to lend that would not depend on the caprice of local big shots.

The government created a new entity to fund these mortgages—Fannie Mae or, as it was officially named, the Federal National Mortgage Association (FNMA). Fannie Mae acted as a middleman between large institutional investors and local lenders, buying and selling mortgages. Whereas in the 1920s banks would hold on to the mortgages and receive funds from investors in participation certificates, under the new system banks would sell the mortgages to Fannie Mae, which, in turn, would resell them directly to investors. Since the mortgage bonds had been valueless without a place to sell them, FNMA created a place where any mortgage—as long as it complied with FHA regulations—could be resold. Within a year, FNMA bought $285,000 ($4.4 million in 2010 dollars) worth of mortgages every day. Whereas a local savings and loan was dependent on local investors, Fannie Mae could resell those mortgages anywhere in the country. Large institutional investors, such as the New York Life Insurance Company, began to buy the mortgages in large numbers, and those institutional investors would not run scared at the first sign of a downturn. Until the 1930s, the mortgage business had been a local business, but now it became national. Realtors and bankers lobbied for all mortgages to be resold, but Fannie Mae held firm (conventional mortgages would not be resold until Freddie Mac's chartering in 1970).[56] Roosevelt's dream of a low-cost mortgage for Americans was realized. Moffett, who was temperamentally unsuited to political work, retired quickly from the FHA to return to the oil business, but not before telling the president that in just a year, the FHA had generated $351 million in building construction and created 750,000 jobs—all without spending any tax money.[57]

The two financial instruments that had caused the mortgage crisis of the early 1930s—balloon mortgages and participation certificates—disappeared, replaced by long-term, amortized mortgages and the national networks of Fannie Mae. The new mortgage system inaugurated a new stability upon which postwar prosperity was built. With substantial down payments and enough time to pay back the mortgages, foreclosures plummeted. The suburbs, where the postwar American dream would flourish, were built through this new mortgage system. Insurance companies bought billions of dollars in mortgages from Fannie Mae, enabling home owners to borrow to buy their piece of the American dream. Never again would a young couple want for a house simply because they didn't have the money.

If the FHA and Fannie Mae saved the American house, it also, at the same time, saved the American car, that other crucial element of Americans' aspiration. Ickes's plan for public housing in cities would have produced a landscape ripe for mass transit. Instead, the FHA program promoted the 1930s ideal of housing: suburban cul-de-sacs accessible only by car. Better-planned subdivisions would have a more "favorable loan rating" and be easier to sell and finance.[58] The FHA planners preferred colonials and lawns, and their regulations on what determined a "good" investment reflected their ideals. In one fell swoop, W. C. Clark's fears for the U.S. economy, reliant as it was on houses and cars, could be assuaged.

An unfortunate—but significant—side effect of the planners' ideals led their suburban cul-de-sacs to openly condemn occupancy by minority groups, especially African Americans. FHA policies encouraged deed restrictions to ensure all-white neighborhoods, seen as necessary for the stability of the investment. Because of those policies, even well-intentioned racial liberals found it difficult to find financing for interracial or even African-American suburbs. In one simple document, the FHA planning manual created the suburb for whites and the ghetto for blacks.[59] The state has great power to reshape capitalism—for good and for bad.

If the big purchase had been fixed by Fannie Mae, other kinds of purchases remained outside government regulation. Though not nearly as important in terms of credit volume, credit for clothes and other goods constituted the everyday world of credit. Though Moffett may have returned stability to mortgage markets, his own life remained tumultuous. Ironically, after his divorce in 1937, his daughter, described by

Time as "Beauteous Adelaide Moffett Brooks, [the] widowed 24-year-old socialite who sometimes sings in nightclubs," filed for bankruptcy. Owing nearly $10,000, she claimed, "I guess I was too fond of buying clothes."[60] Her story, the story of clothes, department stores, and ultimately credit cards, is the other thread of borrowing that will lead us into postwar America.

CHAPTER FOUR

HOW I LEARNED TO STOP WORRYING AND LOVE THE DEBT (1945–1960)

Tuning in to the first episode of *The Honeymooners* in 1955, suburban Americans gladly watched everything that they had left behind. No longer did they live in the cramped, hot apartments of their urban youth. Freezers that could hold a month's food had replaced antiquated iceboxes. Sitting in their spacious dens, viewers watched Alice Kramden, the exasperated working-class wife, explain to her bus-driving husband, Ralph, what she really wanted and what the suburban viewers already had:

> I . . . want a television set. Now, look around you Ralph. We don't have any electric appliances. Do you know what our electric bill was last month? Thirty-nine cents! I want a television set, and I'm going to get a television set. And what do you care about it? You're out all day long. And at night what

are you doing? Spending money playing pool, spending money bowling, or paying dues to that crazy lodge you belong to. And I'm left here to look at that icebox, that stove, that sink, and these four walls. Well I don't want to look at that icebox, that stove, that sink, and these four walls. I want to look at Liberace![1]

Suburbanites could not only enjoy Liberace, the piano-playing sensation of the 1950s, on their television sets, but everything else that the suburbs offered. Postwar America entered a twenty-five-year boom that, unlike any boom before or since, raised the living standards of the middle more than those at the top. Poverty still abounded, particularly in the cities and the country, but in between, in the suburbs, a new, prosperous America was being created. Though the suburbs exuded conformity, for most people the conformity was welcome. After the hardships of the Great Depression and World War II, Americans longed for comfort and stability. If the monotonous suburbs looked "like Russia with money," as 1950s intellectuals claimed, that money made all the difference. The money that made the difference, however, was not theirs.

The postwar dream of suburban living was made possible through debt. Living in mortgaged homes, driving in financed cars, postwar Americans relaxed at new shopping centers—where they purchased televisions on credit. While many baby boomers remember their parents wheeling that new Zenith into the living room, few know how that television was purchased. That first television set, bought around 1950, was bought, for most people, on credit. Televisions were expensive. In 1946, the first year TVs were on the market, only 0.02 percent of all households had one. Two years later, in 1948, they still cost $440—not including the installation of that rooftop aerial. The volume of television sales necessary to bring down the price relied on consumer credit. Americans didn't have $400 for a television, but they could borrow it. By 1955, two-thirds of households had a nice black-and-white. Americans borrowed so much that department stores, which sold televisions alongside clothes and furniture and which had branched into the suburbs to follow their formerly urban clientele, had more money tied up in consumer charge accounts than in their inventory. Televisions, cars, and revolving credit made everything better than in those cramped apartments in the city.

The borrowing began as soon as you left the city to tour an as-yet-unbuilt development. Looking over floor plans in a small office next to fields of semibuilt houses, prospective home owners reviewed the many borrowing options in easy-to-read pamphlets. Returning veterans could borrow easily thanks to the VA loan program, through which, with nearly nothing down, a family could purchase a new home. Even for nonveterans, the FHA provided easy financing with relatively low down payments. Fannie Mae bought and resold the mortgages for both programs, making all those FHA and VA loans possible. Half of all new construction was federally financed after World War II. Such federal programs provided ready financing for millions of borrowers even long after the war ended. For suburban buyers, mortgages were easy to come by, whether federally insured or not. If a house was good enough to be federally insured, local savings and loan banks would be willing to lend on it. Meeting FHA building standards meant that subdivisions could easily sell off their homes and home buyers could easily borrow for them.

Macy's Sale of
TELEVISION

COMPARE THESE SETS WITH OTHER FAMOUS BRANDS SELLING FOR MUCH MORE AND SEE WHAT BUYS THESE ARE!

$139† $169† $169†

17″ HYDE PARK
TABLE SET,
WOOD CABINET

20″ HYDE PARK
LIFE-SIZE
TABLE SET

17″ HYDE PARK
OPEN FACE
CONSOLE SET

$199† $229† $279††

19″ HYDE PARK
OPEN FACE
CONSOLE SET

20″ HYDE PARK
DELUXE FULL
DOOR CONSOLE

20″ HYDE PARK
3-WAY
COMBINATION

Why do you pay so little for fine quality TV when you buy 'Macy's-Own' Hyde Park?

We buy direct—your price does not include extra handling costs.

We buy in vast quantities—as you'd expect from the World's Largest TV and Music Centre. The savings through this big-buying are passed right on to you.

We sell in vast quantities—more people buy TV at Macy's than any place else in the world. These big-selling savings are passed right on to you.

Add them all together and you'll realize why Macy's can put such low prices on such fine sets

All Hyde Park sets have:

Black-faced tubes that reduce glare, make viewing easy on the eyes.

Built-in tunable antennas.

Wood cabinets have a lustrous hand-rubbed mahogany finish, decorator-styled.

All sets rigidly tested and approved by hard-to-please Macy's Bureau of Standards.

Use Macy's Cash-Time Plan

Macy's gives you the most liberal purchase terms allowed by the latest government credit regulations. Just 15% down puts any of these superb sets in your home. Take up to 18 months to pay; small service charge.

†Add $20 for Federal Excise Tax and manufacturer's warranty for 1 year on picture tube and 90 days on all other parts. Installation and service extra, if desired. AC only.

††Add $30 for Federal Excise Tax and manufacturer's warranty for 1 year on picture tube and 90 days on all other parts. Installation and service extra, if desired. AC.

Sorry, no mail or phone orders.

MACY'S
WORLD'S LARGEST TV AND MUSIC CENTRE—MACY'S FIFTH FLOOR

Also at Macy's-Parkchester • Macy's-Jamaica • Macy's-Flatbush • Macy's-White Plains

See other 14′, 16′, 17′, 19′, and 20′ sets; table models, open face and de luxe full door consoles, 3-way combinations

MACY'S 6% CASH POLICY ON PRICING ITS GOODS: **WE ENDEAVOR TO SAVE OUR CUSTOMERS AT LEAST 6% FOR CASH, EXCEPT ON PRICE-FIXED GOODS**

See other Macy news on pages 13, 19, 24, 79, 82 and 87

Macy's offered televisions on their "cash-time" plan.

Once the house was built and the happy family moved in, they were faced with an immediate dilemma, unique to prosperity: how to fill the house? If Jane Austen knew that a single man in possession of a good fortune must be in want of a wife, the Macy's credit manager knew, just as certainly, that "no woman moves without wanting to redo her new house."[2] To make sure that Macy's and not a competitor got her business, credit was used to lure her into the branch department store. Into the roomier houses came a trove of goods bought, to a large degree, on credit. After buying a home, of course, you got an address and a mailbox next to the curb. In this mailbox, shortly after you moved in, you found your very first Charga-Plate vying for its slice of consumer dollars.

The story of the Charga-Plate didn't begin when postwar home owners moved in to their new ranch houses but far away in New York City, at Bloomingdale's on Lexington Avenue and 59th Street. To understand what was different about the postwar credit card, we have to understand what came before it. From the 1910s to the 1930s, middle-class women shopped at department stores such as Macy's and Bloomingdale's and a hundred other local retailers. What those stores had in common, as they'd had since the late nineteenth century, when the department store was invented, was that they had it all. The department store in the late nineteenth century was the Amazon.com of its time. Before the department store, shoppers had to travel all over town to specialty shops, where, in dark rooms filled with musty shelves, storeowners would show pricey merchandise. At the department store, shoppers moved among columns of marble lit by sunlight beaming through broad sheets of window glass. Goods were encased in perfectly clear displays to be admired and fawned over. A woman could go there for everything from kid gloves to evening gowns. A hundred clerks—often handsome young men—served the vast throng, offering merchandise identical to that of the specialty stores but for far less. Away from the floor, in a room plush with leather, the manager oversaw his many departments, each replicating—and ultimately replacing—a specialty shop.

In the city, the department store offered convenience. One subway or taxi ride and the day's shopping could be finished. There was no need to wade through the slush of a Boston winter. Shoppers knew that the prices were fair. Many department stores, after the advent of phones, even took orders. Perhaps most importantly for our story, department stores—owing to their sales volume—offered copious credit. In those stores, shoppers—generally women—charged their purchases to an account, which was billed at the end of the month. Those charge accounts had to be paid each and every month—promptly. From its inception in the nineteenth century until World War II, this charge account, thought of as a shopper convenience like gift wrap, defined department store credit.

In the 1910s and '20s, another form of credit was developed by department stores: the coupon book. Unlike charge accounts, the coupon book offered shoppers an option not to pay at the end of each month. Like installment credit, payments could be spread out. To get that kind of long-term credit took a long discussion with the credit manager, who would judge you, your budget, and your whole life. The credit manager would be doing you, the customer, a favor. In return for this inspection, a customer could get a coupon book for a very limited amount of money, such as $25. Every time the coupon book ran out, the customer had to go through the same rigamarole, injuring the borrower's pride. For those with less money, begging for credit limited the appeal of the coupon books, which, though widely available, were seldom used.

Moral lectures were inevitably part of meeting with the credit manager. Enforcing repayment fell to the store's credit department, but the credit manager's tone would be considered inappropriate. Rather than just bean pushers, credit managers considered themselves replacement husbands for women shoppers gone astray—almost *in loco husbandis*.[3] In the absence of husbands, credit managers were expected to manage wives' spending. Weak husbands could be called to task by credit managers for not being able to "control" their wives' spending. A credit limit, when it existed, reflected not a credit rating but the extended household authority of a husband, who asked the store to control his wife in his stead.

This idea of the responsible husband and spendthrift wife had long existed as a truth of the middle class. For the working class, however, the gender roles were inverted. Workingmen were considered to be the spendthrifts, passing their time at saloons while smoking cigars. One of the main arguments for Prohibition had been banning not alcohol consumption but the place where so many working-class men frittered away their income: the saloon. In 1915, a few years before Prohibition's enactment in 1920, *The Washington Post* had a Valentine's Day letter contest on the question of "whether husbands or wives were more extravagant." The top letter, from Mrs. Marie Roye, won $1 by writing that "the fact remains that in every city in the world, saloons, redlight districts, billiard rooms, poolrooms, bowling alleys, cigar and cigarette stores . . . are all kept up by men. . . . No matter what women spend frivolously, they have a long ways to go to even up with the not only useless, but pernicious, extravagances of men."[4] Throughout the

1920s, private clubs maintained legal repositories of liquor. Only the so-called workingman's club felt the strong arm of the law. Working-class men, unlike middle-class men, could not be trusted to keep to the budget. Household instructional books and pamphlets of the 1910s and 1920s aimed at responsible working-class wives encouraged them to take the entirety of their husband's paychecks, distributing the cash among envelopes labeled "rent," "groceries," and the like, and returning only a small amount to him to placate him. The idea of women as natural spendthrifts applied only to women with money. Department stores, which catered to the middle class, reinforced this idea of women's spending, but it was only well-to-do women who needed to be controlled.

The credit manager would control a middle-class wife's spending so that the debt would never run too high and

HOW TO MONEY-TRAIN YOUR WIFE

▶ *put the facts on the table, share the decisions*

▶ *budget together (but guard your own lunch money)*

▶ *set a good example, and keep calm at all times*

Articles like "How to Money-Train Your Wife" reinforced the idea that a husband was the only restraint on a wife's spending. Only by training her to budget could her "spendthrift" ways be held in check.

wreck the respectable household budget. Though the credit manager was seen as powerful, in practice he was not. Castigating as he called the customers into his office, the credit manager truly feared that customers would never shop there again or, worse, never pay back the debt.

Despite what customers were "supposed" to do, bills often went unpaid for months, as customers used charge accounts to finance their purchases over a long period of time. Credit managers who were too tight with lending scared off customers. The only thing worse than an unpaid debt was a customer so offended by the collection that she never came back. It was better to write off a bad debt than to, as one financial advice magazine put it, "get a reputation for being hard with charge account customers."[5] Stores needed charge account customers. While regular customers bought something in only 37 percent of visits, charge customers bought something 57 percent of the time.[6] To keep that goodwill, stores sent collection, or "dunning," letters in a choreographed manner, designed to remind borrowers that they had a moral and financial obligation to repay.

While extreme measures could be taken to repossess durable goods, in the softer lines of department stores, debt collection relied on a moral, not a contractual, relationship. Department stores would inevitably lose money if they took every slow-paying customer to court. But money had to be collected somehow. Debt collection was an elaborate dance that began with a gentle reminder. If the customer still did not pay, a follow-up letter used stronger language, as in this example from a 1922 collection guide: "It grieves us to be forced to write you again in the matter of the delayed payments on your account. You have shown no inclination whatsoever to abide by our monthly settlement terms, established for all alike, and after careful consideration of the account, we are obliged to withdraw credit privileges."[7] Even in 1922, when furniture stores regularly employed a team of strong-backed men and a city marshal to denude a working-class apartment, the department store, catering to a more affluent clientele, felt the need to be gentle. The trouble with such letters was that middle-class propriety was very sensitive. A customer who lost her credit at a store might never shop there again—perhaps even loudly complaining to her friends about her ill treatment. Credit could be a public relations nightmare. Slow pays and no-pays were all too common but had to be endured for the sake of customer relationships.

The credit department, like other convenience services, was a money pit. Unpaid accounts paid no interest. When a bill was overdue, the store had to carry the debt. Slow-paying customers and defaulters cost the store money. All customer credit was financed internally, as clothing stores—then known as draperies—had done since they had sold nothing but calico and silk. Like the gift-wrapping department, the credit department was a service the store offered to woo customers in from competitors. It lost money, but it helped sales. Customers with a line of credit shopped at the same store week in, week out.

In 1938, a little-noticed program at Bloomingdale's, the famous New York department store, was about to end the credit department's inferior status and begin to change the ways in which Americans borrowed. In 1938, Bloomingdale's rolled out a new credit program for its customers: the permanent budget account (PBA). "A new type of extended payments," the PBA allowed customers the flexibility not to pay their whole bill every month. Of course, not paying their bills every month was what many already did. The PBA institutionalized an existing practice. The slow pay became standard. It incorporated rule breaking into the rules themselves. In the PBA, payments could run as long as six months. Unlike installment credit, not every individual purchase would be spelled out on contract but aggregated into one bill. Who would want to repossess socks? In return for this flexibility, the store would charge a small amount of interest. No longer would dunning letters go out and offend slow-paying customers. The customers, for the first time, would be in control of their spending and repayment—for a fee. This new kind of credit was called revolving credit, and the PBA was the first time, but not the last, that consumers had access to its possibilities.

World War II initially interrupted this grand scheme as the government instituted widespread credit controls. Like other department stores, Bloomingdale's shut down the PBA program in 1941 along with its other credit programs. The federal government froze charge accounts and installment credit alike to control inflation as commodities ran scarce. Toward the end of the war, however, retailers less law-abiding than Bloomingdale's realized that the government's regulations did not apply to this new kind of revolving credit. By wartime's end, the idea of revolving credit had spread across the country. As peace returned, revolving credit, like the PBA, found its place alongside preexisting forms of credit.

Unlike those other forms of credit, revolving credit was uniquely suited to postwar America. Whatever one's budget, revolving credit made all purchases possible by splitting up the payments over many months. With revolving credit, rich women and poor alike could say, "Charge it!" at the checkout line and hand the cashier a shiny metal Charga-Plate with their account number. There was no need to hand over the installment coupon book and show that you could not afford a "regular" charge account. The other shoppers, and the clerk, would not know the income difference between the rich and the middling. The flexibility of revolving credit eliminated the insulting moments with the credit manager as well. Never again would a woman have to grovel for more time from a male credit manager; she could pay just a small finance charge and take care of it next month. Only once would she have to go up to that well-advertised credit office on the sixth floor. At Bloomingdale's, the PBA changed the moral meaning of borrowing.

In return for this flexibility, shoppers expanded their purchases. The credit manager of Bloomingdale's proudly told his colleagues that if anything, the biggest problem was customers developing a "tendency to overbuy." By 1949, 75 percent of major stores had revolving credit programs, whose 13 percent annual interest rates went a long way toward filling the credit department's money pit. In the competitive retail environment of postwar America, shoppers flocked to the stores that offered them this affordable and flexible form of credit.

Christmas was as opportune a time to go into debt in the postwar era as it is today. "Bloomingdale's Is My Santa Claus!" proclaimed the headline of a 1946 Bloomie's advertisement. Ann Smith, a "gal from the Middle West keeping herself in rent, clothes, meals, and recreation," needed $96 to meet all the demands on her gift list, but "short of winning a quiz program she didn't know how she'd do it." Through a permanent budget account, that's how! Such ads offered credit to meet family obligations. That such advertisements were always directed at women speaks volumes about men. Bloomingdale's ran an advertisement in 1949 offering to help aunts with their "18 children" (nieces and nephews) through

"Bloomingdale's Is

My Santa Claus"

**SAYS ANN SMITH WHO HAS JUST DONE
HER CHRISTMAS SHOPPING WITH A
PERMANENT BUDGET ACCOUNT**

A nn will feel that way about Bloomingdale's long after
the last light is doused on the Christmas tree and the last pine
needle shaken out of her slippers. She was here having
her purchases Christmas wrapped when she explained her
sudden buying power to a friend. After all, a gal
from the Middle West keeping herself in rent, clothes, meals
and recreation on her salary (even though it is a good one)
may find the thought of a visit home empty handed
awfully poor for the spirit.

"I'll have to get them something—even if it's little," she
thought. "If only I could afford an account at the store."
Well, she can and she did . . . next thing you know, with
reindeer jumping practically from her eyes.

**SHE SAW OUR CREDIT MANAGER
AND NOW SHE'S SOLVENT FOR CHRISTMAS**

S he showed him her gift list, dreams for brother Bobby
age 7, Carol age 4, Dad and Mother and Irma, the cook.
Using good judgment and an overflowing heart as buying guides,
she'd need about 96.00. Short of winning a quiz program,
she didn't know how she'd do it. Well, our credit manager
told her. She could open a Permanent Budget Account
for any length of time up to 12 months. Ann chose 6 months.
She will pay 1/6 of the total each month. That's 16.00
plus a small carrying charge and no down payment on any
of the gift items she picked. (Certain household items do
by Federal regulation require a down payment.)

A s Ann pays off her balance, she's good for that much
more spending power. Her credit is permanent for the original
amount for which she opened her account. That's what
makes it Christmas every month with a Permanent Budget
Account and Ann said it for thousands of PBA addicts,
"Bloomingdale's is my Santa Claus."

ANN'S GIFT LIST

For Carol: Pinafore . .	3.98	For Bobby: Roller skates	3.99
Doll	11.98	Slippers . .	3.45
For Dad: Raincoat	19.95	For Mother: Housecoat .	12.95
Pipe	10.00	Evening bag	10.50
For Irma: Pressure cooker .	13.50	Perfume .	5.00

COME IN AND LET OUR CREDIT MANAGER WORK OUT A PLAN FOR YOUR OWN NEEDS. 7th Floor

Entire contents copyrighted 1946 by Bloomingdale Bros., Inc.

BLOOMINGDALE'S • **LEXINGTON at 59th STREET, NEW YORK 22, N. Y.** • VOLUNTEER 5-5900

*Christmas permanent budget account
advertisement (1946).*

the PBA. Overcoming her "seasonal shopping problems," the loving aunt was encouraged to buy that "special one . . . the pert red-headed doll" for $5.98 and "another . . . an exciting Bubble-O-Matic gun" for $2.98 on a PBA.[8] Her $75 limit would more than cover presents for the eighteen children (though it might take until the next Christmas to pay it off!). Credit "makes it Christmas every month with a Permanent Budget Account." Spending her $16 a month for the next six months, "Ann said it for thousands of PBA addicts, 'Bloomingdale's is my Santa Claus.' "[9] But it was the morning after Christmas, as an article in *Life* explained in 1953, that you could hear Santa urge on the real reindeer who pulled his sled: "On Bergdorf! On Goodman! On Neiman and Marcus!"[10]

One holdout in retail, akin to Ford in the 1920s, was Macy's. It was founded by a former Nantucket whaler, Rowland Hussey Macy, in 1858, and the red star from his sailing days became the symbol of the company, representing his personal promise of low prices to his customers. Part of that low price came from his atypical policy of cash-only sales. Before he came to New York, his attempts at running cash-only stores in Massachusetts had ended in failure. But in New York there were sufficient people and competition that a low-price, cash-only store could prosper.

Fast-forwarding to the postwar era, Macy's continued to privilege cash over credit, offering a 6 percent discount to cash buyers. Echoing the Ford savings plan, customers could deposit money in the "Macy's Bank." At Macy's this bank, holding $9 million in 1948, actually worked.[11] The span between deposit and withdrawal was not nearly as lengthy as in saving for a car. Moreover, deposits were another way in which a husband could exert control over his wife's spending.

Jack Straus, the president of Macy's, was no fool. Macy's had a credit department like any other store's. It managed to sell the largest variety of goods in the world and to have the largest store in the world. In Christmas season, as celebrated in 1947's classic *Miracle on 34th Street,* a quarter million people shopped there daily. The real miracle of Macy's was not Santa but its ability to reach out to both cash and credit customers, both of whom were looking for that special deal.

On the outskirts of cities like New York, shoppers and stores made a new life. In 1954, Abraham & Straus, the venerable New York retailer, announced that it was opening the largest department store in the East—but it would be on Long Island, just a five-minute drive from Levittown.[12] Christmas on 34th Street at Macy's no longer meant shopping in the largest store in the world. Coupled with the grand advertisement for the store was an equally grand solicitation for credit. In the suburbs, credit, not cash, would be king. Revolving credit, in the form of the permanent budget account, had arrived.

All suburban credit managers agreed that the key to the success of their branch stores was revolving credit. Revolving credit, particularly for young couples in desperate need of outfitting all their rooms, bound customers to the stores. Families with a mortgage borrowed twice as much as families without a mortgage. Constrained finances did not have to mean going without. Department stores bought lists of new arrivals from utility companies and sent out Charga-Plates. Despite the lack of credit applications, these shoppers, screened only by neighborhood, turned out to have the same default rates as other suburban shoppers. Suburban department store shoppers were roughly the same: homemakers under thirty-five years old, with two to three children and a higher income than those who still lived in the city. The fresh Charga-Plate arriving in the mail would entice that newlywed into Macy's.

Credit mattered more to suburban department stores because one of their main urban services—delivery—was no longer relevant. The downtown department store's success, much less that of the mail-order catalog, was predicated on the tremendous hassle of shopping in both the city and the country. Carrying all those goods home from the store or riding one's horse to the store took all day. Delivery, in the era before widespread automobile ownership, was essential. In the new suburbs, delivery mattered not a whit since to live there you needed a car anyway. Branch stores of the downtown department stores were built in shopping centers at the intersections of highways. Though many of the examples were in the Northeast, these developments were national. The Texan department store Sanger's built its branch seven miles from downtown Dallas at the intersection of highways 67 and 80 on the loop around the city. The branch stores had all the parking customers demanded. From 1945 to 1955, the parking lots of Federated Department Stores increased in area from 65,000 to more than 2.5 million square feet. For the first time, department stores devoted more square feet to parking than to merchandise. Credit promotions, important in the city, became essential in the suburbs.

By the 1950s, department stores cared less about protecting customers from their own desires than selling merchandise. The protective credit manager of the 1920s was totally absent in the era of revolving credit. Since the average charge sale was three times the average cash sale, stores pushed credit for all the customers. Since the new forms of revolving credit became profitable, for the first time, when the monthly interest rate was raised to 1.5 percent, no longer were credit managers worried about limiting customers' borrowing. The more credit issued, the better the overall profits of the store. Federated Department Stores was the first to abolish limits on revolving credit, in 1958, but other stores quickly followed. The customer, not the credit manager, decided how much to borrow. Such an arrangement gave customers the flexibility they wanted (as well as escalating borrowing costs) and the stores the large sales volume they wanted. These revolving credit accounts, called option accounts, for the first time gave shoppers the option of paying back their debt or not. No longer would accounts be past due; borrowers would just get finance charges. By 1960, most major retailers consolidated all their credit plans into option accounts.

Flexibility in repayment was essential for postwar consumers because so much of their income was already allocated to mortgages, car payments, and the like. How did postwar Americans balance all this borrowing? With budgets. Budgets had been promoted by scolds and know-it-alls since the turn of the century as the best way to deal with consumption. Primly outlined accounts detailing the smallest dollar spent, budgets are supposed to rein in our insatiable desires and free-spending ways, rendering our economic life orderly and moral. Yet budgets have all the authority of a New Year's promise. Since we make them, we can break them. The first good sale at Barney's, and out goes the budget! Contracting for a budget through credit might seem like a good way to discipline spending. Instead of allocating a certain amount every month to a grocery bill, which can vary, why not sign up for a frozen food plan to fill the freezer, as many households did in the 1950s? Both freezer and food could be paid for every month on installments together, making the expenditures budgetable.

Even following a budget is not a sure recipe for financial safety. Counterintuitively, the real danger of budgets is not in breaking them but in believing in them. Aren't budgets supposed to help us maintain our finances, to keep us on track? They are, but though a budget can be clear-cut, economic reality can be far messier. Confusing the order of the budget for an orderly world is the first step toward the precipice of bankruptcy. William Whyte, before he wrote his best seller, *The Organization Man,* denounced the "budgetism" of the young middle class not for its prudence (he was no libertine) but for its lack of prudence. Instead of controlling their spending and saving money, young couples borrowed on the installment plan as much as they could, fitting the monthly payments into a budget. Neatly arranged as monthly payments, the budget legitimized installment borrowing. Budgets, for Whyte, were the "opiate of the middle class," dulling them to the dangers of overspending. The interest was still paid to lenders, depleting these young couples' savings. Whyte, who came of age during the Depression, warned the young couples of the 1950s that such faith in the steadiness of the future was foolish. This critique of budgets runs counter to generations of financial planners, but its evidence surrounds us today, when well-planned borrowing has collided with sudden market downturns and unemployment. The danger of budgets, ultimately, is believing that they will tame not only you but the world around you.

For most of the postwar generation, however, Whyte's

warnings proved wrong. The economy had been tamed. Budgeters of the 1950s lucked out. Unlike today, the stability of the economy then allowed borrowing to the very limits of one's budget. Incomes grew, and jobs were rarely lost. Instead of ruining them, borrowing helped postwar Americans leave the ruins of the Depression far behind.

In the stably growing economy of the postwar era, more Americans could borrow than ever before. A 1953 article in *Life* ranked forty-two occupations according to their riskiness. What made someone a low risk was the "steadiness, not size, of [their] income." People with fluctuating incomes, like lawyers, ranked lower than might be expected. At the bottom of the list, at 42, was farm laborer, that old standby job of fifty years earlier. With their low, seasonal wages and a tendency to drift, collecting a debt from them would be difficult. Good credit required a stable job. Some unfortunates, even during the postwar boom, could not make ends meet. With all the newfound opportunities to borrow, lenders also began to learn new ways to get their money back. With revolving credit, as with the permanent budget account, the debt itself needed to be collected; repossessed toys had no value.

Suburbanites at every income level borrowed more than their equivalents in the cities. Naturally, debt collectors, such as Walter Muller, flocked to that quintessential suburb—Levittown—to ply their trade. Muller had begun his career in the credit department of the Philadelphia department store Strawbridge & Clothier but by the 1950s had been running his own collection business for some time. His rates were typical: in most cases, he took half of whatever he collected. Focusing on larger, older uncollected bills whose debtors had already moved—"skips"—Muller offered department stores

HOW GOOD A CREDIT RISK ARE YOU?	
(1954)	
1. Business Executive	22. Lawyers and judges
2. Accountants, auditors	23. Traveling salesmen
3. Retail managers	24. Plumbers
4. Chain store managers	25. Police and firemen
5. Doctors and dentists	26. Carpenters
6. Engineers	27. Guards and watchmen
7. Farmers (owners)	28. Farmers (tenants)
8. Army and Navy officers	29. Truck and bus drivers
9. Office workers	30. Enlisted servicemen
10. College professors	31. Unskilled factoryhands
11. Railroad clerks	32. Janitors
12. Skilled factory workers	33. Section hands
13. Post office employees	34. Plasterers
14. Railroad trainmen	35. Barbers
15. Hotel, restaurant managers	36. Coal miners
16. Schoolteachers	37. Common laborers
17. Clergymen	38. Bartenders
18. Nurses	39. Musicians
19. Public officials	40. Domestic servants
20. Retail sales people	41. Painters
21. Printers	42. Farm laborers

A list of credit risk by occupation.

more than the nothing they were going to get without his services. He framed his collections in moral terms, explaining that "the thing that gives me pleasure is getting these people to face responsibilities, getting them to start a different kind of life."[13] Moral suasion and hounding were the main tools that Muller and other debt collectors employed. Repayment of the debt was what mattered—not the underlying merchandise. Manufacturing was efficient and store markups were high, so the real cost was in bad debt losses, not the cost of the goods. By outsourcing the debt collection, stores could keep annoying debt collectors at arm's length. No self-respecting person would complain about a debt collector coming to her house, even if she might complain about Bloomingdale's refusing her credit.

Though the 1950s family lucked out on budgets, they also knew that they had something even more powerful than luck on their side: the tax code. Before World War II, the tax code did not matter for middle-class Americans. Between the tax brackets and the standard deduction, income taxes were paid only by the wealthy. Over the course of the war, however, the federal government steadily raised the rates and lowered the tax brackets to pay off the enormous federal debt. After the war, the high taxes remained. The top bracket (inconceivable today) was 91 percent for nearly the entire postwar period. Even for those below the top bracket, federal taxes had for the first time become something for everyone to reckon with.

But though the middle class now had taxes to pay, it also had deductions to take. As today, all the interest on a mortgage could be subtracted from a family's yearly income. Unlike today, however, not just mortgage interest but all consumer interest could be deducted as well. Though mortgage interest was the largest interest paid for most middle-class families, adding up all the interest on Cadillacs, furs, and televisions still made a sizable dent in the yearly tax bill.

All forms of interest were deductible because when the income tax was created in 1913, through the Sixteenth Amendment, interest was nearly always a business expense. Consider who could legally borrow at that time. Since small-loan laws did not yet exist, everyday borrowing was on the gray or black market. Farmers mortgaged their land, entrepreneurs borrowed for their businesses, but in one's personal life, there was no borrowing to be had. The idea of personal borrowing was inconceivable to the framers of the tax code, and thus all interest was deductible.

Only when the income tax began to encompass everyone after World War II did the interest deductions begin to affect taxes—and for the postwar home owner, they were fantastic. All the interest paid could be deducted. What incentive, then, was there not to borrow? Only those who took the standard deduction—that is, most renters—lost out. For home owners who took the mortgage interest deduction, the deduction effectively cut the cost of their borrowing by a third or a half. Interest on top of that was also subsidized. Borrowing wasn't saving, but it was not nearly as pernicious as it would have been in the absence of the deduction.

Unsurprisingly, between tax incentives and rising incomes, the middle class borrowed far more frequently than either the poor or the rich. Through this borrowing, it created a lifestyle of fantastic material affluence. Minks and boats, houses and cars, televisions and radios, all formerly the province of the well-to-do, became the norm for the middle class. Americans embraced debt. The percentage of households using credit rose after World War II, from 38 percent in 1949 to 54 percent in 1958. For the middle class, the moral valence of debt began to change. Learning to love the debt involved not only things but ideas. Scolding intellectual journals such as *The New Republic* and *The Nation* may have printed articles like "Do You Owe Too Much?" and "Charge-Account Prosperity," but more mainstream publications such as *U.S. News & World Report, Newsweek, Good Housekeeping,* and *Changing Times* ran just as many articles during the postwar period examining the current "debt crisis"—and ultimately taught people how to use it to their advantage. One credit executive remarked that the meaning of credit had changed from being a sign of being unable to pay with cash to being a sign of being trusted, even a "mark of character."

Revolving credit was department store credit, and it was for *everyone*. Department stores that took advantage of this new revolving credit system experienced fantastic sales growth. It's no coincidence that the stores that most fully exploited the new charge systems—Filene's, Abraham & Straus, Bloomingdale's, Foley's, Burdines, and others—grew in the postwar era to become America's largest retail conglomerate: Federated Department Stores. Even its nearest rival department store conglomerate, May Department Stores, was composed of avid revolving credit retailers such as Marshall Field's, Kaufmann's, Meier & Frank, Famous-Barr, and Lord & Taylor. In the 1950s, these department stores followed their customers out to the suburbs, offering revolving credit to furnish all those new suburban homes. With revolving credit, more people could borrow at department stores than ever before. You didn't need to be able to pay off a purchase this month. Whereas charge accounts had been associated since the 1920s with high-end stores, by the early 1960s, the majority (61 percent) of consumers surveyed believed that there was no difference in quality between stores that offered revolving credit and those that offered only charge accounts. In the new democracy of debt, all levels of consumption could fit into the budget. Permanent budget accounts, the forerunner of today's credit cards, were here to stay.

Historians circulate an anecdote that in 1950, Diners Club founder Frank McNamara, realizing he'd forgotten his wallet while enjoying a fine New York steak dinner, thought to himself, "Why should people be limited to spending what they are carrying in cash, instead of being able to spend what they can afford?" More likely, in fact, is that when Frank McNamara returned from New York he got the idea from listening to his wife on the car ride home. (It would not be until the early 1970s that Mrs. Frank McNamara, a married woman considered an economic dependent, could apply for credit in her own name. The credit control in the family that had existed under the credit manager continued under revolving credit as well.) If a Mr. McNamara could use his Diners Club card at a few select New York supper clubs such as the Copacabana and the Latin Quarter, Mrs. McNamara could use a charge card in nearly every department store in the entire country.[14] As late as 1961, only 1 percent of stores took universal bank cards. Americans shopped at department stores more than at any other retailer, and the stores' credit, not banks', was what mattered most. The real history of credit cards begins with department store charge accounts in the 1930s, not Diners Club. Credit cards were really invented to sell housewives' dresses, not businessmen's steaks.

Though Diners Club is often hailed as the trailblazing first step on the road to credit, even a Federal Reserve report published in 1957 to detail the entirety of consumer credit to policy makers, hundreds of pages in length, detailing minutiae of all forms, neglected to mention Frank's "invention." Alongside Diners Club, major banks, including Bank of America and Chase Manhattan, had launched universal credit programs in the early 1950s. As envisioned by the bankers, the cards could have been used anywhere. Yet they were not. They failed within a few years, and bank credit cards were taken off the market. As Mrs. McNamara could have told them, Bloomingdale's didn't take any card but its own.

If all these kinds of credit seemed the same to customers, for retailers, they were not. Behind each purchase stood a complex network of firms that provided the money for the lending, which was usually hidden from the customer. Insurance companies bought VA and FHA mortgages. Automobile finance companies took on car debts from the dealers. For department stores and other retailers, however, the expansion of consumer borrowing presented a serious dilemma. The majority of sales were now done on credit, but providing that credit ate up profits. The profit margins on credit, while real, were slim—only in the single digits—compared to the profit margins on merchandise, which were all at least 30 percent. The capital of department stores was tied up in barely profitable consumer credit when it could be invested in more lucrative merchandise. If a department store has more money invested in credit than clothes, is it still a department store or is it a bank? Lending could never be as profitable as selling but stores found it difficult to get financing for consumer debt.

Few banks were willing to lend money to the stores to finance the revolving debt. What would the collateral be? A pair of slacks? Many banks demanded strict accounting for what money was lent for, and in the flexible world of revolving credit, such reckoning was impossible. When a customer paid $20 on a $100 debt, were the slacks being paid off or the television? The solution to this puzzle, discussed in the next chapter, transformed the U.S. retail landscape, preserving the supremacy of department stores for a while but also allowing revolving credit, more generally, to expand throughout the economy. Once department stores could resell their debt, so could any retailer. Without a lock on credit and delivery, department stores lost the edge of unmatched service that had made them successful. The customer loyalty that revolving credit was intended to create lasted only as long as department stores were the only place to get revolving credit. The firm grasp of department stores on revolving credit ended as a new kind of store emerged in the early 1960s: the discount store.

CHAPTER FIVE

DISCOUNTED GOODS AND DISTRIBUTED CREDIT (1959—1970)

In 1963, the Harvard Business School professor Malcolm McNair addressed a roomful of department store accountants in a Philadelphia Sheraton. Though they listened politely, it is hard to imagine that they really believed him when he told them that the most successful retail model of the last hundred years, the department store, was over. "In the past ten years," McNair said, "the traditional department store has been facing two major challenges: first, the problem posed by the trend to suburban living; and second, the problem presented by the meteoric rise of the discounter." Though nimble chain department stores, such as those owned by Federated Department Stores and May Department Stores, had branched into the suburbs to follow their customers, it would not be enough to escape the discount meteor.

The rise of the discount store marked the fall of the department store. Discounters, such as Target, provided the convenience of department stores but at lower prices. Few discount stores, unlike all department stores, offered credit to their customers. At the same time, an old kind of retailer that had been sidelined by the department store in the nineteenth century reemerged: the specialty store. Specialty stores, such as The Gap, provided a narrow selection that focused on just one customer segment, with a deeper inventory than any one department of a department store could possibly provide. Between these two retail developments the centralized shopping of the department store waned and new kinds of credit arose to fill the needs of this new, decentralized landscape of consumption.

In the late 1950s and early 1960s, new discount stores popped up all over the country. Though today we think first of Wal-Mart, Target, and Kmart (all founded in 1962), hundreds of such discounters—now forgotten—dotted the landscape. Nearly three thousand discount stores spanned the country, but most of them were one-store operations, such as Big M in Miami and Big C in Cincinnati. (Evidently, using only the first letter was cheaper.) For those at the top of the department store game, as well as those starting out at the bottom of the discount store business, McNair's meteor was not news at all. They all had their own telescopes and could see what was coming.

Target, for instance, was founded by Douglas Dayton, the youngest son of an esteemed line of midwestern retailers. Douglas's father and grandfather had successfully steered Minneapolis's Dayton department store chain to success. Douglas, like many others involved in department stores, noticed the disturbing difference between discount and department store sales. Whereas department store sales had risen 27 percent during the 1950s, discount store sales had risen 700 percent. Douglas, like other department store heads, made the plunge, opening the first Target store in Minnesota. And yes, even then people called it Tarzhay.[1] Douglas maintained the quality of his department store at discount prices, and though the name might have sounded French—reflecting the better quality of its discount goods—the store was all-American.

The first discounters of the 1940s and 1950s bought factory seconds—possible only in a system so productive that even slightly irregular goods could be discarded. Lodged in abandoned industrial buildings such as former mills and factories, discounters had clothes, shoes, and everything else heaped throughout a vast industrial space. The discounters of the 1950s had a suspicious reputation for shoddy goods, which "caveat emptor" would not even begin to cover. Yet shoppers still flocked, greedy for lower prices as the inflation of the mid-1950s gave everybody sticker shock. The discounters had more in common with nineteenth-century wholesalers than Target today. But they performed a vital function, showing consumers and retailers alike that there was a demand for cut-rate merchandise.

The new discounters of 1962, however, marked a break with those hucksters and wholesalers. Their low prices relied on organizational innovation, not sleight of hand or damaged goods. Modeling themselves on the supermarkets of the 1920s and '30s that had crowded out the old grocers, the discounters ran a cash-only, self-service business. Rejiggering prices and service in the new era of cheap transportation and production, discounters reinvented U.S. retail by de-skilling traditional sales work and cutting prices.

The discount store's rise was made possible by the collapse of an older retail model braced by law—in this case the fair-trade laws of the 1930s. State legislatures had passed the laws during the early 1930s in response to what was called the "chain store menace."[2] Chain stores, all too familiar today, were the hottest things in town in the 1920s. In 1920, chain stores sold 4 percent of all goods; by 1929, they sold 20 percent. Alongside installment credit, chain stores represented the most striking transformation of American consumption in the 1920s. The anti–chain store movement—perhaps the last gasp of populist politics—could be found in every state. One wing of the movement, led by Representative Wright Patman, a Democrat from Texas, pushed for an outrageous tax derived by multiplying the number of stores by the number of states in which a store resided. Echoing the politics of the 1890s, Patman wrote, "Will the country's interest be promoted in a better way by the million and a half retail stores being owned by more than a million local citizens, or will the country be better off if these million and half retail stores are owned and controlled by a few?" The Great Atlantic & Pacific Tea Company (A&P)—which even to this day is the nation's largest chain store ever—would have paid $471 million in taxes under Patman's plan, despite having profits of only $9 million.

Though a few states passed more restrained versions of Patman's plan—taxing companies by the number of stores that they operated but without the insane multiplier—more important were the widespread fair-trade laws. Fair-trade laws allowed manufacturers to set prices for their products in a state. If manufacturers had a set price agreement with even one retailer, other stores could not discount that product. Chain stores, despite their higher volumes, could not demand a lower price from manufacturers. For price-protected goods, the lower manufacturing costs resulted in profits for the manufacturers, not lower prices for customers.

The end of manufacturer-controlled pricing began with a thirty-eight-year-old New Orleans grocer named John Schwegmann, who, having worked in his family grocery since the age of fourteen, believed that "by keeping prices low the public [would] reward [him] by buying more."[3] He refused to cooperate with the pricing schemes of liquor manufacturers and went to court to fight for his right to set his own prices. The court agreed. Beginning in 1951 with *Schwegmann Bros. v. Calvert Distillers Corp.,* which struck down Louisiana's "non-signing" provision, the fair-trade laws in forty-five states began to wobble. Emboldened by his victory, Schwegmann became the poster child for free pricing, continuing his fight in *Eli Lilly & Co. v. Schwegmann Bros. Giant Supermarket,* which pushed for the right of retailers to set their own drug prices.[4] By 1958, one of Schwegmann's top executives was testifying in Congress before Arizona department store owner—and archconservative—Senator Barry Goldwater. To a retailer like Goldwater, the discounters' cost of goods was only 7 percent of their revenue, compared to department stores' average cost of goods, which was nearly ten times as much. Goldwater told the executive, "If we could get merchants in this country to operate this way at seven percent, you will be the saving grace for the merchants in this country."[5] Cheap goods meant high profits for retailers—or so Goldwater thought. Whether or not the fair-trade laws saved merchants, discounters certainly killed department stores like Goldwater's.

Macy's, which never signed agreements with manufacturers, seized on this opportunity in 1951 to cut its prices by 6 percent for nearly six thousand items, kicking off a price war in New York. Though the next year Congress reaffirmed the validity of fair-trade laws through the McGuire Act—which empowered states to bind nonsigning retailers such as Macy's—the stage was set for the slow death of the fair-trade laws. The McGuire Act only allowed states to have "non-signer" clauses; it did not require it. By the early 1970s, only twelve states still had fair-trade laws on the books.[6] In 1975, President Gerald Ford finally ended the forty-year experiment in manufacturer-controlled pricing with the Consumer Goods Pricing Act, "enabling," as he wrote in his signing statement, which sounds oddly like an advertisement, "consumers in all 50 States to shop for the best products at the lowest possible prices."[7] There was not a clean end to the fair-trade laws, but there was a clear rise in free-market pricing in the 1950s and 1960s that allowed discounters to take advantage of lower manufacturing costs. Without price stability, manufacturers had to look for other ways to cut costs—such as manufacturing overseas—to maintain profitability. Even with such movements, manufacturing profits took a hit, which in turn made other forms of investment, such as finance, more appealing.

The discount store grew so fast not only because of its prices but because of the way it changed how Americans shopped. Incomprehensible as it is, self-service in stores did not exist until 1917, when an enterprising southern grocer named Clarence Saunders reorganized his store, Piggly Wiggly, to allow customers to select their own food from the shelves. The innovation, obvious today, was so novel in 1917 that Saunders actually patented it. Self-service allowed customers, for the first time, to buy on impulse without any oversight by clerks. Though self-service spread through the grocery business in the 1920s, eventually forcing even the largest grocery chain, A&P, to adopt the model by 1930, other types of retail stores resisted it. Merchandise was too expensive to have grubby-handed customers pawing it. The high cost of manufacturing meant a high cost of goods. Department stores kept clothes safely behind counters, and highly trained employees served customers.

*Clarence Saunders first patented the
self-service store in 1917.*

In the world of cheap goods—manufactured in the U.S. South or even overseas, where cheap land and nonexistent unions allowed manufacturers to cut costs—some merchandise could be broken, stained, torn, ripped, and manhandled by customers. It didn't matter; it was cheap. Instead of gazing through glass-paneled counters, customers could flip through racks. In many customer surveys, self-service actually outranked low prices in why customers preferred the discounters. Self-service (40 percent) was the most cited reason—even more than price (23 percent)—consumers who liked discounters shopped there.[8] Retailers also had cause to like self-service. Without the need for well-trained employees, wages could be cut. Whereas downtown department stores paid 30 percent of their sales volume in wages, discount stores paid as little as 8 percent. Self-service, it was thought, also encouraged impulse buying since shoppers could emotionally connect with freely caressed merchandise. Centralized check-out meant that a customer paid only once, not many times throughout the store, thus trimming the moment of pain. In this world of cheap goods and de-skilled labor, discounters could thrive. Their prices could be lower yet still profitable. For discounters, innovative merchandising drove growth, while department stores relied on credit to expand sales.[9]

One discounter, however, stood apart from the rest, and, unlike Kmart and Target, it began without a department store or dime store parent company. At its outset in 1962, this discounter was so small-time that it was not even mentioned in a comprehensive national survey of all the discounters in the United States. This outfit, barely distinguishable from the others at first, settled on a different way of doing things. While other discounters focused on cities, this retailer aimed at the country, counting on the new postwar compression of space brought about by the highway system, and then the con-tainer ship. In Japan, production was being reinvented. Toyota had just perfected "just-in-time" production, where, instead of piles of carburetors and shocks waiting to be installed, the carburetors and shocks arrived at the factory just before they were put into cars. As Toyota's inventory costs dropped to nearly nothing, the costs of production plummeted. Inven-tory, after all, should always be thought of as an investment with a zero-interest return. All those carburetors and shocks sitting around cost money, in that they tied up capital that could not be invested profitably elsewhere. Toyota invented just-in-time production, and the rest of the world, since that day, has struggled to keep up. Just-in-time production enabled a lower-cost manufacturing process by eliminating unprofitable stored inventory—parts arrived at the factory "just in time." Less well acknowledged is that at that same moment, in the United States, an equally important innovation occurred—just-in-time distribution—and every other retailer in the world continues to this day to catch up to the company that perfected it: Wal-Mart.

Wal-Mart grew for many reasons, but none of them involved credit. Yet credit's absence, as for Ford, had startling ramifications for both Wal-Mart and American consumers. From the outset, Sam Walton did not offer his customers credit. Unlike the discount descendants of large department stores and five-and-dimes, Wal-Mart began from the ground up. Sam Walton had stores and merchandise, but he did not have the capital or expertise to offer credit. The store's low prices reflected the larger lack of service. No free gift wrapping. No complimentary delivery. No money-losing charge accounts. Though the credit practices didn't win customers, the prices did. But prices weren't—despite what we might assume—everything.

As in the rise of the department stores, homemakers' need for ease drove the change. A survey of suburban discount shoppers from 1961 revealed what motivated the shift to discount stores. Regardless of class, moms love a deal—but especially for their own clothes and those of their children. Even though they continued to buy their husband's clothes at department stores, discount store shoppers virtually abandoned department stores for women's and children's clothes.[10] For most shoppers the discount appeal was just as much about the shopping experience as about price. Among the younger set, self-service was actually preferred because it "spe[d] up shopping and let the customer browse without interference."[11] Salespeople didn't act, according to one discounter, as "the customer's conscience. The customer no longer had to justify to herself or anyone else a purchase that she would enjoy making." Not interacting with staff meant not being watched, which in turn allowed shoppers to dress comfortably—a consideration almost inconceivable today, when we wear jeans to everything—but 1961 was a more formal time. One discounter remarked that his clientele "like to shop us in a very leisurely way. If a person wants to shop in a department store they usually cannot walk in in slacks or shorts.... In a discount store, you can see all types of people...the slacks...the shorts...the pedal pushers, or even dungarees."[12] As another said, "We're working on breaking down all the traditions." When you can go shopping in shorts, is there any going back? Convenience extended beyond attire. In the suburbs, you could go shopping at night, while downtown the stores were open late only one night a week.[13] Discounters may have lacked the formal convenience services of department stores, like credit, but they offered other informal conveniences that mattered just as much.[14]

The discounters that came out of existing retailers, such as Kmart, tended to offer credit, while those invented as discounters, like Wal-Mart, did not. Only half of discount stores offered credit in the 1960s, but even then, few customers used the stores' credit plans. Though the majority of department store purchases were charged by the mid-1960s, only 13 percent of discount store purchases were. Few stores had the volume to run such a service profitably. The lack of credit at Wal-Mart and many other discounters marked a break in the long history of coupling retailers to credit. Though retailers had long been able to resell their customers' debt, the customers still got the credit at the retailer, creating customer loyalty. The discount store, on the other hand, told consumers to look elsewhere if they wanted to borrow.

Whereas department stores had promoted their own credit departments and policies, many discounters had a far more ambivalent approach to consumer credit. Part of what kept prices so low at Target, Douglas Dayton explained in 1969, was that it offered "no credit." Self-service enabled low payrolls, suburban locations enabled vast big-box parking, and the lack of credit enabled capital to be invested in expansion—not customers' bills. Unlike other discounters, Target sold no large appliances, completely breaking the link between its business and that of the 1950s mill stores. And it did take checks. "That," Dayton said, "is the way we want it to be."[15]

The appeal of the discounters, despite the lack of credit, weighed heavily on the minds of credit professionals. Among discount shoppers, 60 percent considered charge accounts important.[16] If it was important to 60 percent of the shoppers who did shop at the discounters, imagine how important it was to those who didn't shop there at all! A *Life* magazine study in 1962 found that the "charge account facilities [were an] important reason for shopping in department stores."[17] Credit had become a primary reason to shop at department stores. Price certainly wasn't. But was quality?

The biggest challenge to discounters, the survey concluded, was the lingering perception of lower-quality goods, aided and abetted by the junk heaps found in the discount stores of the 1950s. Though only a small percentage of regular discount store shoppers believed the stores had lower-quality goods, infrequent shoppers cited low-quality goods as the most important factor in avoiding discounters.[18] If a store could "successfully impress customers with the quality of merchandise and its competitive value, [then] there remains a very large additional market."[19]

Meteors move quickly. By 1961, since the previous survey two years earlier, discounters had begun to shed the perception of lower quality while keeping the low prices. The ease of returns helped, aided by the fact that the layouts of the new stores appeared more like those of the familiar department stores than the series of heaps in the old mill stores. Margins on discount goods were lower—closer to 20 percent, rather than the traditional department store margin of 35 percent. But the new discounters reorganized their inventories. By focusing on the goods that could be sold in high volume at lower prices—such as dresses—and eliminating the inventory-clogging items rarely bought—such as sewing supplies—they could cut prices. In just one year, from 1960 to 1961, discount store sales rose 65 percent.[20]

If the discount store meteor had been named by scientists, they would have called it Kmart. The biggest discount store in the 1960s was Kmart, which leveraged the legacy of its parent company's tradition of quality to become a discount giant. Like the other discount stores, one visionary was behind the shift: Harry Cunningham. Working his way up from stock boy, Cunningham became the president of S. S. Kresge, a venerable chain of dime stores. Kresge, by the late 1950s, was cash-rich but growth-poor. Various attempts to grow the chain produced additional volume but not additional profits. Discounting offered another way of doing business, and when he became president in 1959, Cunningham seized the opportunity to remake Kresge.

Cunningham was able to use all that cash to explode out of the starting gate. For a time, Kmart was a meteor of its own.

While 60 percent of discounters were one-store operations, Kmart opened eighteen stores in just its first year, 1962.[21] Kmart, like Target, was started to defend a retail chain. Its sales volume per store grew as fast as the number of stores it operated. Between 1963 and 1970, Kmart increased its sales volume per store eighteen times. The fastest-growing department store, J.C. Penney, grew its sales volume only four times.

With deep pockets and organizational experience that other discounters lacked, Kmart was able to expand nationally from the very beginning, strategically picking cities with fewer discounters, such as Atlanta and Detroit, and avoiding heavily served areas, such as Chicago, New York, and Boston. In those cities, however, Kmart clustered, placing stores roughly five miles apart to encircle a city. Detroit, for instance, got eight Kmarts nearly all at once, enabling a synergy between their advertising efforts, as well as increasing the efficiency of their supply chain. By 1965, Kmart had more stores than any other discounter in America. By 1967, it had a higher sales volume—a little over $1 billion—than any other chain.[22]

Kmart also broke with the department store's shopping center model. Many shopping centers excluded discounters, since they attracted a disproportionately lower-income group. Where to open a store? Surveying the demands of a population could be expensive. But, of course, as one discount store owner suggested, "the easiest thing to do is to open up near a shopping center because you know darn well they made an expensive survey and, if they thought it is right, it must be right."[23] Kmart turned its exclusion into an opportunity, opting instead for freestanding locations with its own 1,000-car parking lots—the first big-box stores.[24] Shoppers appreciated the free parking, which was largely absent at downtown department stores.

In some ways, Cunningham rode the baby-boom wave. Young people and young families came of age at a disproportionate rate in the mid- to late 1960s, and it was always the young who needed good deals. The good deals also helped those of more moderate means. Opinions on discount stores strongly reflected income differences. In the early 1960s, while 67 percent of households earning under $5,000 shopped at discount stores more than half the time, only 43 percent of households earning above $5,000 did.[25] The good deals reflected not only a shift in generational culture but an already slowing prosperity. The cheap manufacturing would, soon enough, produce fewer of the good-paying jobs that made shopping at department stores possible.

By the end of the 1960s, Cunningham had proved the future of retail was in discounting. The blue-light special was still in the future, but Kmart's parent company, S. S. Kresge, bet the proverbial farm on Kmart, sinking millions of dollars into its expansion, siphoning dollars out of its dime store business. When other dime store chains went down in the 1970s, Kresge survived in its new guise as Kmart.

While discounters cut at the department store from below, other stores began to pop up that struck at department stores from above. For lower prices, customers turned to discount stores, but for better service and selection, they turned to specialty chain shops. While discount stores took care of shoppers looking for a bargain, specialty chain stores gave shoppers greater inventories. Specialty shops had continued, even with the department stores' dominance, but they did not become chains until the 1970s. Even more than the discount stores, specialty stores reveal the centrifugal forces tearing the department store apart. Consider that the department store of the nineteenth century had consolidated all the different kinds of shopping under one roof in the name of lower prices and better service. By the 1960s, those different kinds of shopping began to spread out again, as shoppers, now mobile in their cars, could flit from store to store more easily. At discount stores, shoppers found lower prices. At specialty stores, they found a better selection. The department store broke apart for the same reason it had come together a century earlier.

The Gap, for instance, was founded by Donald Fisher in 1969. At first it sold only used LPs and Levi's jeans to the youths of San Francisco. Folk and rock played over loudspeakers. This new retailer had a focused but deep inventory. Unlike department stores, whose capital was tied up in credit, The Gap had 75 percent of current assets invested in merchandise inventory.[26] Unlike most places that sold Levi's, The Gap offered any size you wanted. If you were short or tall, fat or skinny, the Levi's you wanted were there. If you were young in 1969, you wanted Levi's and nothing else. Donald Fisher was born in 1928. He was no baby boomer, but he saw the rising potential of that generation's spending. Catering to this niche group and providing exactly what they wanted, stores like The Gap began to displace the clothing of the department stores. By 1974, The Gap had introduced its own lines of clothing, manufactured in Asia and domestically, to reduce its dependency on Levi Strauss.[27] By 1977, the little shop in San Francisco had expanded to 248 stores across the country. The postwar one-style-fits-all gave way to the generational niches of today.

The primary competitor of The Gap, as its financial filings attest, was the "units of large national department, specialty or discount, store chains which [had] considerably larger sales and assets."[28] Yet despite the David-and-Goliath quality of The Gap versus Federated Department Stores, it was The Gap that turned out to have the advantage—and it knew why. In the first few years of The Gap, Fisher hired senior management from both traditional department stores (Roger Markfield from Macy's) and the new discounters (Jack Eugster from Target).[29] For it and the other new specialty chains, the depth of selection, the store locations, and the inventory control all made them competitive. Like Wal-Mart, The Gap invested early and deeply in computerized inventory control.[30] Every size was always available in every store. In 1969, it accomplished this inventory control by having salespeople tear off a part of the jeans' sale tag that listed the style and size and toss it into a box.[31] Every day Fisher knew exactly what had sold—and what buyers wanted. Within a few years, this was done by computers tracking purchases. The Gap's management knew what boomers wanted and sold it to them in places where they wanted to be. Most of what The Gap sold was Levi's (69 percent in 1977), but it built on that foundation.

And on cash. A Gap employee from the early days remembered that "back in the early seventies, credit and charge cards were not widely used. . . . So at the end of the day you could see how much was sold in an undeniably concrete way: a wad of cash. There was the kind of cash flow that instilled confidence in the entire enterprise."[32] Stores like The Gap didn't offer credit as department stores did, but they didn't need to. The young people they catered to didn't have credit cards, any more than the working-class people who shopped at discounters did. Cash was king.

The rise of working women—at least among the married middle class—led to a revolution in fashion, as older women dressed for the office. Ann Taylor, along with other stores such as Talbot's, found a new niche in a changing economy. Fashion reflected a cultural shift—casual at home, elegant in the workplace—as well as an economic shift of women at work. The discount store supplied clothes for home, while the specialty store supplied clothes for work.

The Gap offered the self-service of a discounter but with better merchandise. So did Ann Taylor and Brooks Brothers. Jeans of every size were arrayed on a wall so that a self-conscious shopper didn't have to have her waist measured by a too-loud clerk.[33] Clerks managed, but did not protect, the inventory—refolding it after it was handled but allowing customers to toss as many pairs of jeans as they liked on the floor of the dressing room. Specialty retailers across price points operated the same way.

The department store, then, began to fragment under this competition, as lower-cost or better-selection retailers took on each department one by one. Basement overstocks became Wal-Mart. Children's became Target. Men's became The Gap. Businesswear became Ann Taylor, Talbot's, and Brooks Brothers. Each specialty store offered better prices and inventories than the department store—but did not offer credit.

Caldor was a typically successful discounter that didn't offer credit. It was founded in 1951 in Port Chester, New York, by a World War II veteran named Carl Bennett, who named the store by combining his name and that of his wife, Dorothy.[34] By 1963, Caldor was solidly in the top one hundred discounters in the country, with annual sales of $15.5 million. But its growth was nothing special. Its sales, like those of the entire discount store industry, had grown 65 percent from 1962 to 1963. Moreover, the largest discounters, such as E. J. Korvette, had annual sales of $257 million. More distressing, no doubt, was that while Caldor sold $2.5 million worth of goods per store, Korvette was able to sell $12.2 million.[35] How could Caldor compete better?

Americans loved low prices but they also loved revolving credit. Customers with charge accounts bought more than cash customers, even when they paid cash—and that could not be ignored in the competitive field of discounting. Shoppers also paid closer attention to advertisements of stores where they had accounts. For stores like Caldor, which relied primarily on a weekly color circular in the local newspaper to attract shoppers, these differences mattered. As they became desperate to attract more customers, revolving credit began to spread outside department stores. Consumers began to expect revolving credit at all kinds of retailers, even at places where installment credit had traditionally financed their purchases, such as appliance dealers. As the discount stores' lower prices rippled through the suburban economy, competition increased. Credit was an important weapon against the more successful stores, but Caldor couldn't finance its own credit.

By the mid-1960s, retailers wanted to know how they could boost sales without offering credit themselves. In their monthly magazine *Discount Merchandiser*, store managers could read a report by the management consulting firm Touche Ross that credit, despite what they had heard, was not profitable.[36] Of course, Touche Ross vastly underestimated the interest rate that stores charged borrowers—a hypothetical 6 percent versus a real 20 percent—in a fit of from-the-hip assumptions only consultants could be paid for. Yet the main point of the report, which was widespread in the industry, was that sales, not credit, drove profits, and if stores could find a way to increase the former without offering the latter they would be better off.

Discounters had to be convinced that offering credit would help them, as they had done pretty well with just bare-bones service. In 1962, as all the new discounters started up, Bernard Korn, a credit executive with a New York finance company, laid out the advantages and disadvantages of lending to customers in the *Discount Merchandiser.*[37] The advantages for discounters were the same as for department stores: increased customer loyalty, higher spending, and more frequent shopping. But the challenges for department stores were multiplied for discounters. On every cut-rate sale, they had to pay for the same billing machines, accounting costs, and collection fees as a regular store—but with already slimmer margins. Korn estimated that stores that offered six-month revolving credit—the only kind he thought made sense by 1962—would need additional capital equal to 40 percent of the sales volume. If a store sold $1 million in a year, it would need to borrow $400,000. A store would need to look outside itself for the necessary capital. If that store could borrow from a bank at 6 percent—no mean feat—then just the interest on the plan, before all the overhead, would cost $24,000 a year. A discounter's increased revenue would need to cover the cost of interest, as well as all the other costs of such a program. The tricky thing about a credit program, though, is that it is all or nothing. If a store had a little extra cash, it could experimentally invest in some additional sweaters. But if a store launched a credit program, it could very quickly devour all of a retailer's capital. Instead of borrowing $400,000, a store might suddenly need $4 million! What Korn encouraged, where possible, was to make arrangements with a local finance company to resell the debt.

Much more than department stores, discounters like Caldor relied on outside firms to provide credit to their customers. Whenever bank cards penetrated a new market, department stores resisted them but discounters welcomed them. But during most of the 1960s, credit was run through the store and financed by a third party. A 1966 survey found that 80 percent of discounters' credit plans were run by outside financial institutions. Credit providers could be local banks or national finance companies, but either way, the private label provided a relationship between the store and the customer, driving sales. Take, for instance, the relationship of Caldor and General Electric, which typified the way in which discounters offered credit, if they offered credit at all.

Caldor's credit dilemma was solved by the unlikely industrial giant General Electric. General Electric had profitably manufactured lightbulbs and washing machines since the dawn of the electrical era, selling its products through specialized dealerships as well as regular stores. Like automobile manufacturers, General Electric helped its dealers finance their sales inventories, as well as underwriting customers' purchases of all those washing machines. Financing dealers' inventories helped GE keep its factories humming twenty-four hours a day year-round and forced the dealers to pay for all those gizmos sitting on the shelves (rather than in GE's warehouses). And of course, financing the installment credit of consumers helped sell goods, which helped GE make money from manufacturing.

Despite the virtues of credit for General Electric, the financing business was not sexy. The unit of GE that handled the credit was called General Electric Credit Corporation (GECC), and, for executives, it was a career stopper. Year after year, since GECC's founding in the 1930s, it had reliably helped the important part of GE—the part that manufactured things—expand its profits. Yet the profits of GECC itself remained relatively stagnant. Without profit growth, it was a good place to end a promising young executive's career.

All that changed in 1961. Shoppers who had become used to buying a little bit here and there on revolving credit at department stores balked at filling out a new installment contract for each new washing machine or vacuum cleaner. While GE's sales continued to expand, credit sales actually fell. So GE rolled out a new revolving credit program in 1961. Revolving credit for durable goods flew in the face of the conventional wisdom that revolving credit was for soft goods such as shoes and socks. But shoppers wanted what they wanted, and GE was happy to give it to them.

Installment credit didn't pay anyhow. Most of GECC's write-offs by the early 1960s were not for unpaid debts but for unsellable repossessed goods. The highly productive manufacturing that made goods cheap enough for the discount store also meant that there was no longer a viable resale market. The world of cheap goods not only destroyed traditional retail, it also destroyed traditional credit—as well as the occasional lunch. Consider the plight of a local refrigerator dealer in 1959, who, in addition to the misfortune of having to attend a credit manager's convention, had to sit next to H. A. Jaffe. Managing the credit department of the New York–based department store chain S. Klein, which had heavily promoted the use of revolving credit by its customers, Jaffe had considered the changing nature of credit deeply. He knew that installment credit was perfect for a world of expensive, durable things. If you missed a monthly payment on a refrigerator, the debt collector could come and get the refrigerator. In a world of expensive goods, that refrigerator could be resold, although perhaps at a discount, and some of the outstanding debt could be repaid. This refrigerator dealer seated next to Jaffe at lunch was the biggest in the state, proudly selling twenty thousand refrigerators a year. Making small talk, the dealer told Jaffe that for every refrigerator sold, he had to register the installment contract at city hall, so that, in case of default, the refrigerator could be repossessed. Every time he registered a contract, it cost $1. Perhaps a better accountant than conversationalist, Jaffe simply asked him how many refrigerators he had repossessed that year. Staring dumbfounded at Jaffe, the dealer got up from the table, saying, "Oh, you, you spoiled my whole luncheon. We have repossessed twelve and spent over $20,000 on recording fees through the year!" For cheap goods in an era of near-constant repayment, repossession and installment contracts were money losers. Many stores stopped filing their contracts and even stopped repossessing, since the goods could not be resold, and simply used the threat as a psychological lever for collection.

Collecting the debt, not the merchandise itself, was what mattered. The merchandise, once sold, was basically worthless. GECC's dilemma, then, was not unique. Repossession and resale—outside of cars and houses—could not replace repayment of debt. Without the ability to reclaim the value of the debt through resale, there was no advantage to the lender of having a secured installment loan. A borrower might as well have an unsecured revolving credit account.

Revolving credit required much more capital than installment credit, as it could not be easily resold to finance companies. Though department stores had led the way, habituating consumers to borrow on their cards and innovating organizational techniques to make revolving credit profitable, other retailers balked at investing their capital in their customers' debts. More important to the rapidly expanding discounters was where a borrowed dollar would best be invested. Banks could finance more stores, or they could finance receivables. Even specialty chains, such as the regional J. B. Robinson Jewelers, benefited. Without financing its own customers, the chain was able to use its capital to expand from two stores to thirty-one between 1969 and 1977.[38] Financial institutions—like GECC—took notice. Unlike most retailers, GECC had access to large amounts of capital.

Also unlike most retailers, General Electric had a fabulous bond rating. GECC financed all the loans by issuing corporate debt. The bonds would pay 5 percent a year, but until the early 1960s, GECC could charge its customers only the price for installment credit of about 6 percent a year. With revolving credit, GECC could charge customers what department stores did: 20 percent a year. Suddenly GECC became wildly profitable.

Within a few years, GECC found that its credit sales recovered. And because of the higher interest rates on unsecured debt, its profits actually increased. The once stagnant GECC became a hotbed of activity. GE opened regional computing centers to track all the debts, compute the complicated interest on the loans, and automate collections. General Electric didn't do things halfway and found itself with more capacity to process revolving credit than its dealers required.

Exactly at the moment when GE had the capacity to lend, discounters found themselves with a need to borrow. In 1966, GE began to offer its credit services to retailers that were in need of a credit system but lacked the ability to process the loans or provide the capital. It offered private-label credit services to retailers, especially discount retailers. Caldor could offer the "Caldor credit card," but GE would take care of everything. Caldor could profit on the sales, and General Electric would profit on the loan. It was a win-win.

Consider, however, the meaning of this new direction for GECC. When GECC was founded, it facilitated the profits of manufacturing. Finance was a means to an end. With the rise of private-label consumer finance, however, finance became an end in itself. GECC helped sell not just GE products but all products, even those made by competitors. Consumer finance became a source of profit in itself, not a means to profit from manufacturing.

A dollar is a dollar. For the investor the source does not matter, even if the larger consequences for the economy could be dire. Every dollar GE invested in consumer debt was a dollar not invested in a factory. GE factories had been the mainstay of the good postwar jobs. Consumer finance, in contrast, created high-paying jobs for a few at the top and a lot of low-paid clerical work for everybody else. The middle ground of middle-class manufacturing jobs began to disappear.

The private-label schemes of General Electric and other finance companies enabled discounters to match the department stores' credit offerings. By the late 1960s, department stores offered little to budget-constrained customers besides credit. Their prices were higher. Credit at discount stores was just as liberally granted by department stores—though surreptitiously financed by GE. In 1960, department stores, the leading category of retailers, had four times the sales volume of discounters, but only five years later discount stores had a higher sales volume than any other kind of retailer, including department stores.[39] The high-priced, centralized retail era had ended. Since then department stores have struggled to define their niche.

There was, however, an alternative to private-label credit: bank credit cards. Bank credit cards had failed in the 1950s because they were impossible to use at the places where people wanted to shop—department stores—and because no bank executive knew how to run a credit card business. By the mid-1960s, the practices developed to run the department store business were widely known. Bank cards offered discounters many of the upsides and none of the drawbacks of running their own credit programs. Bank cards might not increase loyalty, but if shoppers liked a store's prices, they would return and spend more—using the bank's capital. Banks and their specialized credit personnel would screen out the bad risks and take care of the expensive billing and collections, which for the bank would be cheaper because of economies of scale. The only real disadvantage was that the bank took a cut of every sale; but weighed against the advantages, it was hard to see how it could be a bad idea.

The problem with bank credit cards was that so few people had them. Though credit spread out spatially, it did not spread out economically. For the wealthy, who frequented the new specialty chains, bank cards began to displace retail credit. Though the bank cards of the 1950s had focused on traveling businessmen, bank credit cards of the 1960s began to spread into the hands of well-to-do homemakers. Consumers loved the ease of use; they were able to borrow at any of their favorite stores. But though credit cards were everywhere by 1970, they were not for everyone. Middle- and working-class people longed to shop on credit at the new niche stores with Master Charge or BankAmericard, but their finances remained tied to the old retail stores such as Sears, Roebuck. Half of American households had a Sears card in 1979, and one-third had a J. C. Penney card.[40] Like

GE, Sears funded its credit operations through the bond market. Its captive finance company, Sears Roebuck Acceptance Corporation (SRAC) began to issue bonds in 1959 to fund Sears customers' credit. Like GECC, SRAC quickly became a profit center, earning over $100 million a year by 1967.[41] The Sears card could be used only at Sears and was thus just like the store credit of old. For many young Americans, their first—and frequently only—credit card was from Sears. Bank credit cards, which could be used in many stores, remained in the wallets of the well-to-do. Discounters, then, continued to offer credit through finance companies like GE because most of their customers couldn't get bank cards.

Average people were simply too risky to give bank cards. In 1975, only half of Americans had bank-issued credit cards.[42] Capital, as always, was limited. Lending techniques could not profitably ascertain the creditworthiness of more mundane borrowers. Though it is hard to believe today, even the most profitable credit cards only broke even. In the late 1970s, a combination of legal and economic changes and entrepreneurial vision would transform the credit industry to make credit cards nearly synonymous with consumer credit for everyone. For more Americans to get their piece of the plastic dream, lending techniques would need to be refined and new sources of capital found.

Once Master Charge and BankAmericard went national and began to penetrate deeper into the population, as will be discussed in the next chapter, discounters could begin depending on plastic to finance their customers' purchases and focus on what they did best: selling. Once the credit card became ascendant, discounters could abandon their credit programs. By the mid-1970s, for instance, Kmart no longer offered credit to its customers.[43] As retailers' margins eroded from the competition of the discounters, their credit operations could not absorb losses. Breaking even was no longer good enough. Though many retailers had profited on their credit operations since the 1950s, those profits still did not equal those of selling. When merchandising was successful, it always provided a retailer more profit than finance did. Kmart eliminated its credit program because investing money in its racks of clothes made more money than investing in its consumers' debts. Retailers that knew how to run their businesses, like Kmart in the 1970s, should always have made that choice.[44] The new distribution of retail required a new distribution of credit that centered on the consumer, not the store. While shopping became more decentralized, credit—at least for those who had access to bank cards—could become more centralized.

At the end of his career, once he had retired from Harvard Business School, Professor Emeritus McNair summarized his thinking on postwar retail and the rise of the discount store: "Too many dollars are tagged before they are ever received, and one of the consequences is a greatly increased receptivity to price bargains. . . . Hence we find the seemingly incongruous situation of rising incomes and . . . a heightened interest in bargain merchandise."[45] Rising incomes had enabled Americans to borrow more than ever before. But because they locked up all their future income in houses, cars, and furniture, they needed everything else to be cheaper. Borrowing claimed dollars before they came in, and Americans could no longer afford to pay full price. The meteor that McNair had so presciently predicted had struck, but it was not a discounter meteor after all but a meteor made of credit.

CHAPTER SIX

BRINGING GOOD THINGS TO LIFE (1970–1985)

As credit cards began to enter society in new places, *The Wall Street Journal* followed their emergence. Many stories focused on people who should not have had cards. The systems in place to keep cards among the well-to-do sometimes didn't work. A Pittsburgh grocery clerk in 1965, for instance, on receiving a card through a background check error, flouted his card to a reporter, declaring "How about this? Just like the rich people."[1] Credit cards connoted class—and classiness. With cards, you could live the life you always wanted. The ultimate story of this sort happened in 1959, just as travel and entertainment (T&E) cards were about to begin to lose their ground to the bank cards. The adventures of a $73-a-week clerk from the Lower East Side named Joseph Miraglia illustrated both the limits and the possibilities of credit cards. In one month of orgiastic spending he ran up a $10,000 bill while entertaining himself across three countries, four girl-friends, and one rhinestone-collared cocker spaniel.

It all began in September 1959, when Joe happened to duck into a fancy New York restaurant and spied a pile of travel and entertainment card applications for "men of responsibility." He filled out Hilton Hotels' Carte Blanche application—complete with his real salary—and to his surprise received a card a few weeks later with a letter that told him "this card is your key to every luxury Hilton has to offer." Indeed it was. Beginning with the Waldorf-Astoria in Manhattan, Miraglia hit Montreal, Las Vegas, and Havana before running out of steam. He bought fur coats, fine wines, dogs, meals, suits, and even silk shirts from the same tailor as Cary Grant. With only the cash he won at the craps tables and some checks he wrote against the card, he lived, as he said, "like a millionaire's son."[2] When the police caught up with him, he simply said, "I always wanted to see the world, and I like nice things."[3]

Although Joe could live the high life on his Carte Blanche card, he couldn't live a normal life. A traveling businessman with a Carte Blanche could eat in a few swanky restaurants, buy his wife or mistress a fur coat in an affiliated shop, maybe even get a suit from a neighborhood tailor who had a relationship with the hotel, but he couldn't go to Kmart. He couldn't buy groceries. Only places that catered to the expense account crowd took American Express, and for everything else there was cash. Yet while Joe could spend $10,000 to live like a millionaire, it would have been nearly impossible for him to spend $10,000 to live like a middle-class person—much less a working-class guy from a Lower East Side tenement.

The way we use credit cards today—to pay for groceries, fast

food, and coffee—was heralded as futuristic in the 1960s—
a hallmark of a wondrous cashless world of tomorrow! It
would be a distributed landscape of credit where cards would
replace cash. One of the reasons this vision of the future
seemed so impossible was because of the very real technological limits on where credit could be used and the moral limits
on where it should be. Joe's story reflected those limits, and
the story we are about to examine shows how those limits
disappeared. How the credit card changed from a plaything
for the rich into an everyday accessory explains a great deal
about why so much credit suddenly became available for the
average American in the 1980s.

There have always been Joes who wanted some better
things, but there have not always been lenders willing to give
them credit. Americans began to borrow much more in the
1970s, not because we all suddenly became spendthrifts but
due to many structural changes in the economy, a few indus-
trious young executives, and one chance shift in the law.

The postwar period had been a time of remarkable growth
and stability. Slowly, inexorably, that world fell apart in the
1970s, as the international economic order shifted from
postwar recovery back to global competition. The seemingly
unending demand for U.S. dollars in the postwar period,
when the whole world wanted to buy U.S. goods, gave way to a
dollar that was less in demand. The economic dislocations of
the 1970s—inflation and deindustrialization—fundamentally
stemmed from this return to normalcy. The stable growth of
the postwar period that had rewarded budgeting and borrowing fell apart. With surging inflation and stagnating pay, real
wages began to fall. Making up the gap, more married women
than ever before entered the workforce, trying to make ends

meet. But consumers also began to rely on borrowing to make up the widening gap. Since World War II, the amount borrowed by Americans had been rising, but the amount they could pay back—from good-paying postwar jobs—had kept pace. In the 1970s, that carefully budgeted balance between rising debt and rising income came undone.

At the same time, the demise of department stores created a new opportunity for bank credit cards to flourish. Though most Americans' retail credit in the 1970s was still from Sears or Macy's, more shopping occurred at places like Kmart. Discounters and specialty chains had displaced department stores. While their lower prices and deeper inventories lured shoppers away from department stores, credit was still needed, if not to solidify customer loyalty, then simply to put off until tomorrow what could not be paid for today.

The early 1970s witnessed the beginning of a titanic shift in the American economy, but the cultural attitudes with which Americans greeted the new decade reflected the past. By the early '70s, bank credit cards had spread across the country. In every city, at least one bank offered plastic. Yet their use was still only for a few, and those few diverged not only in income but in outlook from those who did not have credit cards. A 1968 sample found that only 17 percent of Americans had credit cards, as opposed to the 62 percent who had gasoline company cards. Men who used credit cards, moreover, were disproportionately affluent, urbane, and more likely to agree with statements such as "I like to think I am a bit of a swinger."[4] The credit card reinforced a lifestyle of aspiration for better things, even for the boss's job. Those who didn't use credit cards had more restrained lifestyles. Men without cards disproportionately believed that "hippies should be drafted," that "liquor is a curse on American life," and that "a woman's place is in the home."

Those who didn't use credit cards were not only disproportionately poorer, they also saw the world differently. Their economic outlook was less optimistic. They didn't believe in investing in stock nearly as much as those who had credit cards. But they also didn't believe they would be executives in a few years or that their family incomes would go up. The optimism that underpinned the credit expansion in the postwar period found its expression in the credit card, and those without that optimism continued to find credit use "unwise."

Unsurprisingly, given how credit was so completely intertwined with women's everyday life, more women than men found borrowing acceptable. Though 62 percent of credit card–having women thought it was "good to have charge accounts," only 33 percent of credit card–having men thought it was good. More women who didn't use credit cards (41 percent) thought that "it is good to have charge accounts" than men who did (33 percent)! Credit was more of an everyday experience for women than for men, and where credit was used, it was appropriate. The habit of using credit made it more legitimate, so more women thought it was okay to borrow. Appliances were okay to borrow for; swimming pools were not. Morality followed the money. So if we are to understand the shift in how Americans judged the use of credit, we need to understand not just what they said but what they did.

Since the mid-1960s, Americans had found it easier to acquire credit cards. Big coastal banks such as San Francisco's Bank of America and New York's Marine Midland Bank offered cards, but banks in Phoenix and Pittsburgh did as well. Everywhere, it seemed, banks were getting into the credit card business. Deposits had been piling up in the commercial banks' coffers ever since the first certificate of deposit (CD) was created in 1961, drawing in funds that had traditionally been put into smaller savings and loan banks. For banks, credit cards seemed ideal. Merchants would pay the banks a cut of everything they sold, and consumers would pay them interest. It was a win-win.

Yet, from the get-go, banks had stumbled. In the early 1950s, they had attempted such schemes and had, within a few years, closed up shop. The bank programs of the 1950s failed for many reasons. Banks relied on income from merchants more than from borrowers; merchants got their money faster, but at a stiff price. On average, banks gave merchants 95 cents for every dollar charged. Skimming off 5 percent of every purchase was as lucrative as charging customers interest. Retailers without capital or inclination to lend paid the 5 percent in the hope that it would increase sales volume. Limited to conventional consumer credit rates, banks took a high cut of each credit transaction, limiting the appeal to merchants. At the same time, they relied on merchants to promote the programs, as stores had traditionally promoted credit programs. Yet, unlike with traditional programs, stores had little incentive to reject bad credit risks. With the default risk on the bank and not the retailer, retailers didn't provide as much "negative information" as the banks would have liked.[5] Promotional costs were high, since this form of credit was brand-new.[6] Perhaps most important, the programs could not capture economies of scale. The per transaction costs were extremely high and, without sufficient scale, made profits impossible. For small transactions, low processing costs were the key to success.[7] The programs flopped.

While bank cards failed, T&E cards—which superficially seemed very similar—flourished. The business behind the two cards couldn't have been more different despite their surface similarities. Though T&E cards were profitable, their scope was limited. American Express, Diners Club, and other travel and entertainment cards remained relatively exclusive. Few members earned less than $10,000 a year in 1967 ($66,200 in 2011). T&E cards charged annual fees. Merchants who catered to travelers knew that credit cards were competitively necessary and that they could never offer credit to people from the other side of the country—or the world. Most important, the cards were issued by nonbank institutions and relied on the bond and commercial paper market for lending capital, not on savers' deposits.[8] Few retailers participated in the programs—airlines, hotels, and restaurants that catered to expense accounts. Despite the similarities, bank cards and T&E cards were fundamentally different. A universal bank-financed card, the aspiration of the early 1950s, remained elusive. To succeed, banks needed a scale of lending that was not possible through incremental growth.

The banks confronted a serious chicken-and-egg problem: retailers wouldn't accept a credit card until many of their customers demanded it, and customers wouldn't apply for a card until many of their favorite stores allowed them to use it. Somehow banks had to simultaneously get retailers to offer credit and shoppers to have cards. And that had to happen nearly instantaneously!

As in the 1950s, the credit card emerged out of the relationship between commercial banks and local retailers. The same pros and cons applied in the 1960s as in the 1950s. Finding retailers willing to accept cards, however, proved easier than getting cards into the hands of consumers. Unlike traveling businessmen, everyday shoppers didn't expect to have access to credit everywhere. Locals already had credit at the stores where they expected it. Expectations of where credit was appropriate mattered. People didn't lack credit in their neighborhoods; they needed it in places they hadn't already gone—both distant shops and in stores that had not traditionally offered credit.

Convincing people to expect to be able to borrow for groceries was harder than convincing grocers to offer credit. People's ideas of what kinds of purchases were okay to borrow for and what kinds were cash only were shockingly inconsistent. According to data from 1968, most credit card users felt it was okay to borrow for appliances, furniture, clothing, gasoline, and sewing machines but not for furs, restaurants, jewelry, hobbies, or groceries. Both appliances and jewelry are durable. Both gasoline and groceries are nondurable. Both furniture and furs are expensive. Both gasoline and hobbies are inexpensive.[9] What decided the acceptability of borrowing was not the thing in and of itself but whether borrowers had used credit before to buy it. Acceptability was driven by not reason but by experience.

Banks pushed their existing customers to adopt their credit cards. Initially, these local credit systems, or bank interchanges, as they were known, strained against the constraints of the local market. The banks with the largest preexisting retail networks thus had a decisive advantage in the chicken-and-egg problem. Bank of America, with its presence across California, began with sufficient territory to overcome the initial problems that the New York banks couldn't. Banks of every size had credit card programs, but it was the largest banks that had the most clients and thus the largest initial networks. Bank of America, in particular, had a long history of consumer finance across California and easily transitioned into this new form of lending. In September 1967, for instance,

58 percent of all credit card debt was in the California Federal Reserve district. New York, that long-standing bastion of financial innovation, had only 13 percent of the balances.[10]

Bank of America (BofA) launched BankAmericard in 1959. It was a disaster. It grew too quickly, and its explosion meant that good as well as bad credit risks received cards. There was widespread fraud. Bank of America, confident in the program's promise, kept up despite losses and by 1961 was able to run it profitably, proving the viability of bank credit cards.[11] Regional banks looked to the BofA as a model for their programs. "When [BofA] turned the corner," a spokesperson from Pittsburgh's Mellon Bank said, "we could see what a well-run program could do."[12] Pittsburgh's Mellon Bank offered its first credit card in 1965. It was not alone. Seeing BofA's profits, other banks launched their own programs in the mid-1960s, anxious not to be left behind. After all, BofA had already enrolled 1.2 million people when those other programs started up.[13] Each city initially had its own network of banks that issued credit cards.

For smaller banks, the only way to solve the chicken-and-egg problem was to start with customers, not merchants. To create an instant supply of credit card–wielding consumers, many banks mailed out unsolicited cards. Take, for instance, the experience of Marine Midland bank, a relatively large New York bank. In 1966, the bank tested two different ways of promoting its credit cards: it mailed out 33,357 applications and, at the same time, 731 credit cards. The kinds of people receiving the credit cards and those receiving the applications were not different, except in how they responded to a card in the mail versus an application in the mail. Though 19 percent of the cards were in use within sixty days, only 0.7 percent of the applications were even returned! The cards got twenty-seven times the response of the applications. Marine Midland could only conclude that direct mailing was the only practical way to get shoppers to use credit cards. The choice to use a card depended, most of all, on whether it was in your hands.[14] Unsolicited cards got a much better response rate than applications.[15] Whether or not the recipients used the cards, banks could tell retailers—in an effort to convince them to join their network—that all the holders of unsolicited cards were only waiting for a place to shop.

As the BankAmericard network grew, the pressure to join increased. From 1968 to 1969, the number of merchants that accepted the card increased from 394,000 to 646,000. From 1965 to 1966, in contrast, the number of merchants had increased only from 50,000 to 61,000. Borrowing through BankAmericard surpassed $2 billion—an increase of $1.2 billion in just one year. BofA's announcement in 1966 that it was extending its network nationally made the other banks' need to act all the more desperate.[16] With the expansion of the network outside California, Louis Lundborg, the chairman of Bank of America, noted that BankAmericard "[would] be the first totally bank-oriented credit card" available nationally.[17]

Licensed banks would administer their cards independently from BofA, but borrowers would be able to use the cards anywhere BankAmericard was accepted. BofA would provide not the lending capital but the network on which the lending could occur. Though shoppers could use their BankAmericard wherever they saw its insignia, the actual operation was a bit more complex than just borrowing from BofA. Retailers would remit the charge slips to their bank, which in turn would pay the store. Then the bank would send the slip to the cardholder's bank, which would pay the retailer's bank. All the slips moving around required a high degree of coordination and compatibility. Credit card numbers needed to be the same length. Just as important, the amount paid to merchants needed to be standardized. Like standardized railroad track gauges, the standardized credit network allowed capital to move around the country. In return for providing the network, Bank of America would receive an initial licensing fee as well as a cut of future earnings from the local bank. As a gold rush mentality kicked in, enthusiasm ran roughshod over prudence. Chicago, in particular, for many years was shorthand for how aggressive lending could go seriously wrong.

In Chicago, the aggressive move of some banks into the credit card field had particularly calamitous results, highlighting the challenges facing lenders in the 1960s. In Chicago, as in many regions, a group of banks banded together in 1966 to form the Midwest Bank Card System.[18] Though each bank enrolled its own clients, a card issued by Bank A could be used at a retailer affiliated with Bank B. In that way, a network effect could be created similar to that enjoyed by much larger banks such as BofA. Customers and retailers alike would find Bank A's and Bank B's cards more convenient than either one of them independently. And when a bank got a customer in 1966, it would probably keep that customer even after BankAmericard came to town. Balances could not be rolled over from card to card as easily as they are today, and as long as you had a balance you were hooked.

Eager to lock down Illinois before Bank of America got there, the banks issued five million plastic credit cards willy-nilly in November 1966.[19] First National Bank of Chicago's enthusiasm was evident as it bought out the perennial Oscar Meyer billboard by the Loop, replacing the hot dog sign with its slogan: "FirstCard: The Nicest Thing Since Money."[20]

Though FirstCard might have been nice for customers, for the banks, their blitzkrieg assault on spending habits was a strategic error. The banks made three crucial mistakes. Mistake number one was that the Chicago bankers, in their hunger for customers, lost their traditional risk aversion, mailing cards to anyone who did not have a bad credit record. Though a good credit record meant that someone was creditworthy, not having a bad record could mean that—or it could mean someone just didn't have a record at all. Mistake number two was not checking for overlaps among mailing lists. Every one of the seven hundred banks had a list of its own customers, which would have been trouble enough, but each bank then went out and bought mailing lists of people who did things that signaled wealth: owned stock, drove expensive cars, owned businesses, had club memberships, and the like.[21] One small-business man with a few shares of stock, a recent car purchase, and membership in the Chicago Commerce and Industry Association received seven credit cards on the same day. He was no doubt prudent, but even if he was good for one card, he could have easily maxed out seven.[22] Another man received eighteen credit cards, including ones for his sons aged nine, eleven, and thirteen.[23] The limits on most cards were relatively low—$350 (about $2,300 in 2011 dollars)—but though most people might have been able to handle the credit limit on one card, few could handle the credit limit on so many.[24] Mistake number three was announcing that millions of credit cards were all to be put in the mail at once, during the busy run-up to the holiday season, when mailrooms were staffed by low-paid seasonal temps. Chicago's criminal element absconded with cards stolen from mailboxes and, in some cases, mailrooms. One Chicago store owner was approached by a "gangland emissary bearing a bale of credit cards" who proposed that they fill out fraudulent charge slips together.

While nationally banks charged off 2 percent of all debt, in Chicago nearly 6 percent of all debt was uncollectable.[25] The eager-beaver banks had to recall all those cards, and though they did not hold the recipients responsible, they did attempt to hold retailers accountable for all the fraudulent card usage. Though the Chicago snafu was outrageous, the national average of 2 percent was still double the highest historical losses lenders incurred on personal loans and installment credit.

Fraud was rampant not just in Chicago but everywhere. Even though the Chicago banks were able to generate $80 million in revenue nearly overnight, the bad-debt losses made profits impossible. To expand so quickly, banks had relaxed their standards of creditworthiness. The Chicago debacle was the most egregious, but not particularly extraordinary. Newspapers and magazines reported that the uncreditworthy, from disreputable "narcotic addicts" to innocent children, received cards with their names already embossed on them.[26] Only 20 percent of banks investigated the credit records of potential applicants before mailing them cards (credit reports such as those offered today by Experian and Equifax were a decade away). Without point-of-sale technology, credit cards were used with carbon paper, and stolen cards were not discovered until the fraudulent slips were submitted. Spending sprees on stolen cards became epic. Banks kept records on the accounts, of course, but accessing them required calling someone and having him or her look up the record in a computer, which was expensive in terms of both labor and equipment. For large purchases, some banks required an authorization. But for everyday purchases, usually under $50, there was no such requirement. Charges could go on for a month before all the slips were added up and the thief was discovered.[27] Ill-gotten cards circulated for months, as thieves knew that only charges over $50 would be checked with the bank. Money was simply stolen "$49 at a time."[28] Chicago's kind of widespread abuse underscored the pitfalls of the credit card's universality. As *Better Homes and Gardens* told its readers in 1967, credit cards' greatest advantage was "versatility," allowing shoppers to "purchase goods and services—from corsages to car repairs—at any retail establishment." In 1967, when Chicago was fighting off the advance of BankAmericard, *Better Homes and Gardens* told its readership that "more than 60,000 merchants in Illinois, Indiana, and southwest Michigan" accepted bank cards, enabling consumers to borrow whenever they might be in the greater Chicago area.[29] Unlike with a traditional charge account, where a shopper applied in person for credit, the anonymity and universality of credit cards—the very features that made them appealing—also made existing systems to control fraudulent and excessive borrowing obsolescent.

Endless court cases made their way through the dockets as victims of credit card fraud found themselves liable for hundreds of dollars in charges. Unlike today, when credit card companies can easily transfer the risk of such theft to third parties, banks endured the losses themselves and often forced the victim to pay them back, even if the card had been stolen from the mail in one of the bank's neighborhood blanketing campaigns. But as competition among issuers rose in the late 1960s, banks decreased cardholders' liabilities, and retailers and banks were stuck holding the bag for fraud.[30] To further shore up the system, Congress banned unsolicited mailings in 1970.[31] Over the first few years of the 1970s, banks unveiled the magnetic stripe on the credit card. Rather than a number being manually keyed into a register or a carbon imprint being made, a card could simply be swiped. A computer could then connect that account to a central computer. This innovation, which made each transaction instantly traceable, enabled banks and retailers to end the rampant fraud of the 1960s.[32]

Not all spending sprees, like Joseph Miraglia's, were due to intentional fraud. More typical was the case of an Atlanta janitor, earning $55 a week, who received a BankAmericard in the mail from First National Bank of Atlanta. In a few months he racked up more than $3,000 in debt. Like many other people accustomed to the firm control of the credit man, this janitor thought that if the bank was willing to extend him the credit, he was good for it. He was not. For BankAmericard his default and eventual bankruptcy were a calculated risk, but for the janitor, First National Bank's easy credit ruined him.[33] As one government official remarked, banks used "a statistical approach . . . rather than individual analyses of the financial responsibility of applicants."[34] Banks expected some people to be unable to pay and to go bankrupt, but the cost of verifying the creditworthiness of all borrowers exceeded the cost of writing off the bad debt. The risks that a large institution could bear and the bankruptcies that individuals could endure, however, were rarely the same.

Many working-class Americans, like this janitor, were less able to handle access to credit cards because their entire lives they had had to beg and scrape for credit access. A bankruptcy attorney told a story of a couple with "menial jobs" who came into his office one day. Going over their spending, he found all the usual purchases except for one: an $1,100 electronic organ. They had bought it because it "made 'nice music.' " The attorney then asked them why they had bought it when they were already underwater with their other obligations, to which the "husband turned to [the lawyer] somewhat in anger and blurted out: 'If I couldn't afford it, why did they let me have it?' " On some level, many borrowers trusted salesmen too much and lacked the financial skills to decide for themselves what they could afford. Particularly for banks, their conservative image made borrowers believe they could spend the credit that was offered them.[35] In a cash economy, where you can buy only with what money you have, financial skills don't matter as much as in a credit economy, where a few bad choices can quickly destroy a couple's life.[36] Betty Furness, President Lyndon Johnson's special assistant for consumer affairs, described the credit card as the "modern Aladdin's lamp" through which all of one's dreams could come true. Yet she also believed that with wider access to credit cards, "those least equipped to cope with credit . . . become the hopeless addicts."[37]

Though banks tended to give credit cards to the well-to-do, some people of the working and middle class also had access. Those borrowers used credit cards very differently from the wealthy. The lower the class of the shoppers, the more likely they were to use credit cards as a form of installment credit rather than convenience credit. Only 18 percent of lower-class credit card users paid off their balances every month, compared to 48 percent of upper-class users.[38] What is surprising about those numbers is not that the wealthy could pay off their balances but that less than half did! Many of those who had money—and those who didn't—used credit cards in the same way. Still, most of the wealthier borrowers paid their bills every month. In the 1950s, the well-to-do generally paid off their credit in a month or two in comparison to a national average time to repayment of about a year and four months.[39]

Credit cards were used like installment credit, but with much higher interest payments.

Wider access came in the late 1960s as the regional credit networks coalesced into BankAmericard and Master Charge. It is hard to conceive that in 1967 the Federal Reserve found it remarkable that Connecticut and Massachusetts had two credit card systems linked together. The network synergies of California enabled BankAmericard to go national, and, following that, everybody else had to either get with the program or start their own. In response, eighty-one other commercial banks in California banded together to form a competing credit network—Interbank Card Association—soon to become Master Charge.[40] Master Charge banks learned from BankAmericard's mistakes and incurred fewer bad-debt losses. Through all the promotions of the two systems, Californians became more exposed to the new plastic than any other Americans. One-fifth of independent California retailers honored credit cards, 50 percent higher than the national average.[41]

The rest of the country followed California. It wasn't until 1969 that New York banks issued BankAmericard and Master Charge. Even then, the second largest bank in the country behind Bank of America—Chase Manhattan—still did not offer a credit card.[42] In 1968, less than 10 percent of banks offered credit cards.[43] The consolidation of a national system took a few years, but the advantages of joining a network became apparent, even if it meant sending along some of the profits to Bank of America. A few local programs remained in New York City and in certain states such as Georgia and Michigan, but by the early 1970s, most banks were aligned with either BankAmericard or Master Charge,[44] which dramatically increased the usefulness of credit cards. Credit cards took off because of those new networks.[45]

The network effect is evident in the proliferation of card programs from 1967 to 1968 as BankAmericard and Master Charge spread. In September 1967, 197 banks offered credit cards, and by June 1968—just nine months later—that number had more than doubled, to 416.[46] Yet despite the greater availability of bank cards, most retail borrowing (93 percent) remained through the store and not the bank.[47]

Master Charge turned out to be good for BankAmericard, which was threatening to look like a monopoly. Whenever credit networks attempted to prevent retailers from accepting competitors' cards, the Justice Department stepped in to restore competition—or at least duopoly.[48] With strong competition from at least one other group, the national networks were allowed to exist. Even the Federal Reserve considered the credit networks a possible "natural monopoly" where the benefits of one or two networks outweighed the benefits of competition.[49] In fact, what BankAmericard and Master Charge did was make a national credit distribution system, like power lines, and allow any bank to produce capital for that network, like a power plant. In the view of many economists, this is the most efficient way to run a network, be it electricity, railroads, or credit. The networks enabled even small banks to profitably run credit cards in a way that without BankAmericard or Master Charge would have been impossible—by adding the value of a network to the value of their capital.

The network not only made retailers and shoppers want to join, it allowed a scale of lending that was unprecedented. What made this possible was that BankAmericard was backed not just by Bank of America but by thousands of banks across the country. BankAmericard was the first credit card issued by banks using only bank capital. The potential capital available from banks, both in their own coffers and what they could borrow from capital markets, far surpassed anything that even GE or Federated could raise. It was the franchise quality of BankAmericard and Master Charge that made the credit revolution possible.

Retailers naturally wanted to tap into that existing network to draw in the most customers. For small businesses, in particular, the advantages were legion. The elimination of receivables and all the capital tied up in unpaid bills had a real consequence. For instance, C. F. Baumann, of California's Bermuda Pools Service, loved credit cards because they reduced his unpaid bills by 50 percent. The owner of a small Atlanta slacks retailer, The Bottom Half, liked that he got paid by BankAmericard whether or not the customer paid Bank of America. The fee he paid the bank was less than his previous bad-debt losses.[50] Though it may have reduced their overall profitability, for many growing small businesses cash flow can ultimately matter more. Suppliers today want cash, not a pile of IOUs. Small chains, such as local grocery store chains, found that they could once again offer credit, something stores hadn't done profitably since the 1920s. Customers tended to buy more and buy more regularly, eliminating the payday inventory crunch that many grocers faced.[51]

In Buffalo, for instance, E. H. Gugliotta managed a small shoe store that regularly lost business to the department store down the street. As soon as he began to participate in Marine Midland's credit card program, his "store went into the black and it's all because of the credit card. People used to look into the window and then keep walking . . . now they see the credit card deal and come in." Shoppers also tended to buy two or three pairs at a time instead of just one.[52] Small stores and independent chains benefited the most from the credit card, enabling them to compete with the big stores.[53] Credit cards helped a more decentralized retail landscape to flourish. In New York alone, Citibank enabled more than 21,000 retailers to offer credit to their customers.[54] Overnight, credit returned to the New York economy. That corner grocery that had had to cut off credit in the 1920s could offer it again. By 1970, 90 percent of the retailers accepting credit cards were small businesses.[55] The big chains dominated the sales volume, but the little shops used credit to compete. For retailers who could not offer credit like the big department stores did, whether fancy clothing boutiques or neighborhood pet shops, credit cards allowed them to compete more aggressively for every consumer's dollar.[56] By 1970, 600,000 retail outlets accepted either Master Charge or BankAmericard. The Master Charge and BankAmericard networks, started only in 1967, were in nearly every state.

Though department stores and their retail progeny still offered credit based on the institution of the 1950s—the credit subsidiary—Americans found hundreds of thousands of alternatives made possible by BankAmericard and Master Charge. Yet for all the worry, all the attention, credit cards accounted for only 2 percent of consumer debt in the early 1970s.[57] Compared to retail credit, car loans, and home mortgages, it was a statistical fluctuation smaller than the Christmastime bump in borrowing. Credit cards could be used everywhere, but they still weren't used as more traditional forms of credit—yet.

Despite the low numbers, something seemed different about credit cards, not the least of which was how quickly they had penetrated the American marketplace. By 1970, around 40 million Americans had credit cards, nearly all of which were either Master Charge or BankAmericard. While credit card lending grew, other forms of borrowing proved more difficult, particularly after the credit crunch of 1966 nearly choked off American mortgage lending. A letter to the editors of *Life* magazine in 1970 from an Angeleno named C. C. Copley described the situation facing the United States far better than nearly any scholarly or journalistic analysis of the looming credit crisis facing the country. Copley explained that "businessmen with solid credit ratings have difficulties in borrowing for such legitimate causes as plant expansion, meeting payrolls or building seasonal inventories. . . . At the same time, we, as consumers, are enticed, cajoled and arm-twisted to buy nickel and dime items and luxuries on the installment plan. There is no money shortage there! Of course, the 18% interest is an irresistible bonanza for the banks."[58]

For most banks, credit cards were not an irresistible bonanza. Lenders wanted to expand, but the law and costs constrained them. The seemingly inevitable profits were sapped by fraud, default, and mismanagement. What seemed like an opportunity to print money turned out, for most banks, to be a drain on resources. Processing all the paper credit slips was expensive. As more banks joined the networks, the correspondence became more complicated.[59] For most of the 1960s and 1970s, credit cards' profitability was blah, despite their higher interest rates. If First National Bank of Atlanta was typical in its introduction of BankAmericard in 1968, it was also typical in that the credit card dragged down its earnings for several years.[60] Even at Citibank, which was always in the vanguard of lending, credit cards were a mixed bag. From 1967, when it introduced a credit card, until 1971, the credit card unit was in the black for only a few months.[61]

Though consumers demanded more credit, banks found themselves limited by the law. In the mid-1970s, banks were hemmed in by usury laws, which capped interest rates. Beginning with Arkansas in 1957, the states, which since the 1920s had raised usury limits, began to lower them again. In 1970, a turning point came when the Wisconsin Supreme Court found that the state's usury limit of 12 percent applied not only to cash loans but to retail credit as well.[62] Historically, usury laws had constrained only cash lending, not installment or revolving credit. This interpretation, coupled with the increasingly strict usury laws, slowly turned the screw on lenders' profits. In New York, for instance, Citibank could lend money at only half the interest rate (10 percent) that Macy's could charge. In Minnesota, in 1973, Marquette National Bank charged its BankAmericard holders a membership fee because the legal lending rate of 12 percent "doesn't," according to bank vice president Jack Bell, "allow us to make a satisfactory profit."[63] Minnesota retailers, such as Dayton's department stores, stopped their revolving credit programs. BankAmericard suspended new applications.[64]

With such low rates, it was hard to make money if there were any defaults. Even just keeping track of who owed what to whom cost too much. Higher-risk borrowers necessitated higher interest rates. Most retailers could not stop lending for fear of choking off sales, but they could revert to older forms. Dayton's in Minnesota, for instance, shifted its revolving credit customers back to installment credit.[65] But banks, without the profits of selling merchandise, simply could not lend. For the expanding credit card market, interest rate regulation—controlled by individual states—determined the chance of either success or failure. In 1978, Citibank and every other credit card issuer's luck changed.

Though the largest banks can seem to dictate the development of finance, small banks, such as Marquette National, can sometimes make a difference as well—particularly in matters of regulation. In a seemingly insignificant case—now called the *Marquette* decision—the Supreme Court unintentionally dismantled all the usury laws of the United States. While the decision was obvious and simple, the consequences were not. An enterprising Nebraska bank had been soliciting credit cards in nearby Minnesota. Minnesota, at the time, had lower interest rate caps than Nebraska. Since the Nebraska bank could charge a higher interest rate, it could lend to riskier customers. Marquette had stopped issuing new cards since Minnesota had capped the interest rate.[66] Naturally, the good citizens of Minnesota, and the banks of Minnesota in particular, were not happy at seeing their laws undermined by Nebraska. The Supreme Court, in a unanimous decision, sided with Nebraska. Since residents of Minnesota could legally go to Nebraska and borrow money there, the residents of Minnesota should not be penalized, as Justice William Brennan wrote, for "the convenience of modern mail."

Without state sovereignty over interest rates, South Dakota and Delaware, states not known for their financial services industries but that lacked interest rate caps, quickly drew the attention of the coastal banks. A bank in either could lend anywhere. Citibank, the indomitable New York bank, began to consider its options. Citigroup's chairman, Walter Wriston, after taking local movers and shakers pheasant hunting and promising myopic local bankers not to compete for their oh-so-profitable South Dakota clients, moved Citi's credit card operations from Long Island to South Dakota. Behind Citibank's transition was the technologically savvy young executive John Reed, who believed that consumer finance could be the future of the traditional commercial bank. From 1973 to 1984, he headed Citibank's consumer finance division, leading Citibank's then-pioneering initiative to give credit cards to customers who had no other relationship with the bank. Getting a credit card had nothing to do with being a depositor. Reed envisioned consumer finance as something unto itself. After *Marquette,* when interest rates could float freely in a nationally competitive market, this possibility became a reality as interest rates quickly rose. Real profits, after millions of dollars in losses during the 1970s, became a possibility for the credit card business.

With the change in the regulatory environment, banks could lend at whatever rate they chose. Even if the state no longer restrained their rates, the market did. Mature competition between Master Charge and BankAmericard, now called Visa, kept merchants' discounts low, which kept the banks' revenues down. Booming interest rates made funding consumer credit expensive, which kept costs high. On both sides, profits were threatened. Even as opportunities seemed to blossom in the credit card industry, bankers were apprehensive about the cards' future profitability.[67]

In 1971, the head of credit of J. C. Penney told *BusinessWeek* that "the telephone rings almost every day, with bankers trying to talk us into changing our policy [of not allowing bank cards]. Our answer is always no, but admittedly we're in a better position than most retailers to resist the pressure."[68] Yet the underlying economy was changing, and department store credit no longer made sense. Department store credit had flourished in the prosperous postwar economy. It had been easy to lend when most people got annual raises and kept their jobs. The 1970s economy of rising unemployment and stagnating wages made deciding to whom to lend more

Credit cards slowly displaced store credit in the 1970s.

challenging. Moreover, banks and stores wanted opposite practices from their borrowers. Banks wanted interest, which meant slow repayment, and stores wanted more sales, which meant quick repayment.[69] With budgets tightened, the banks and borrowers' interests were more aligned. With the rise of distributed credit, department stores lost one of their key competitive advantages over specialty chains and discount stores.

Department stores resisted the bank cards every step of the way. In the middle of the decade, one-fifth of the top one hundred department stores had begun to accept the high-status American Express card, but most stores continued to refuse Amex as well as Visa and Master Charge.[70] By the end of the 1970s, however, many department stores began to reconsider their credit programs. While a minority of high-end stores, such as the ultraluxe Neiman Marcus, maintained their programs, other stores began to accept bank cards. Young people, raised with discounters, focused on finding the best prices and had less store loyalty than their parents.[71]

In the fall of 1979, despite being in a better position to resist, J. C. Penney was the first national department store to take Visa or MasterCard, but others soon followed.[72] The economics of credit had changed. Bank cards were able to profit from interest paid by borrowers, not just a cut of the merchant's revenue. Issuers were able to cut merchant fees from 4 percent in 1975 to 2 percent in 1979, so department stores needed to weigh the cost of offering their own credit against the bank cards' lower fees.[73] Equally important, both banks and retailers realized that banks could more easily shoulder bad debts than stores could.[74]

As the economy pushed and banks pulled consumers toward longer repayment periods, department store cards predicated on quick repayment were no longer viable. Stores could no longer afford to lend. By 1979, Federated Department Stores admitted that it no longer made money on its cards, but at the same time, as its head of credit said, "they are our link to the customer."[75] By 1977, more than half of all department store sales were on credit, and stores felt they had no option.[76] The VP of retail sales for American Express observed that department stores "consider their charge account base to be the lifeblood of their business."[77] So much effort and money had been invested in offering credit over the years that it seemed unbelievable that the department stores should give up their store cards. After all, credit had acted as a barrier to entry for many of the stores and kept out the competition. If their customers could easily use BankAmericard, the stores would once again need to compete more openly on price—which more vitally threatened their bottom lines. Even Federated, which had "vowed" never to allow bank cards, tested outside credit in its Miami stores, forcing other retailers, such as Dayton Hudson, to "look closer" at their credit programs.[78] The successful experiences of their competitors, more than any argument, swayed big retailers to accept bank cards. Like their customers, retailers had entrenched ideas as to how credit should work.[79] Stores that accepted bank cards actually got new business.

While credit card rates rose, so did interest rates throughout the country. Shortly after the *Marquette* decision, in 1979, President Jimmy Carter appointed Paul Volcker the chairman of the Federal Reserve in an effort to stamp out the inflation that afflicted the economy. Volcker raised interest rates to slow the economy and dampen inflation. He was successful but in the process caused the recession of the early 1980s.

Banks' high cost of borrowing drove the final nail into the coffin of the usury laws. Even states that still had usury laws on the books could not seriously expect the banks to borrow from the Federal Reserve at 20 percent and then lend that money to consumers at 6 percent. In places where banks were restricted, loans ceased. Banks that lent money lost money. In Texas, the usury limits were flexibly pegged to the discount rate, yet lending still ground to a halt. One Houston banker, E. Michael Gatewood, told *The Wall Street Journal* that "loan demand is literally dead." With high rates of inflation, rational consumers should have borrowed, but the high numbers shocked potential borrowers. Gatewood observed, "there's obviously psychological impact when you talk about high interest rates. The consumer is just not interested in going into debt. People are concerned about the economy, and it goes right down to their individual credit."[80] Even the group historically most likely to borrow—newlyweds—was cutting back. A recent California bride, Marcie Leonard, canceled eleven credit cards and postponed buying furniture on install-ment because "prices are just too high and credit charges are exorbitant."[81] Rather than borrowing more, people borrowed less as inflation climbed.

The high interest rates presented credit card companies with a golden opportunity. Credit card interest rates had risen alongside other interest rates, but when the recession ended in 1983 and all the other interest rates fell, credit cards maintained their high—23 percent—rates. It was then, in 1983, when Citibank's bets of the 1970s paid off handsomely. Rather than drop the interest rates and return to their tradi-tionally affluent clientele, credit card lenders began to lend to riskier—and more profitable—borrowers. The time of credit cards for everyone had arrived. For John Reed, the success of credit cards led to his success, as he assumed the chairman-ship of Citibank in 1984.

By then, Master Charge and BankAmericard had long since divorced themselves from the banks that created them. As Master Charge, and especially BankAmericard, consoli-dated their credit networks, member banks increasingly resented sending a slice of their profits off to a much larger competitor. In California, for instance, Wells Fargo did not want to issue cards with its rival's name on it.[82] Beginning in 1970, member banks slowly bought out BankAmericard from Bank of America. In 1977, BankAmericard was renamed Visa.[83] Master Charge's name change to MasterCard followed in 1979. The credit networks had completely separated from the capital sources.

While John Reed remade Citibank, another young executive named Jack Welch rode the new credit economy to power. In 1977, Welch was given the reins at GE Credit, the division that managed all those revolving credit accounts. With $11 billion in assets at the beginning of the 1970s, the division had a lot of possibility but was not at the sexy center of GE's manufacturing, which had been building earth-shattering engines, in fact the first-ever jet engines, since World War II. With space shuttles and jets filling the skies and swelling the hearts of patriots, it was hard to convince people that light-bulbs and credit cards could possibly compare. Taking the profits from selling lightbulbs and investing them in debt, Welch began to shine at General Electric. Three hundred fifty retailers maintained private-label credit programs through GE in 1979.[84] By 1980, GE Capital had $70 billion in assets, including $9 billion overseas.

When Jack Welch took the helm at GE in 1981, based to a large degree on his success in consumer finance, his vision was clear: "Finance is not an institution—it has to be the driving force behind making General Electric the most competitive enterprise on earth." Older divisions, including the lighting division, which he had managed during his rise to power, would be continued, but the profits would be reinvested in financial products. Divisions that were losing profitability, such as the one that made toasters and clocks, were sold. U.S. manufacturers could not compete with low-cost products from Asia. By the mid-1980s, 70 percent of nonautomotive consumer goods came from Asia, brought across the Pacific in container ships. The general electrical products that had given GE its name were no longer even made by the company. The purpose of GE was to make money. Welch no doubt agreed with U.S. Steel president David Roderick's assessment in 1979 that "the duty of [U.S. Steel's] management is to make money, not steel." Unfortunately, although making money is good for U.S. Steel, making steel created more good-paying jobs for average folks.

It is hard to convey the kind of generational revolution that this kind of financial thinking amounted to. U.S. Steel had beaten the Nazis. American jet engines intimidated Communists. Turning the great centers of American manufacturing into financial companies, which, as Henry Ford would have been the first to assert, produced nothing, was appalling to many CEOs, who prided themselves on making *something*. In a joint interview in 1996, *Fortune* magazine asked Jack Welch and Roberto Goizueta, then the CEO of Coca-Cola, about the rest of the decade. For Welch the answer was clear: "I think, without question, that financial services, because of the opportunities available, will become an increasing mix of our business. That is absolutely going to happen." The CEO of Coca-Cola demurred, surprised: "I would never find excitement in the financial services. I dislike to produce something that I could never touch." Though GE's profits grew, its manufacturing in 1995 was 10 percent less than in 1980, the company having closed 43 percent of its factories. In 1980, the year before Welch took control, GE employed 285,000 people in the United States. In 1998, as the company financialized, it employed only 165,000. For Welch, and for successful U.S. corporations, the rise in profits from turning manufacturing capital into financial capital mattered more than all the good-paying factory jobs—and he had no choice. CEOs have a responsibility to shareholders to produce more profit. A dollar invested in debt made more money than a dollar invested in a factory. The benefit was clear. For the country as a whole, however, the rising profitability of finance came at a devastating cost as the largest U.S. industrial corporations began to see finance as the road to growth. More money, it seemed, could be made by financing purchases than by making goods to be sold.

If the increase in borrowing only underlined Americans' economic troubles, for lenders, the borrowing boom of the 1980s proved immensely profitable. Though John Reed's consumer finance division had lost tens of millions of dollars in the 1970s, the hundreds of millions earned in the 1980s more than made up for the loss. The growth of General Electric's financial divisions revived the stagnating company and led Jack Welch to be celebrated as one of the country's greatest CEOs. Credit cards had become tremendously profitable, reorienting commercial banks and manufacturing companies toward consumer finance as never before.

Banks of all sizes pioneered credit in the 1960s, but by the 1980s large banks were again in control. Though any bank could tap into the MasterCard and Visa networks, only the largest issuers had the economies of scale to make it profitable. The largest card companies could offer interest rates 4 percent lower than those of their smaller competitors.[85] While small banks, with less than $25 million in assets, averaged 203 loans per credit employee, banks with more than $500 million averaged 1,702 loans per credit employee—eight times as many loans, substantially lowering labor costs.[86] By the early 1980s, the top fifty issuers owned 70 percent of the outstanding balances. Citibank, GE, and other large financial institutions were poised for success.

Credit cards had come a long way in only a decade—from 10 percent of receivables in 1968 to 35 percent by 1977.[87] To keep this expansion going would require more money to lend. Even as Reed and Welch remade the industry, the basic stuff of credit—capital—remained scarce and expensive. In the 1980s, an old idea that had long remained dormant—securitization—would be applied to the newest form of credit, flooding the Visa and MasterCard networks with money to lend. GE, Citibank, and other finance companies could help the Joseph Miraglias across the country bring good things to life—but how long that good life would last would be another question. Once people started using credit, it was hard to stop. Miraglia was let off in 1959—the judge evidently considered his actions to be youthful indiscretions—but, like everything else having to do with postwar credit, the case portended things to come. In 1984, Miraglia perpetrated what *The New York Times* called the "largest credit card counterfeiting ring ever encountered in the New York metropolitan area."[88] He did a year and a half in federal prison. It remains unclear to this day whether his credit rating suffered.

CHAPTER SEVEN
IF ONLY THE GNOMES HAD KNOWN
(1968—1986)

In a bizarre, yet telling, Freddie Mac advertisement in the American Bankers Association journal in 1984, the CFO of Freddie Mac, Leland Brendsel, his houndstooth coat bounded by garden gnomes, claimed to commune with "the gnomes of the secondary market, our omniscient associates." According to the advertisement, the gnomes had brought the dark secret of securitization—the collateralized mortgage obligation (CMO)—to Freddie Mac. Remember the participation certificates from the 1920s and how they had contributed to the mortgage crisis of the Great Depression? For forty years, such bonds had been largely absent from the economy because of their inherent instability. Beginning in 1968, for the most noble of motives, they were brought back with a new name—mortgage-backed securities—but the same old problems. The mortgage-backed security and its successor, the CMO, transformed U.S. finance through the process called securitization, which, like the participation certificates of the 1920s, turned consumers' debt into investors' bonds.

Though clearly the result of an advertiser pulling an all-nighter, the gnomes reflected the basically supernatural qualities of the CMO, which seemed to violate the laws of nature, turning ordinary mortgages that were difficult to resell into easily sold bonds. Even gnomes in Europe and Asia would buy them! The CMO appeared to solve all the problems Freddie Mac and Fannie Mae faced. New investors could be found for all these long-term mortgages now transformed into short-term bonds. With a new supply of investors, S&Ls could readily resell their mortgages to Freddie and Fannie, which no longer had to worry about their debt ceilings. Subterranean, beyond the light of auditors, the gnomish mystery of securitization granted possibilities inaccessible to the natural world—or at least to traditional banking. Securitization offered a way out of the constraints of capital faced by banks in the 1980s, but through a lightless tunnel whose exit remained uncertain.

Congress resurrected the mortgage-backed security in the Housing Act of 1968 in order to solve the urban crisis. After the urban riots of the 1960s, policy makers desperately looked for new sources of capital to invest in America's inner cities. At the same time it created a program to invest those funds in mortgages for the poor—the Section 235 program. Overseeing the connection between these two programs were Fannie Mae and Ginnie Mae. In the same housing bill, Congress privatized Fannie Mae and spun off Ginnie Mae (the Government National Mortgage Association, GNMA). Fannie Mae's budget had grown over the years, as had its debt, and privatizing it would take all its mortgages off the federal balance sheet. Johnson had spun off Ginnie Mae to allow

THE GNOMES CHART OUR PROGRESS

FREDDIE MAC HAS SOLD MORE CONVENTIONAL MORTGAGE SECURITIES THAN EVERYONE ELSE COMBINED.

When Freddie Mac opened its doors in 1970, there was no national secondary market for conventional mortgages. We created it. Today, more than 50% of all conventional mortgages are sold in the secondary mar-

Freddie Mac buys and pools mortgages, then sells securities backed by them. This is not an offer to sell or a solicitation of an offer to buy PCs or CMOs. PCs and CMOs are sold only by means of an offering circular. PCs and CMOs are not guaranteed by the United States or by any Federal Home Loan Bank and do not constitute debts or obligations of the United States or any Federal Home Loan Bank.

ket. And Freddie Mac continues to be the dominant force in that marketplace.

How could one company start an industry? Actually, we have had some help. The gnomes of the secondary mortgage market, our omniscient associates, have made significant contributions over the years—particularly with regard to our securities.

There's no better example than our Mortgage Participation Certificate (PC), the first conventional, mortgage pass-through security. Valued for its quality, liquidity and attractive yields, our PC has linked investors to lenders like no other security of its kind—with over $62 billion sold.

But the PC's success didn't stop Freddie Mac—or the gnomes—from

Leland Brendsel,
Executive Vice President
and Chief Financial Officer

exploring other ideas. In 1983, we issued our Collateralized Mortgage Obligation (CMO). A record-breaker at $1 billion, its initial offer was the first significant introduction of a current-coupon mortgage security with some call protection. So, not surprisingly, the CMO has appealed to a wide range of institutional investors.

The gnomes say that nothing represents Freddie Mac's commitment to innovation better than our securities. We certainly agree. Write Leland Brendsel, Executive Vice President and Chief Financial Officer, for more information. The conventional secondary mortgage market has come a long way since 1970. And its growth has only just begun.

THE GNOMES KNOW℠

Freddie Mac
Federal
Home Loan
Mortgage
Corporation

Communications Services
1776 G Street, N.W.
P.O. Box 37248
Washington, D.C.
20013-7248

© 1984, FHLMC. This advertisement and the Freddie Mac gnome characters are the copyrighted property of the Federal Home Loan Mortgage Corporation.

Circle 135 on Reader Service Card

The gnomes understood the new financial instruments, even if no one else did.

government a free hand with policy. Becoming two institutions, Fannie Mae (keeping the name) would continue to facilitate the secondary mortgage market while the newly made Ginnie Mae would handle the "do-gooder" stuff by subsidizing mortgages to low-income families; the subsidies—if not the mortgages themselves—would remain on the government's balance sheets. Moving mortgages off the government books allowed more money to be spent in the subsidization of low-income housing. Fannie Mae, however, would remain strictly off the books. Its goals, which Congress hoped were not incompatible, were to push for middle-class housing and a modicum of profit. Together, Ginnie Mae, mortgage-backed securities, and Section 235 would redefine the U.S. mortgage system—and determine the future of American finance.

As the postwar prosperity of the 1960s slid into the stagnation of the 1970s, Wall Street acquired a renewed prominence. For two generations after the Great Crash, Americans had looked with disdain on finance in general and the stock market in particular. Production, not finance, had made the United States a superpower. American steel, in the form of ships, planes, and bullets, had beaten back the Nazis. By the 1980s, it was finance, not production, that was making investors billions of dollars. The creativity of bankers, however, was hamstrung by those pesky regulations that had safeguarded the economy since bankers had last been in control during the 1920s. Many of the "new" financial instruments of the 1970s and '80s—such as the mortgage-backed security—had actually existed in the 1920s and earlier and then had subsequently been eliminated for their contributions to the Great Depression. As the postwar prosperity built on manufacturing faded in the 1970s, giving way to the stagflation of high unemployment and high inflation, policy makers began to reconsider those regulations—particularly when the local banks appeared to be on the verge of folding because of the rapid rise in interest rates. Mortgage-backed securities became an easy fix not just for poor borrowers but for lenders' portfolios. The solution for the poorest Americans and the solution to fix America's banks were one and the same: securitization. Like the "easy fix" of the Section 235 program, the "easy fix" for the banks—and especially savings and loan banks—had unexpected consequences.

Since the Great Depression, mortgage markets had enabled the great stretch of the American suburban sprawl. Replicating California across the country, oddly snow-drenched ranch houses defined prosperity. But while the suburbs prospered, the cities fell apart. Mortgage capital flowed out to the suburbs, where FHA and VA loan guarantees made the loans risk-free and high-yielding. In cities, where FHA maps outlined African-American neighborhoods in red, federal loans could not be easily had. Red-lined neighborhoods were cut off from the capital that flowed freely in the rest of the country. Home repair became difficult for want of funds. Reselling homes became even harder as institutional mortgages were either expensive or impossible to get. The same system that produced the prosperity of the postwar suburb also produced the penury of the postwar ghetto.[1]

In the mid-1960s, the ghettos exploded. Race riots had traditionally involved white workers protesting integration, but the mid-1960s gave race riots a new color, visible on television sets across the country. This color terrified white policy makers, who, living in Washington, witnessed firsthand the effects of the riots as the city burned in 1968.

Though the precipitating cause of the riots in Washington was the assassination of Dr. Martin Luther King, Jr., the underlying frustration gave rise to a very particular kind of riot. Rioters didn't march to the Capitol building and burn it down. They didn't march to Bethesda and torch middle-class, white homes. Instead, they lashed out at their own commercial districts. This anger, you see, was born of a specific economy that existed, by 1968, only in the black ghetto.

In the ghetto, the world of the Fat Man and the Skinny Man still held sway. Debt networks that made credit cheap for white people in the suburbs did not extend to the inner cities. There, credit was still personal, expensive, and arbitrary. Home sellers typically had to finance their buyers, who could not get mortgages at a bank. Corner grocery stores still kept their accounts in thick bound-leather books behind the counter. As appliance stores financed their own customers, installment credit and repossession, disappearing in the suburbs except for cars, remained a part of daily life. Interest rates, through concealed costs and add-on charges, could be ten times the interest rates of the suburbs. The repossession of barely functioning, overpriced televisions meant not only the loss of the money paid but also humiliation—and subsequent anger. The antiquated credit system helped set the stage for the riots.

When the riots broke out, according to *The Washington Post,* rioters focused their ire not on distant stores that denied them service but on the local ones that provided them with service—expensive, extortionist service. Though we remember the images of rioters leaving stores with televisions and diapers, the real story took place inside. Before the riots, credit relations were inflammatory, and during the riots—before the looters left with stereos—they burned the records of their installment contracts.

Credit, then, was doubly at the center of the urban riots

of the mid-1960s: an absence of mortgage credit choked off housing, while an abundant, but exploitative, charge and installment credit system inflamed the anger of the rioters. To policy makers, the obvious solution was to connect the inner city to the larger networks of capital that had made the suburbs stable and prosperous for the past thirty years. Suburbanites had watched their home values grow for a generation. Rarely does a policy solution appeal so broadly and appear so obviously correct. Investment bankers, such as George Whitney of the Investment Bankers Association of America, testified before Congress that "money alone is not necessarily the solution to this problem. There has to be a mechanism to transfer ownership to the people who are hopeful of helping themselves."[2] A lack of community ownership, observers on the left and right believed, had led to the riots. Conservatives and liberals alike wanted to extend ownership in the inner city, hoping it would stave off a repeat of those terrifying events.

Finding capital to invest is easier said than done, however. Seeing the instability, big banks would not lend. Even inner-city banks, minding their fiduciary responsibility, invested their depositors' money in suburban mortgages. Modeling lending programs on the FHA loan system, Congress created a program to channel capital into the cities and reduce the risk to the lender. To do this, Congress brought back the mortgage-backed security to fund a new lending program: Section 235.

Owning a home went beyond investment, however. These new home buyers, policy makers believed, would take a greater pride in their communities and themselves. Indeed this moral transformation underpinned the political appeal of the program. President Johnson told Congress that expanding home ownership would "increase responsibility and stake out a man's place in his community. A man who owns a home has something to be proud of, and good reason to protect and preserve it."[3] The very first page of the HUD Section 235 handbook defined the program's purpose as "to enable lower income families to become owners of homes and thereby experience the pride of possession that accompanies homeownership."[4] The political agenda of fashioning a contented, responsible citizenry mattered as much as or more than wealth formation.

Mortgage professionals applauded the Section 235 program as a way to rebuild U.S. cities. Section 235 was government housing that respected free-market institutions, rather than substituting for them, as in government-owned public housing. The president of the Mortgage Bankers Association of America (MBA), Everett Spelman, believed "the position that the legitimate function of the federal government is to aid private enterprise, not to replace it. The most recent and important example of this [outlook] is the interest subsidy programs—the Section 235 and 236 programs."[5] MBA's director of public relations observed that "billions of dollars have been spent on public housing. But public housing never provided a complete answer to the problem of housing the poor, and never gave anyone a stake in the capitalistic system. Section 235 does."[6] The belief in ownership was not a partisan value but an American one. One mortgage banker declared that Section 235 "answered the [rioters'] cry, 'Burn, baby, burn' with 'Build, baby, build!' "[7]

Section 235, in this regard, was only one of several programs initiated in 1968 to restore the flow of capital to low-income urban areas. But of those programs, Section 235 was the most important in that it was the largest and had the longest-run consequences. The federal government's role in housing in 1971, when federal programs subsidized 30 percent of housing starts, was shockingly higher than the 4.4 percent subsidized in 1961, and, according to Nixon administration officials, "much of the increase in housing units . . . occur[ed] in section 235."[8] Government-sponsored mortgage debt accounted for 20 percent of the overall increase in mortgage debt in 1971.[9] While in operation, Section 235 marshaled mortgage-backed securities to transform hundreds of thousands of Americans from renters to owners. Section 235 created such an upswing in housing that by 1972, the president of MBA could declare it the "principal system" for low-income housing.[10] Poor Americans across the country left rented quarters for what they believed would be a true piece of the American dream.

The dream, like many of the Section 235 houses, was built on a shaky foundation. The hope of the buyers and the policy makers was quickly undermined by the problems that gripped the Section 235 program. To understand why Section 235 unraveled, one must understand how it worked on the ground. Nearly every assumption that middle-class policy makers had about the buying and selling of houses crumbled under the Section 235 program. Freed from conventional market pressures, absent administrative oversight, and with considerable profit incentives, the appraisal, brokering, and building of houses under the Section 235 program were unlike any that congressional policy makers had encountered with their own home purchases. The conventional housing market relied on well-informed, competitive market actors buying and selling. In the Section 235 program, the buyer's ability to choose among well-priced houses did not exist for a variety of reasons, and in that lack of choice, the reality of

Mortgage companies provided Section 235 loans . . .

... that Fannie Mae and Wall Street investment banks resold as bonds

Section 235 came to mock the dream of both policy makers and home buyers.

Section 235 promised nothing less than to rebalance the scales of American economic inequality.

The mechanisms of Section 235 appeared straightforward. Section 235 loans allowed buyers with little or no savings to buy new and used homes. The program provided billions of dollars in financing for millions of homes during its operation. Eighty percent of the funds were earmarked for families at or near the public housing income limit.[11] A home buyer who qualified for the program would receive an interest subsidy every month such that the government would pay all the interest above 1 percent. Sliding-scale down payments, which reached as low as $200—two weeks' income for the median Section 235 buyer—would enable even the very poor to own a house.[12] If a borrower defaulted, the government would pay off the balance of the loan. Home buyers could borrow up to $24,000 as long as FHA house inspectors declared the property to be in sound condition. After having bought a home, their monthly rent payments would become, instead, equity. Section 235 would build wealth. FHA administrators such as Philip Brownstein believed the Section 235 program "[broke] down the remaining barriers to the fullest private participation in providing housing for those who are economically unable to obtain a decent home in the open market."[13] By definition, Section 235 lent to borrowers who could not get a mortgage from conventional lenders. The program intentionally sought out the riskiest borrowers, whom Brownstein described as "families who would not now qualify for FHA mortgage insurance because of their credit histories, or irregular income patterns."[14] Section 235 buyers had no normal access to home financing. The program offered them their only chance for home ownership.

While policy makers assumed that market pressures would provide accurate pricing and quality control—as it largely did for middle-class housing—the subsidies of the Section 235 program skated over the differences between the inner city and the suburbs. The market-based mechanisms of the suburbs, which relied on savvy purchasers with many buying opportunities, did not exist in the city. Market prices, moreover, could not exist without a market, and by setting properties apart institutionally and financially, the prices Section 235 buyers paid no longer reflected the market but an arbitrary number determined by a FHA appraiser. Though the FHA appraiser's manual would have liked to define value as "the price which typical buyers would be warranted in paying," the Section 235 buyer, by definition, was not typical, and there were frequently no other buyers.[15] The FHA pricing method, relying on "substitution" of "comparable" houses and elaborate punch card data analysis, could not provide accurate prices.[16] Without good pricing information, Section 235 buyers—trusting the FHA's reputation—paid what the appraiser told them to.

FHA staff appraisers may have lacked prices but more than made up for it in a shocking surplus of preconceptions. Rather than being experienced construction professionals, FHA appraisers had an education that consisted of only nine months of intermittent "generalized instruction" and on-the-job training with other inspectors.[17] Perhaps more important, few white appraisers wanted to spend time in the black inner city. Inspectors were rarely from the neighborhoods for which they were responsible, and they loathed going there. Local FHA offices had to rotate the Section 235 appraisal responsibilities among the inspectors to keep the staff happy.[18] Such rotation necessarily led to less skillful appraisal. Appraisers minimized the time spent in inner-city neighborhoods and complained about having to go at all. Appraisers' work reflected their contempt for the buyers. Though some defects might have been overlooked, it is impossible to understand an appraiser overlooking two floors covered with dog and human excrement, as one FHA-approved home in Pittsburgh was.[19]

Appraisers who worked for the FHA had a dead-end job with little opportunity for advancement and looked on their jobs as stepping stones to the more lucrative private sector. Appraisers interviewed by federal investigators spoke comfortably of having received bribes. Beyond graft, however, was the pervasive feeling, as one appraiser felt, that the only "good jobs" were in the private sector with mortgage companies and real estate firms.[20] Rather than "civil service," an FHA job was "basically a patronage job" reinforcing local networks and connections. Appraisers solidified those connections and furthered their careers by issuing positive reports. Little wonder, then, that many of the most egregious Section 235 scandals relied on appraisers' turning a blind eye.

In the inner cities of Philadelphia, Washington, D.C., Detroit, and elsewhere, houses were bought by speculators, given a superficial refurbishment, and then quickly resold at an inflated price through the Section 235 program. Urban homes were old, and the rehabilitation done on many of them could only be described, as it was in congressional investigations, as "cosmetic."[21] An investor would put in a few hundred dollars' worth of work—painting over old wallpaper, perhaps—and reap immediate resale returns of several thousand dollars. In Paterson, New Jersey, for example, a real estate speculator in league with an appraiser earned between $7,650 and $18,200 per house flipping fifteen properties. In eleven of the fifteen cases, the same FHA staff appraiser, who later lost his job over the controversy, had evaluated the property. Only a few months later, investigations found code violations in ten of the fifteen houses, with several exceeding a hundred violations per home.[22] Those fifteen properties constituted only one-quarter of all the Section 235 properties in Paterson that violated the building code, and they were not aberrant.[23] Speculators' repairs added little value. The difference between the purchase price and the selling price was far more than the cost of repairs. Perhaps most important, saddling new home owners with massive and necessary repair bills, discovered only after settlement, all but guaranteed foreclosure. A busted water heater, whose installment purchase would add $10 or $20 a month, could break a family's razor-thin budget, as it did in the case of one Washington, D.C., family.[24] For many home owners, the mortgage was at the limit of their ability to pay. The faulty appraisal process left many Section 235 buyers in precarious financial circumstances.

Though Congress had intended the Section 235 program to function within the normal housing market, in practice, the agents constructing the housing market—the brokers—fashioned a market different for Section 235 buyers than for normal buyers. Restricted by brokers to a limited pool of houses, lacking experience in home ownership, and possessed of no alternatives, Section 235 buyers were the antithesis of suburban buyers, save for their ambition to own a home. Before Section 235, according to congressional investigators, most of the people buying and selling in inner-city neighborhoods had been "primarily real estate speculators out for a fast buck."[25]

Builders too took advantage of the program. The federally subsidized homes bought in suburban Everett, Washington, to which black buyers had access typified the situation home buyers faced under the Section 235 program. In Washington State, the Section 235 program was tremendously profitable and, according to housing experts, " 'carr[ied]' the real estate market," accounting for, in some counties, as much as 80 percent of all home sales.[26] Such volume came at the cost of home buyers' equity. In Spokane, Washington, a home buyers' activist survey found that 90 percent of Section 235 home owners did not believe their house was worth what they had paid for it.[27] The houses had electrical (41 percent), plumbing (48 percent), wall (42 percent), furnace (36 percent), and floor problems (37 percent), just to name a few.[28] Built with the cheapest materials and slapdash methods, the buildings could not last long, much less the thirty years of the mortgage. The siding, for instance, could be pushed in with only the slightest of pressure.[29] The hollow-core front doors were only a quarter of an inch thick. Inspectors described the springy floors, which, lacking crossbeams, were akin to "trampolines." Overflow valves drained not into the sewer but into the ceiling. Though perhaps adhering scholastically to the building code, these construction standards were atrocious. One of the main problems, the House Banking and Currency Committee investigators found, was the total absence of communication with local code authorities. Simple acts of communication would have righted many of the program's wrongs.[30] Adherence to building codes, a matter taken for granted by policy makers, went overlooked in the Section 235 program, which operated outside the conventional housing market pressures of the suburbs. The shoddy construction prompted observers to wonder if the program, intended to end urban slums, was instead creating slums anew.[31]

Builders defended their actions, however, by blaming the new buyers, claiming that they had brought the slums with them. Many problems with Section 235 buyers, particularly the high foreclosure rates, which ran as high as 25 percent in some locales, were blamed on the new home owners' "personalities and backgrounds." The problem of the culture of poverty, some warned, was more difficult than the problem of financing. Robert Gray, the director of public relations for the Mortgage Bankers Association of America, wrote that "you can legislate a good low-income housing program but you cannot legislate the personalities and background of the people who operate it, nor the people who move into the homes."[32] Home owner knowledge, in the critics' views, was male knowledge born of growing up in owner-occupied housing. Black renters, in particular, could not be responsible home owners. The trope for all these discussions was the "welfare mother with young children."[33]

While bankers and inspectors blamed "the type of people" who bought through the Section 235 program, the problems ascribed to the culture of poverty were in fact the problems of shoddy construction and overly trusting buyers who believed the FHA appraisers. Builders' claims that the problems with homes arose because "the homeowners [did] not maintain their houses" were difficult to reconcile with the lack of cross-beams.[34] Feeling betrayed by both the government and the real estate industry, many Section 235 buyers simply gave up. In Everett, for instance, nearly half of the Section 235 home buyers just walked away from their houses. Those who remained wanted to leave but, according to investigators, did not "because of the fear that it would damage their credit."[35] The twenty-seven families that did default on their mortgage in that Everett subdivision left the government with houses that could not be sold for the amount owed.[36]

Rip-offs were not unique to Everett. In all areas, opportunistic brokers took advantage of first-time home buyers. Poorer buyers, brokers believed, would be easier to deceive. Brokers, particularly, targeted those living in public housing because, as a Denver broker remarked, "compared to where they're coming from, they want whatever I show them."[37] As one Philadelphia broker put it, the Section 235 buyers got only "the really crummy houses, the lemons."[38] In desperation, the broker believed, "the 235 buyer will buy literally anything."[39] Many brokers saw the Section 235 program as an opportunity to unload unsellable properties.[40] Only when the seller, as one St. Louis broker insisted, is "in trouble with his house" would he sell through the Section 235 program. The program presented a tremendous opportunity for tapping a virgin market of buyers. In St. Louis, a broker printed 12,000 postcards to mail to potential customers, who, for this broker, were mostly black and in public housing.[41] A government survey found that, indeed, in St. Louis and Philadelphia, one-third of Section 235 buyers were on public assistance, the majority of them receiving Aid to Families with Dependent Children, or AFDC.[42]

While home buyers lost money on fraudulently priced housing, speculators in urban housing could reap extraordinary profits, relying on friendly appraisals to qualify the housing for Section 235 financing. Investigations found similar stories across the country. Internal audits conducted by HUD showed widespread overpayment by consumers and overvaluation by HUD officials.[43] Overvalued houses would eventually cost the government more money in subsidized interest and betray the trust of low-income home buyers saddled with mortgages for homes that could never be sold for the price they had paid. In nearly half of the audited houses bought under the Section 235 program, the values were, according to the internal audit, "too high."[44] Fraud didn't end with local appraisers and brokers.

Though the Section 235 program was created in Washington, it was funded on Wall Street. While government-insured mortgages had been traded since the 1930s, the mortgages had always been bought and sold individually. Mortgage-backed securities pooled those mortgages together so that investors could handle them as large bond issues, with interest payments and premiums backed by a house's value rather than a company's assets. Like the participation certificates of the 1920s but on a far grander scale, mortgage-backed securities made investing in mortgage debt effortless. Managing individual mortgages was tricky, but buying bonds was straightforward. The original mortgage lender—the "originator"—kept track of the borrower, and the bondholder collected the cash.

The same kind of company that sold FHA loans was still in the middle—the mortgage company. Though brokers sold the Section 235 houses, the actual mortgages did not come from local banks. Few banks were involved in the program. Ninety percent of Section 235 loans originated with specialized mortgage companies, whose only business was lending money and then reselling the mortgages.[45] According to the Mortgage Bankers Association of America, Section 235 loans, in 1970, made up three-fourths of all mortgage company business.[46] Though investors received the mortgage-backed security, the mortgage company would handle all the complicated details of actually collecting the interest and principal payments and then would pass them along to the investor, after collecting a service fee.[47] Crucially, between the investor and the mortgage company stood Fannie Mae, which bought and bundled two-thirds of all Section 235 loans.[48] While mortgage companies assembled the pools of mortgages for bundling, Fannie Mae backed and orchestrated the sales, lending its aura of government insurance to the process. Few private financial institutions wanted to buy the mortgages directly, but when they were repackaged as mortgage-backed securities, investors could be found. With mortgage-backed securities, these proto–subprime loans could find investors in national and international capital markets. Making mortgage-backed securities work, however, required pools of hundreds of mortgages. To resell their mortgages to Fannie Mae, mortgage companies needed to create huge volumes of loans.

In their zeal to bundle mortgages to meet the minimum pool sizes required for Fannie Mae bundling, some mortgage companies falsified credit histories.[49] In April 1973, HUD, at the request of the Senate, investigated mortgage companies that lent predominantly to low-income borrowers. Auditing 1,309 mortgages issued by 250 mortgage companies, the investigators found a stunning record of fraud and deception among a substantial portion of the mortgagees. Sixty mortgage companies, or one-quarter of the total, had provided "incorrect or false mortgage credit information."[50] Mortgage companies would intentionally omit other debts, as well as lawsuits, in an effort to help potential Section 235 home buyers qualify for a mortgage. In nearly 10 percent of cases, the mortgage companies allowed the buyers to avoid paying the down payment, either by paying less than the fully required amount or allowing a third party to pay it. While skipping the down payment misled investors and perhaps helped the borrowers, 33 mortgage companies in 917 cases, or 70 percent of cases, charged "unearned, unallowable, or excessive fees."[51] Mortgage companies helped borrowers get into the house they wanted but made sure that they paid for it. Lending money at arm's length without reliable federal standards enabled too much capital to flow into this noble but mismanaged program. The only people who didn't know what was going on—at first—were the investors who bought the mortgage-backed securities and the government agencies that subsidized the mortgages.

At every step of the home-buying process, Section 235 buyers encountered another appraiser, broker, builder, or banker seeking to defraud them. Deception in the Section 235 program emerged from the explosive mix of an opportunity for profit, an absence of institutional oversight, and a lack of market discipline—in a series of events eerily similar to the those of the subprime crisis of 2007–2009. Quickly after it started, horror stories surfaced in the press, and Congress began to investigate abuses. Even as Section 235 remade mortgage finance, the program fell apart. The Department of Housing and Urban Development (HUD), at the behest of Congress, investigated its operations in 1970. The resulting report asserted that, instead of helping poor Americans to acquire a stake in the economic system, "the federal funds in this program are ultimately going to the speculators, the real estate salesmen, and the mortgage companies who finance the speculator" and not into owners' equity.[52] Though the report described many shortcomings in the program, because the investigation was conducted internally by HUD, which oversaw the program, many members of Congress doubted the report's veracity. So Congress released a second independently conducted, and even more damning, report on January 6, 1971.[53] Though initially HUD secretary George Romney denounced the report as "inaccurate, misleading and very incomplete," only eight days later he suspended the Section 235 program.[54]

With this suspension Section 235 effectively ended. "Who to blame?" was the essential question surrounding the Section 235 program. Was its failure born of individual malfeasance or the very structure of the program? The goal of the program had been simple enough—to subsidize mortgages—yet at every turn, it seemed, the tacit assumptions of policy makers had been undermined by unexpected speculators' incentives or institutional failures. While acknowledging the fraud cases, mortgage bankers such as Everett Spelman asserted that "the individuals who have violated the law should be . . . prosecuted. However the dishonest behavior of these individuals does not represent a defect in the concept of these programs."[55] HUD secretary Romney, less forgiving perhaps, attributed the failure of the program to the underlying naiveté of Congress. The failure of the program was not, he insisted, due to the administration of the program but the program's basic goal of providing home ownership to the lowest-income families. Romney believed that "neither the FHA nor anyone else had an adequate understanding of the problems inherent in an effort to place low-income families in a homeownership situation."[56] Lending to extremely-low-income home buyers was inherently precarious, since, as Romney pointed out, "any temporary loss of income or unusual expense amounts to a financial catastrophe." Putting such people at the mercy of the rigid mortgage system was foolish because "it makes no serious provision toward leniency." The uncertain financial lives of the poor were met only by the steady, unyielding demands of the mortgage. Though the FHA encouraged lenders to give borrowers "greater forbearance," if home owners missed more than three months of payments and could not pay back missed payments, the house would still be foreclosed on.[57] Subsidies could alter the costs of mortgages, but no subsidy could alter the practices of mortgages. Section 235 failed not only because of opportunists but because home owners could not build equity in an overvalued house, no matter what the terms of the mortgage. Whether that inflated value came from corrupt inspectors or easy-credit mortgages is, in the end, immaterial to those home buyers' lives. The program to help the inner city lasted only a few years, plagued, as it was, by fraud and corruption. At the most basic level, policy makers avoided the underlying problem of income inequality by focusing on the apparent easy fix of housing credit.

Though Section 235 failed, the mortgage-backed security

succeeded. Fannie Mae continued to bundle mortgages into mortgage-backed securities and sell them to investors. Fannie Mae confused public and private like no other institution. Though it still acted in the "public interest" during market downturns, liberally buying mortgages and supporting the housing industry, it did not dampen expansions, pushing growth even in the face of inflation.[58] Though ostensibly private, Fannie Mae remained subject to the Department of Housing and Urban Development, particularly through HUD's control over Fannie's debt ceiling. During the Republican '70s, HUD's authority went unused. Privatized Fannie Mae paid a good 13 percent return to its shareholders and remained bullish on the economy. Since Wall Street and not Congress provided Fannie Mae with funds, its obligation was to "show performance" to its stockholders—or so went the reasoning of its management.[59] During Republican administrations, low-income housing was put on the back burner, even as Fannie Mae grew in importance. By 1977, it had more assets than all but five U.S. corporations. Unlike all other "private" companies, though, Fannie Mae could swap debt with the Treasury to give it some liquidity. Despite all the talk of being private, Fannie Mae operated as an off-the-books government entity—a creature of accounting magic.

Enter Freddie Mac. Freddie Mac, chartered in 1970, was exactly the same as Fannie Mae except that it handled conventional mortgages instead of federally insured mortgages (FHA, VA, and the rest). During the 1960s, conventional mortgages had displaced federally insured mortgages as the predominant way home buyers borrowed, but there was no secondary market for them, as there was for FHA or VA loans. When Congress created Freddie Mac to resell conventional mortgages, it too took on the mortgage-backed securities model, calling them "participation certificates" like the mortgage-backed securities of the 1920s. By the mid-1970s, mortgage-backed securities supplied up to half the volume of mortgage debt. During the 1970s, Freddie Mac fashioned a national secondary market in conventional loans that produced the same effect as Fannie Mae's.

For the middle class, conventional mortgages had become more important than federally insured mortgages, and it was here that the stagflation of the 1970s really hit home. As the American economy slid into double-digit inflation in the mid-1970s, interest rates began to climb to cover the rising cost of lending money. Lenders with a large fixed-rate mortgage portfolio, like savings and loan banks (S&Ls), also known as "thrifts," which took in short-term deposits and lent out long-term mortgages, were hammered by the rise in interest rates. The thrift business in the postwar era was nearly as straightforward as the old joke that bankers followed the 363 rule: pay depositors 3 percent, lend to borrowers at 6 percent, and be on the links by 3 P.M. Unfortunately, the rapid rise in interest rates in the late 1970s complicated that enviable job. In Michigan, for instance, one of the largest mortgage lenders was Standard Savings & Loan Association. Founded in the nineteenth century as the Workman's Saving and Loan Association, it had prospered along with nearby Detroit for most of the twentieth century. Like many other banks, it lent low during the prosperity—and felt the sting as interest rates rose. By 1981, on average, it had to pay 11.4 percent to its depositors while only getting 10 percent from its mortgages—losing 1.4 percent! It hadn't lost money since 1893, yet now it was bleeding dry. The resolution of this defect would bring about the savings and loan crisis of the 1980s and solidify securitization as the true foundation of American borrowing.

According to the president of Freddie Mac, Kenneth Thygerson, the S&Ls' share of new mortgages fell from 60 percent in 1976 to 42 percent in 1982.[60] Without access to cheap capital to lend, S&Ls were collapsing, and Freddie Mac was the only way to save them. Thygerson saw this restructuring of the mortgage industry as a "dramatic transition similar to the one that followed the Great Depression." In 1982, like so many S&Ls, Standard sold $1 billion of its mortgages to Freddie Mac. Using that cash, it could lend mortgages at the current market rates and raise that 10 percent. The vice president of mortgages described the mortgage sale as being "taken out of the darkness."[61]

In the late 1970s, some enterprising banks tried to get in on securitization. Bank of America once again led the pack in innovation, offering the first private-issue conventional mortgage-backed securities in 1977, but was quickly followed by Washington Mutual (WaMu) as well as an assortment of S&Ls.[62] Salomon Brothers, the venerable investment bank that had assisted Fannie and Ginnie in launching their mortgage-backed securities, sold BofA's securities as well.[63] By 1980, individual investors could buy mortgage-backed securities just like the big institutional investors did. It was harder for individuals, of course, since the lowest denomination of bond was $25,000, just like the Ginnie and Fannie bond issues, but some investment banks provided "odd lots" of bonds for those who wanted them. By this point, large banks had caught on to the appeal of mortgage-backed securities and were issuing them against their own holdings. BofA's bonds didn't have a federal guarantee but did have private insurance against default. The insurance was essential to reassure investors against foreclosure or a rapid collapse in values. Lee Kendall, the president of Mortgage Guaranty

Insurance Corporation, which insured most of the bond issues, told *Fortune* that "the insurance was devised to cover 1933 conditions."[64] Even if the insurance companies somehow folded—inconceivable!—the mortgages that filled BofA's pools were "backed by a home that is worth at least 25% more than the value of the mortgage."[65] Despite those assurances, buyers demanded a higher yield than on the mortgage-backed securities of Ginnie, Freddie, and Fannie. Private mortgage-backed securities lacked a federal guarantee and, like the participation certificates of the 1920s, couldn't be resold.[66] Only Ginnie Mae, Fannie Mae, and Freddie Mac bonds enjoyed a strong secondary market. The value of moving that debt off the balance sheets, however, made mortgage-backed securities an attractive option for the largest banks.

But the S&Ls could not survive for long even with the higher-interest mortgages in their portfolio. Even at 11 percent, savings flowed out of the banks as it became cheaper than ever before to invest in the stock market through mutual funds. With the bull market of the 1980s firmly under way, even small-timers fancied themselves big-shot investors.

Facing the collapse of S&Ls—the banks most dependent on fixed-rate mortgages—across the country, Congress passed the Depository Institutions Deregulation and Monetary Control Act (DIDMCA) and the Garn–St. Germain Depository Institutions Act of 1982 in order to expand thrifts' access to deposits and expand the kinds of financial products they could offer. DIDMCA repealed mortgage interest rate ceilings, no matter what state law said.[67] The 1982 act followed up by allowing all banks to write adjustable-rate mortgages.[68] The changes brought S&Ls into the more volatile economy of the 1980s, but it also made it easier for S&Ls to resell their mortgages to Freddie Mac. Pundits called this "deregulation," but it did not remove government from the markets; it just changed the nature of the relationship.

One way to handle the crisis was to make the interest rate on mortgages adjustable. Adjustable-rate mortgages had been available in Europe for a long time, but in the United States—because of the widespread FHA system—most mortgages were fixed-rate. Many banks in the early 1980s offered ARMs—and even included lower-cost "teaser" rates to make the first few years easier on the borrower.[69] Despite the lures, most borrowers wanted the stability of a fixed-rate mortgage. Even in the high-interest-rate era of the early 1980s, overall only 11 percent of mortgages were adjustable.[70] For thrifts, however, ARMs peaked quickly.[71] By 1984, ARMs made up 68 percent of all S&L mortgages, but as interest rates fell through the 1980s, borrowers returned to fixed-rate mortgages. Deregulation allowed S&Ls to venture into this new kind of lending and to charge higher interest rates—both of which allowed them to survive—but it was the securitization of fixed-rate mortgages that mattered in the long term, allowing lenders to grapple with their existing portfolios and continue to lend when interest rates fell. Securitization, more than ARMs, sheltered the U.S. mortgage system.

After 1980, the new regulations allowed thrifts not only to buy but to sell in vast numbers to Freddie Mac. Selling off mortgages to Freddie, however, meant taking a loss. Even with deregulation, thrifts lost $5 billion in 1981.[72] Better to cut the losses than go under. S&Ls sold billions of dollars' worth of mortgages to Freddie Mac, which promptly issued bonds against them. The deregulation caused a massive surge in the mortgage-backed bond market, but S&Ls' desire to sell exceeded Freddie's ability to resell.

Since its inception, Fannie Mae had resold mortgages

but always had a large inventory of unsold mortgages that were said to be "warehoused." David Maxwell, appointed president of Fannie Mae in 1981, pushed for ways to reduce the warehousing of mortgages. Reducing that inventory became his number one goal.[73] Any mortgages that were not turned into mortgage-backed securities—and there were many—encumbered Fannie Mae with the same problems as the S&Ls had. In 1981, Fannie Mae had $56 billion of such mortgages with an average yield of 9.5 percent, while borrowing cost 17 percent![74] In the first six months of 1981, Fannie Mae lost $146 million—a far cry from 1976, when it had earned $126.8 million.[75] At the same time, S&Ls increasingly relied on Freddie Mac to stabilize their balance sheets. More than half of Freddie's loan growth during the early to mid-1980s came from swapping debt with S&Ls.[76] S&Ls issued mortgages and then swapped them for mortgage-backed securities from Freddie Mac. S&Ls could reduce their risk through diversification, but they still incurred a substantial risk that if interest rates shifted, they could lose lots of money—quickly. Fundamentally, thrifts' long-term lending and short-term borrowing were incompatible in the volatile economy of the 1970s and '80s. New ways to sell off mortgages needed to be found.

Congress changed the federal law limiting old mortgages to only 20 percent of Fannie Mae's and Freddie Mac's portfolios, but that would only be a short-term fix. With the limits removed, the agencies bought $8 billion in S&L mortgages, but something else needed to be found to give them the liquidity that the S&Ls needed.

Financiers may not have built the jet, but with deregulation under way they certainly could build new financial instruments. Like the jet, the CMO was the product of public-private

HIGH-YIELD MORTGAGE SECURITIES

How to get a piece of the action

Securitization turned real houses into abstract cash flows with higher yields than government bonds.

collaboration. In June 1983, Freddie Mac, in association with the investment bank Salomon Brothers and the commercial bank First Bank of Boston, issued a genuinely new financial instrument: the collateralized mortgage obligation (CMO). While the mortgage-backed security and its antecedent, the participation certificate had paid all investors in the same way, the CMO managed to create many different kinds of securities out of one mortgage through the "tranche."

In 1984, John and Priscilla Myers found their dream house—a split-level ranch on a wooded hillside outside Lancaster, Pennsylvania. In the distance, ducks could be heard squawking and deer could be seen in the evenings at the edge of the forest. A prudent middle-class guy who marketed gasoline for a living, John Myers wanted a fixed-rate mortgage. So they went to their local savings and loan to get a $47,000 mortgage to buy the house. Yet with all the interest rate volatility, the bank could not hold on to a fixed-rate mortgage. What could the bank do?

Tranches were truly a magical solution to this problem, able to turn a simple thirty-year mortgage into short-, medium-, and long-term investments—all with a range of risks and returns. While a mortgage-backed security produced a long-term bond that mimicked its origins, the CMO cleverly turned a long-term mortgage into a range of bonds—from the extremely short term to the long term. Through high-speed computers, investment banks could divide the interest and principal payments on a mortgage into a series of securities, each called a "tranche," that would receive different amounts every month. Each of the different tranches received a different share of the payback from the mortgages. Short-term bonds received a lower interest rate but a faster repayment, while long-term bonds received a higher interest rate but a slower repayment. Shorter-term securities received their repayments more quickly, with a lower interest rate and lower risk, than the longer-term securities, which shouldered a greater default risk and received, as recompense, a higher interest rate. Bewildered? Even to contemporary bankers, the system was mysterious. Only the gnomes really understood, but in practice what it meant was that banks could keep writing thirty-year mortgages and use one-year bonds to fund them. Magic? Maybe. But it meant that all those warehoused mortgages could be sold off. The liquidity problem of Fannie, Freddie, and Ginnie—as well as all the S&Ls in the country—could be resolved. Americans wanted fixed-rate mortgages because they fit neatly into a budget, and with the CMO financial institutions could provide them without incurring the risk that interest rates would fluctuate unexpectedly. The magic of CMOs was that the mismatch of long-term lending and short-term borrowing could be solved.

A CMO enabled the Myerses to buy their house. John may have borrowed the money at the local S&L, but his mortgage was sold off and repackaged as a CMO. The possible owner of his CMO could even have been the Middle Eastern oil tycoon whose gasoline he marketed. He sent his $514 payment every month to the S&L—which remained the servicer of the loan—but he didn't know who actually he owed money to—and he didn't care: "as long as Priscilla and I were able to get the money for the house . . . we were happy." By 1985, two-thirds of new mortgages were funded by mortgage-backed securities and CMOs.[77] Leland Brendsel, perhaps heeding the gnomes' advice, pushed aggressively for international investment in CMOs, issuing, in 1985, a CMO intended for international investors that he hoped would be "paving the way for the expansion of mortgage-related securities market around the world."[78] Salomon Brothers managed the international issue of the bonds just as easily as it managed Freddie Mac's domestic bond issues.

"Mortgage money will never again be unavailable," announced Richard Pratt, the head of mortgages at Merrill

Lynch.[79] The CMO tapped into a whole new category of investor. Though Fannie Mae had dreamed of new investors for mortgage-backed securities since the 1960s, in reality, most buyers had been S&Ls. Despite the plans of Ginnie Mae, pension funds provided less than 1 percent of all mortgage funds by the early 1980s. Thrifts had, from Freddie Mac's first mortgage-backed security issue in 1971, been Freddie's primary buyers—purchasing, until the late 1970s, 95 percent of all bond issues. Only with the CMO did pension funds finally start buying mortgage-backed securities in the volumes that Freddie, Fannie, and Ginnie had hoped. And if there was money to move, there were profits to be made. As early as 1983, just as the CMO was taking off, Salomon Brothers earned 40 percent of its net income—roughly $200 million—from mortgage activity. Mortgages for all, as Pratt said, definitely came at "a price." As old-fashioned savings and loan banks struggled to make profits on mortgage lending, CMOs guaranteed the flow of capital into the conventional mortgage market. The flood of money from pension funds—over $1 trillion by 1985—and other nontraditional investors into mortgage-backed securities gave buyers like the Myerses the ability to own a home.[80]

As interest rates fell, Americans returned to the fixed-rate mortgages that promised predictability. Though lenders would have preferred ARMs—which gave *them* stability—competition from other lenders forced everyone to offer fixed-rate mortgages.[81] And CMOs provided banks with the predictability that whole mortgages could not. Whole mortgages, without diversification, were seen as much more risky. Credit models of 1988 estimated that whole mortgage loans were twice as risky as securitized mortgage loans.[82] Banks that resold their mortgages tended to resell all of them. For instance, in 1986, in the suburbs of Chicago, the little Lyons Savings & Loan Association of Hinsdale, Illinois, offered thirty-year mortgages at 9 percent. In the postwar period, Lyons would have lent the money and held the note until every penny was paid back. In 1986, however, every single mortgage that Lyons made was resold to investors. In just five months, Lyons sold $550 million worth of mortgages. The chief executive of Lyons believed that the lower interest rates were but a respite before the return. Bankers might have remained conservative—in avoiding risk—but their pessimistic outlook pushed them into avant-garde banking.

CMOs spread through the economy, drawing in institutions that had not traditionally been mortgage lenders. The boundary of retail, manufacturing, and finance—already fuzzy with consumer credit—continued to blur. Kmart and J. C. Penney allowed S&Ls to open shop in their stores. Sears, Roebuck set up its own mortgage lending operation (Sears Mortgage Securities Corporation), echoing the trend of becoming a finance company. By the 1980s, Sears owned diverse interests in real estate (Coldwell Banker), investment banking (Dean Witter), and insurance (Allstate).[83] Building on its widespread store card, Sears even launched a national credit card—Discover—as a rival to MasterCard and Visa in 1986. In stores across the country, the Sears credit department became the Sears financial center, offering mortgages, insurance, and real estate services, as well as credit cards.[84] Not to be outdone, GMAC bought the mortgage operations of two regional banks in 1986, to become the second largest mortgage lender in the United States, believing that its purpose was to make possible the "two aspects of the American dream—the strong desire to own a car and to own one's own home."[85] Even GE, through its General Electric Credit

Corporation, offered mortgage-backed securities.[86] Building on their earlier experiences with finance in the 1960s, many businesses shifted their focus to where the money was in the 1980s.

With securitization, American borrowers had cheap access to investors around the world. Oil money from the Middle East financed housing developments in the Midwest. Global finance and U.S. finance aligned to produce a new global economy of debt. Securitization did not result from "deregulation," despite what politicians and pundits might have said. Regulations may have changed to promote a certain kind of financial system, but at no point did the state abandon the market to itself. It was the interplay of public and private—Freddie Mac, S&Ls, mortgage-backed securities—that made these new sources of capital possible.

The newest source of capital, however, proved to be an old one. S&Ls battled for savers' deposits, but that money, by the 1970s and '80s, was going increasingly to pensions, IRAs, and 401(k)s. A huge fraction of CMO bondholders were not plutocrats but working stiffs. In 1981, the Labor Department expanded the limits on mortgage investments by pension funds. In the first offering of S&L mortgage-backed securities, Fannie Mae sold 43 percent of the bonds to pension funds.[87] Pensions wanted long-term investments to match their long-term needs. For union or public-sector pensions, supporting housing also meant good PR with the membership.[88] The losses of the thrifts were the gains of the investors, who could buy bonds with an effective 15 percent yield, which was better than that of AAA corporate bonds then paying 14 percent.[89] The 1 percent difference, coupled with the implicit government guarantee, drove the demand for mortgage-backed securities through the roof. S&Ls could get the capital they needed from small-time savers—but only through the bond markets.

To compete with other investments, S&Ls had to either sell off their mortgages or, in the case of the many hucksters, engage in such absurdly risky lending that they became more Las Vegas than Wall Street, which eventually led to the S&L crisis. The narrative of the S&L crisis that most Americans who lived through it remember is one of outrageous fraud by bank managers. It crushed many small depositors' savings. Though I was a child in Baltimore in the 1980s, I can still clearly remember seeing family friends lined up in the parking lot outside the Old Court Savings and Loan—one of the most notorious examples of bank managers run amok. Despite the sensational explanations, the larger story of the crisis is often ignored. S&Ls, intended to be resuscitated by deregulation, were in fact dead on arrival. Ironically, the government once again turned to securitization to resolve the fallout from all the S&L failures. The Resolution Trust Corporation, chartered by the government in 1989, securitized defunct S&L assets. As part of the new financial regulations of the Financial Institutions Reform, Recovery and Enforcement Act of 1989, Freddie Mac and Fannie Mae took over even more of the mortgage functions of S&Ls, relying on securitization to fund their enterprises.

Nearly a quarter of U.S. S&Ls had failed in the early 1980s, when interest rates rose, but the whole system no longer existed after securitization. The survivors had struggled to remain viable by embracing securitization.[90] In the process, however, they no longer maintained their importance as sources of capital. When Americans saved at thrifts, it made sense to have thrifts hold the mortgage loans. But as American savings found their way into pensions and mutual funds, the S&L's role became more like that of a mortgage company—simply originating and reselling loans. CMOs may have saved S&Ls as businesses, but they also made them into glorified mortgage companies. If S&Ls bought mortgages, they were just like any other anonymous bondholder—nothing special. The real S&L crisis was not a few deregulated hucksters but the complete shift of Americans' savings from banks to markets.

Mortgage and finance companies could just as easily originate mortgages—and many did. In 1984, the same Salomon Brothers that had packaged mortgages for S&Ls and commercial banks sold $100 million in mortgage-backed securities from American Southwest Finance Company. The same secondary mortgage market that saved S&Ls also killed them—at least as they were traditionally run. The S&L crisis showed, ultimately, that S&Ls might no longer be needed. Global bond markets could fill the role of the old neighborhood banker. In a titanic shift in the organization of American capitalism, banks had become service providers, not capital providers.

Policy makers had hoped that the mortgage-backed security would be an easy fix for inequality, spreading the postwar prosperity to everyone. Instead that lofty ambition had produced a value-neutral technology that enabled investment not just in low-income housing but in any kind of consumer debt. As profits in other parts of the economy receded, the profits of this kind of lending exploded. Capital flooded into U.S. consumer debt. Investors found that it was as easy to buy unproductive consumer debt as to put money into productive businesses. Instead of cars, the United States now manufactured debt.

When mortgages became securities, the number of possible investors grew. Rather than just producing mortgages for their own banks, bankers produced mortgages for the market as if debt were a product like any other. It was the same as the shift in farming from subsistence crop to cash crop. Producing for oneself and producing for the market, even if it is still the same corn, results in a very different mentality. Knowing that mortgages could be resold into the capital markets meant that bankers looked for ways to expand their lending that would never have been possible if they had been limited to their own capital. In the era of the CMO, the smart bank could be like the Skinny Man, its vault nearly empty, with a pile of IOUs in a nearby basket. Though in 1883 this meant bankruptcy, in 1983 it would mean prosperity. Unlike the Skinny Man, however, none of the money at risk was the bank's. Investors, who believed in the safety of bonds, and borrowers, who trusted that no one would overlend to them, incurred all the risk. The difference this would make would become clear in the next two decades.

CHAPTER EIGHT
THE HOUSE OF CREDIT CARDS
(1986—2008)

Good parents instill in their children an appreciation of the importance of thrift. Piggy banks, stuffed with grandparents' largesse, abound in kids' pink and blue bedrooms. Dutifully, grandchildren deposit dollars for "college funds," even though, as the parents painfully know, their pittances could not even buy the first semester's books. The purpose of the saving, though, is not as important as the act of saving. Habits inculcated while young can steer adults through a lifetime of responsible decisions. Yet while piggy banks continued for children in the late twentieth century, the actual way Americans saved, both knowingly and unknowingly, bore little relationship with the porcine ceramic atop the dresser. It was this "investing," which displaced "saving," that led so many children to grow up to be debtors.

As the postwar period ended, Americans saved less in banks—piggy or otherwise—than they had before. Beginning in the mid-1960s, Americans rediscovered the power of financial assets. Though bonds had always been popular, stocks, following the crash of 1929, had developed a bad reputation. Time and profit heal all wounds, and by the mid-1960s a new generation was beginning to rediscover the benefits of equity. In the 1970s and 1980s—after Congress revised the tax law—American workers could use newly invented IRAs and 401(k)s to shelter their taxable income for retirement. Unlike the postwar generation, which relied on the defined-benefits plans of large corporations, these employees had to manage their own financial lives. As never before, workers invested those savings in stocks, reading *Money, Fortune,* and other pop success primers to figure out where to put their nest eggs. It worked.

With more savings invested in financial assets such as stocks than in savings accounts, Americans actually grew their wealth twice as much in the 1990s as in the 1960s. Though they borrowed more, the value of their assets grew even faster. Though lambasted for their lack of traditional savings, the financially savvy Americans of the 1990s could look at their capital gains and know that they had much more wealth than their parents did because they had trusted the market. They didn't have to save because now they invested.

Americans could be forgiven for thinking of their homes as being in the same category as stocks. They watched their retirement accounts and house values grow, but though stock prices rose, inflation eroded them. By 1983, stock prices had barely recovered to their pre-1973 crash height, and, after adjusting for inflation, they actually hadn't. For home owners, the late 1970s were a tremendous boon. Most home owners made a bucket of cash during the 1970s from the rapid inflation. Home owners who borrowed in the late

1960s with low interest rates had enjoyed a decade or more of inflation. Inflation might be bad for creditors, but it is great for debtors. Nominally, the house bought for $25,000 in 1970 would be worth $75,000 in 1985, but the home owner would still only be paying the mortgage on $25,000. The $50,000 just sat there.

Though the rising price of houses made for a good "investment," houses were not investments in the classic meaning of the word. Money invested in stocks was put into a business that produced value. Money invested in a house produced nothing. A house was not a farm or factory, just an oversized consumer good. The price might have gone up, but so could the price of snow globes. Mortgages were, however, a good way to save; they created a structured way to put aside a little bit of principal every month. In the boom of the 1980s, investment acquired a new shine, and so too did the "equity" in houses.

Unlike the debt repayment of the postwar period, which relied on rising income, debt repayment of the 1990s relied on rising asset prices. With rising house prices, home owners could borrow against their houses and repay their debts, even if their incomes did not rise. Everyone's house, and the U.S. economy, became a house of credit cards.

The trouble with assets is that to use their value they have to be sold. For stocks, this doesn't present much of a problem, but for houses it does, since unlike stocks, we live in them. Should home owners have to sell their houses to use the houses' rising value? In keeping with the new investment ideas, mortgage bankers of the late 1970s and early 1980s did not think so. Increasingly promoting open-ended home equity lines, banks allowed home owners to borrow, in a revolving fashion, from the equity in their homes. The $50,000 lying fallow could be spent without moving. In the early 1980s, most home owners used their home equity lines like traditional home improvement loans—to fix the roof, to build an addition, and so on. In 1984, as President Ronald Reagan began his second term in office, this traditional use of home equity began to change. Unintentionally Reagan set the wheels into motion to transform our houses from homes into ATMs.

This transformation began, unexpectedly enough, on a television show in 1954. In the mid-1950s, Ronald Reagan was a popular, if undistinguished, actor, except perhaps for the die-hard fans of *Knute Rockne—All American*. Though not a box-office leader on the screen, he was a leader behind the scenes, having been elected the president of the Screen Actors Guild (SAG) in the 1940s. In the 1950s, however, General Electric hired him to tour its factories as a morale booster for its employees. As television took off, General Electric, as one of the largest American corporations, turned again to Reagan to host *General Electric Theater*, which he did from 1954 to 1962. As an employee of GE, Reagan toured the country, espousing GE's point of view, which was, needless to say, more antiunion than SAG's. Explaining his transformation from the leader of one of the most liberal unions in the 1940s to the face of conservatism in the 1980s, he said, "I began to talk more and more of how government had expanded and was infringing on liberties and interfering with private enterprise. . . . It finally grew to the point that one day I came home from a speaking tour and said to Nancy, 'I go out there and make these speeches which I believe—they are my own speeches—and then every four years I find myself campaigning for the people who are doing the things that I am speaking against.' And I said, 'I am on the wrong side.' "[1]

More than just politics, part of being on the wrong side

was Reagan's own experience with his wallet. During his hey-day in the 1950s, the top marginal tax rate, which he was in, was 91 percent. For each additional movie he made in a year, he took home only 9 percent of what he earned. When Reagan took power in 1981, his ideas of politics and taxes came with him, formed, in a large part, by his experiences at General Electric. When his experiences were confirmed by supply-side economic theory, in 1984, he told the Treasury Department to put together a plan of tax reform to give high earners, including hard-pressed movie stars like himself, more take-home pay.

With a broad mandate from the president to fix the tax code, the wonks at the Treasury Department set to work.[2] Over the next two years, politicians and policy makers battled behind closed doors and over martini lunches over what should stay and go in the tax code. At the center of the debates were tax rates and tax deductions. Beginning with President John F. Kennedy's investment tax credit in 1963, tax credits and deductions for private industry had blossomed in the tax code, leaving the middle class, which lacked either the capital or the wherewithal to take advantage of such tax shelters, furious. The economics wonks in the Treasury Department cared less about voter anger than market distortions. The mortgage interest deduction caused housing to be cheaper to buy. Because housing was cheaper than the market rate, the free marketers argued, Americans bought too many houses. Why should homes, as one possible form of investment, be encouraged? People could just rent. In fact, all forms of interest should no longer be deductible. Consumers, after all, were not businesses.

Though Reagan favored tax reform, eliminating the mortgage deduction was nonetheless unthinkable. The reasoned economic argument mattered little to Reagan, who knew that eliminating the deduction would lead to a revolt by home-owning Americans, as well as the real estate industry. While the wonks debated, Reagan gave a speech in May 1984 to the National Association of Realtors, reassuring them that "in case there's still any doubt, I want you to know we will preserve the part of the American Dream which the home-mortgage-interest deduction symbolizes."[3] Mortgage debt had long been thought of as "good" debt, which was why it was protected during the tax reform. Since the 1930s, when the FHA had made good housing a national project, Americans had been encouraged to take out long-term mortgages and buy a house. Owing a mortgage was not just a financial choice, it was a sign of adulthood and the imprimatur of middle-class success. While a mortgage signified maturity, credit cards signified fun. In the middle of the debates stood a few sacred cows: lower tax rates, steady government revenues, and the home mortgage interest deduction. While the deduction for mortgage interest had been tabled, however, all the other distortionary deductions, such as the interest on cars, credit cards, and all other consumer purchases, were still up for debate.

The American Dream of home ownership proved to be one of the most resilient obstacles to Reagan's conservative agenda. Though in principle he was opposed to "big government," all his attempts to rein in Fannie Mae, Freddie Mac, and Ginnie Mae proved impossible. In the mid-1980s, all the agencies reached their debt limits, riding the wave of a resurgent housing market. Reagan's administration—what Fannie Mae president David Maxwell called a "cadre of zealots"—moved to use this as an opportunity to push for totally private alternatives.[4] In 1984, Reagan signed the Secondary Mortgage Market Enhancement Act, which allowed private banks and S&Ls to pool mortgages and issue mortgage-backed securities with the same ease as Freddie and Fannie in an attempt to displace the centrality of the Maes and Macs to the economy.[5] Private mortgage-backed security issues, by corporations such as GE, had totaled only $2 billion in 1983, compared to $70 billion by Freddie, Fannie, and Ginnie. Reagan's policy overrode the state laws preventing pension funds from buying private mortgage-backed securities. The act was part of a broad agenda by the Reagan administration to make the U.S. mortgage market truly private.

Illustrating the gap between "promarket" ideology and business reality, nearly all groups associated with the housing industry—mortgage brokers, bankers, bond traders, builders, and so on—pushed back against the reform. An editorial in *United States Banker* claimed that Reagan's call to "repeal [Fannie's, Freddie's, and Ginnie Mae's] ties to the Federal government in order to compete freely and equally with their private sector competitors" displayed a naiveté about the economy.[6] There was no private alternative. Though buyers and sellers for stocks were easily found, mortgages—always more complicated—had a serious coordination problem. Even the relatively liquid Ginnie Mae mortgage-backed securities found both a buyer and a seller only 60 percent of the time.[7] On a bad day on the NYSE, a mere 2 percent of stock trades would go unmatched. The Maes and Mac worked because they could buy, hold, and resell mortgages—something that never happened on a stock exchange. The secondary market was a market in name only. In practice, Fannie and friends were just traders. Private intermediaries could not take over this role and would almost certainly lock up the system. In this, as in the tax reform, Reagan bent to political and business pressure, authorizing a raise in the debt ceiling of the Maes and Mac in 1986, even as he continued to pursue his tax reform.

When the Tax Reform Act of 1986 was finally passed, the mortgage interest deduction remained, but all other consumer interest deductions were eliminated. Even at the time, policy wonks wondered what would happen now that mortgage debt was so different from other forms of debt. Without the consumer interest deductions, economists reasoned, Americans would borrow less, since debt would now cost more. Their reasoning certainly made sense. Despite their profound respect for economists' reasoning, however, Americans opted to borrow even more.

Behind the scenes, in the halls of Washington and the banks of New York, houses and credit cards—through securitization—became ever more interchangeable. And unlike the credit cards of the 1960s, credit cards could now be used everywhere. The new availability of credit allowed more Americans to borrow than ever before, but in the volatile economy of the 1980s, such access came at a high cost. Bankruptcies rose as more financially precarious people borrowed on their cards, budgeting their payments to the limits of their incomes, trusting that credit card companies would not extend credit beyond their ability to repay it. Though borrowing like this had worked in the postwar period, in the 1980s it did not. Sudden interruptions in income from job loss or illness led to catastrophe. While installment debt default ended with the repossession, credit card default could haunt borrowers for years unless the borrowers declared bankruptcy. Still, borrower optimism abounded even in the direst circumstances. A Harvard University study of bankruptcies in the 1980s found that most debtors, even when faced with the hard truth that they would never be able to repay their debts, struggled on to attempt repayment, unwilling to concede that they had become bankrupt. Most people who lost their jobs in the 1980s, especially the white-collar workers who had the greater access to credit cards, never again found jobs that paid so well but continued to borrow on their cards while unemployed, optimistic that their old salaries would return. The financial reality trumped the moral obligation to repay. Inevitably, reality overtook even the most optimistic of borrowers, leading to an explosion of bankruptcies. By the late 1980s, the credit card went from a sign of affluence to a symbol of degeneration. While talking heads on television panicked about waning morality, the financial structures of profit that had given credit cards to all those bankrupts mushroomed.

Contrary to popular denunciations, the growth of credit card debt in the 1980s continued to be among the upper middle class. Stretching out their payments, affluent consumers caused outstanding credit card debt to skyrocket in the 1980s. Only the most prudent working-class and poor families, with perfect credit scores, could even get credit cards—and then they paid them back. There were potential working-class and poor consumers who, no doubt, could have shown those yuppies how to mismanage some plastic, but they could not get cards. In the early 1990s, the pattern of profligate rich and virtuous poor borrowers abruptly ended, and low-income borrowers began to be as irresponsible as high-income ones.[8]

How could this have happened? People don't wake up one morning and suddenly stop paying their bills. Maybe they do if they lose their jobs, but the change, though it happened during a recession, did so even for those who were employed. What changed in 1991 was not the behavior of existing low-income borrowers but the behavior of riskier borrowers, who, for the first time, had access to credit cards. Borrowers, not borrower behavior, changed. In 1970, only one-sixth of U.S. households had bank-issued revolving credit cards, while in 1998 two-thirds of households did. People hadn't changed; the people who had credit cards had. Around 1991, new credit card companies began to aggressively lend to those who, throughout the 1980s, had been denied credit. The percentage of households with credit cards rose from 35 percent in 1980 to 65 percent in 1991.[9] These new borrowers were poorer and riskier than any before, but credit card companies had, so they believed, figured out a way to handle all the risk. They also believed they had found a nearly endless source of capital. Though the credit departments of department stores of the 1950s and '60s had collapsed under their scarcity of capital, credit card and mortgage companies of the 1970s and '80s faced no such obstacle because of a financial innovation that underpinned this debt expansion. Securitization had come to the credit card and, through its ability to repackage risk, facilitated this new group of high-risk borrowers.

After John and Priscilla Myers moved into their split-level in 1984, they might have watched a shopping channel on their newly installed cable television. Relatively new, the shopping channels of the 1980s offered retail in the living room. The Sears, Roebuck catalog had offered the same thing since the nineteenth century, but not with such lively hosts. Buying the goods on shopping channels, like any other form of retail, required credit. In 1984, one of the shopping channels approached the Ohio-based Banc One about offering its customers credit cards.

Banc One had long ridden the wave of credit innovation. Its largest subsidiary, City National Bank & Trust, wasn't even among the top 150 banks when it became the second bank—after Bank of America—to offer BankAmericard in 1966. Over the 1960s and '70s, City National became one of the leading credit card processors, offering its services to other banks, credit unions, and even finance companies. By 1977, it handled 33 million transactions annually—90 percent of which were on behalf of other banks.[10] Its actual banking assets remained small, but it became a hotbed of financial innovation, always at the edge of new technologies such as point-of-sale machines, ATMS, and electronic banking.

For years Banc One had offered credit cards to traditional upper-middle-class borrowers. The profits of their credit cards in the early 1980s emboldened lenders like Banc One to push into new markets such as television shopping. Banc One agreed to the deal, expecting the channel's customers to have a high but manageable default rate of 5 to 6 percent.[11] Banc One even expected the default rates, at first, to be much higher, before the portfolio was "seasoned" and the good risks were sorted out from the bad. When, after a few months, the default rate held steady at 11 percent, executives began to worry. With $2 billion invested in the deal, executives at Banc One needed to find a way to resell this debt. Two billion dollars, with such high default rates, was too much to lose! No other big institutional lender would want to buy the portfolio of debts as it was too risky. What to do?

In the immediate postwar period, such a situation would have been impossible to resolve. Without the ability to sell all of the debts at once to a third party, there was no way out but to write off the debt—and fire all the executives involved. But luckily for Banc One, the collateralized mortgage obligation (CMO) provided an alternative model.

Pressed for a solution, the innovative, smart guys at Banc One had an idea: why not just treat credit cards like a mortgage? Mortgages could be parceled off and sold as a security, so why not credit card debt? Credit card income was far more irregular, but with enough financial wizardry, something could be worked out. Banc One would retain the servicing income of the cards, but the investors would receive the interest payments—and be stuck with the bill if too many borrowers defaulted.

Two years later, in 1986, Banc One issued the first credit card–backed security, selling $50 million of the portfolio to investors. An unexpectedly risky situation pushed it to find a solution, leading to a financial innovation. The credit card–backed security was a marvel! Without its own capital at risk, Banc One and many other lenders began to realize that their business could divorce the riskiness of the borrower from their own profits. Unconstrained by their own available capital, credit card companies could rapidly expand their lending and sell the debt as securities. The riskiness of borrowers no longer mattered as long as the security could be properly tranched.

Turning mortgages into CMOs offered a model for financiers to turn any asset into an array of securities. Wall Street innovation accelerated, inaugurating an era of financial wizardry unseen since the 1920s. As before, financiers believed that their inventions could not fail and even considered their magic an applied science, naming it "financial engineering." The CMO acted as a prototype for other kinds of consumer debt, not just credit cards and mortgages. Bankers' faith in securitization cannot be overstated. Securitization, by the late 1990s, embraced ever more exotic assets—tobacco company settlements! David Bowie record sales!—enabling borrowing without risking the capital of those directly involved.[12] Securitization offered a nearly magical way for banks to evade the constraints of deposits, capital ratios, and the spirit of government regulations. Securitization enabled an unprecedented rise in borrowing, made possible by the new pools of investor capital.

Securitization could turn any loan into a bond. The slogan "If it's gradable, it's tradable"—popular in the mid-1980s—meant that anything that could be made to look like a bond, that is, given a rating and made to produce regular coupon payments, could be resold.[13] By the late 1980s, that was true. As with mortgage-backed securities, the first investors were large institutions. First Boston Corporation and GMAC securitized auto loans in 1985, and it was only a short time before anything could become a bond.[14] This more general category of securities became called "asset-backed securities," or ABSs. Securitizing debt allowed financial institutions to move debts off their books and thus not have to hold reserves against them, allowing a far greater amount of credit to be extended.[15] Financial institutions could lend far more than they owned. Once lenders' need for capital was reduced, interest rates could be lowered, allowing loans to be made to a wider—and riskier—group of borrowers than ever before.

In 1986, asset-backed securities seemed like a magical fix-all, lowering costs and risks, at least for the lenders, while helping people buy the things they most wanted. Important observers, such as James Connolly, the managing director of the investment bank Salomon Brothers, believed that securitization reduced the overall risk in the U.S. mortgage system: "What we've learned from the mortgage market is that you can reduce default risk still further by carefully underwriting pools of loans that are geographically dispersed." In Connolly's view, "it would take a major economic upheaval for most people to default on their home mortgages, and they're not likely to be more cavalier about their automobiles." Though the United States was one country, it was in reality composed of many semiautonomous economies. Texas, New York, California, and Florida—all states with different economic bases—would all have to enter a recession at the same time for the securities to fail. Bankers knew that such a situation would be unlikely. Oil, finance, computers, and oranges couldn't all tank at once. Could they? In normal situations, "the few defaults can be protected by insurance." Everything failing at once would be inconceivable.[16] Moreover, the new computer models gave Connolly and other investment bankers confidence that they could predict defaults more accurately than would have been possible a generation earlier, allowing them to further reduce their risk and extend more loans. There was no need for the old-fashioned margin of safety.

But there was a need for investment bankers. Though it would take only 1,000 mortgages to create a $100 million asset pool, the same size pool would require 20,000 auto loans or 100,000 credit cards.[17] Putting the elaborate deals together required Wall Street. Computers made the deals possible by rapidly classifying loans—by location, credit rating, interest rate, and size—for assembly into pools. I-bankers had a lot of work ahead of them.

Securitization rapidly overtook the credit card industry. In 1990, 1 percent of U.S. credit card balances were securitized. The demand for securities outstripped the supply. Investor demand, rather than lender supply, began to drive the market. Lenders began to search for more people to lend to. The safest borrowers already had loans, so these searches ended with riskier borrowers. Say's Law of "supply creating demand," long discounted by Keynesians, seemed to be enjoying a renaissance. By 1996, 45 percent were securitized.[18] Seventy-seven percent of the rise in credit card debt from 1990 to 1996 was funded by credit card–backed securities. Americans charged three times as much in 1998 as in 1988. The fastest-growing credit card companies in the 1990s had no depositors at all. Investors, not bankers, lent Americans the credit for their daily lives.

The fastest-growing card issuers in the 1990s were not banks but pure credit card companies that acted like mortgage originators. These companies, such as First USA, Advanta Corporation, and Capital One, lent little capital of their own. Like mortgage companies, they acted as middlemen between borrowers and investors, servicing payments and taking a cut. Like mortgage companies, they relied on securitization for their capital. Since card companies lent to the riskiest customers, their portfolios had a substantial default risk, but with enough tranches and insurance, even a risky corporate bond could become AAA, appropriate for pension fund investors. In 1994, Advanta secured all of its $2 billion in credit card balances.[19] By the late 1990s, more credit card debt was securitized than owned by banks.[20]

Investors embraced the bonds. With AAA ratings and a better yield than Treasury bonds, credit card debt was a no-brainer. The new flow of capital produced odd bedfellows. While unions struggled to keep jobs in the United States and many American businesses found it hard to get a bank loan, unions and businesses could agree on one thing: credit cards for everyone. In the mid-1990s, the Bank of New York pitched members of the AFL-CIO a special card. Offered through Union Privilege, which negotiated discounts for union members, the card featured the profitable lack of a grace period but had a relatively low interest rate of prime plus 5 percent (13.25 percent in 1996).[21] In 1996, for $575 million, Bank of New York sold the union credit card debt—with $3.4 billion in receivables—to the subprime lender Household International, a deal that elevated Household to the seventh largest credit card issuer in the U.S.[22] Though the 2.2 million unionists who held the card may have found it difficult to organize for better wages, they could at least be sure of getting a gold card with "free car-rental insurance, roadside emergency auto service, a retail purchase-protection plan, and extended product warranties" that protected them as consumers in a way that Reagan-era unions could not protect them as workers.[23] And of course, all those hard-won union pension funds earned a good return by investing in their own members' debt. Credit cards offered by the AFL-CIO brought an ironic ring to the slogan "membership has its privileges."

Securitization made it easy for not only Americans but overseas investors to invest in consumer debt. In 1989, Citicorp issued its first credit card securitization for foreign investors, the "Euro issue."[24] Within a year, all the other big credit card issuers followed suit. With their AAA ratings and relatively high yields, the bonds were in high demand for foreign investors. In May 1990, Citicorp issued its first "global issue" of $1 billion of credit card–backed securities.[25] The other big lenders, such as First Chicago and Household, also issued global issues— $1 billion and $800 million, respectively—over the summer of 1990.[26] In the first nine months of 1990, $8.4 billion in U.S. credit card receivables, or 21 percent, were issued abroad.[27]

Though the profitability of a dollar invested in credit card debt fell in the early 1990s, consumer debt investments remained twice as profitable as banks' business investments.[28] The falling profits centered on two seemingly incompatible facts: increased default and increased repayment.

Borrower default increased simply because card companies lent to riskier people. New borrowers needed to be found to meet investor demand and sustain growth. Unlike traditional banks, pure credit card companies had no other business, and with so many issuers competing, all the reliable cardholders had long been tapped out. The 1991 recession brought a rise in charge-offs from 3.5 percent to 5.5 percent in just two years.[29] To a Moody's senior analyst, the rising charge-offs were not at all surprising, since "issuers have gone to riskier and riskier accounts, trying to expand the market."[30] But credit card companies had a new way to handle the riskier loans—and even make money off the bad debt.

In an unexpected way, the S&L crisis enabled credit card companies to lend to riskier borrowers. When the Resolution Trust Corporation sold off the nonperforming loans of defunct S&Ls, in an effort to reclaim some of the lost capital from that debacle, it created a taste for bad debt and companies that could process it. Credit card charge-offs, for instance, along with all those bad S&L loans, could be dumped into this market.[31] For instance, the number one company in the business in 1993, Tulsa's Commercial Financial Services (CFS), began in 1990 by buying $1 million of bad S&L debts for 0.76 cents on the dollar, or $7,600. In eighteen months, the company collected 3.5 cents on the dollar, or $35,000. That was not a lot of money, but the rate of return was still very high if it could be reproduced at a larger scale. CFS quickly focused on bad credit card debt. According to industry specialists, $1 billion in bad credit card debt was securitized and sold in 1992.[32] In 1992, Citicorp, though not a failing S&L, sold $367 million in bad debt. Buyers believed that 20 percent returns were realistic. Buying the debts for 4 cents on the dollar, even meager collections could yield high returns.

Bad debt securitization became good business. CFS led the way. Standard & Poor's gave its bond issues an A rating. CFS's core business was buying bad debt from the top twenty-five card issuers and collecting it.[33] In 1997, the company reported profits of $190 million on $1 billion in revenue.[34] With twelve securitizations totaling $1.46 billion by 1998, CFS had turned bad debt into investable securities.[35] It securitized the bad debt for the same reason that credit card issuers securitized good debt: the loans went off the books. William Bartmann, the president of CFS, explained that securitization was "a very effective tool for business planning purposes [since] it literally frees up all the money to buy the next group of loans."[36] Securitization took bad debts off an issuer's books just as effortlessly as it took off good ones.

By the late 1990s, for every fourteen dollars lent, one dollar was uncollectable.[37] Like any other form of securitization, using tranches, the bonds could be given a good rating by sequestering the highest default rates into high-risk, high-return tranches. With such an easy way to sell off bad debts, defaults were no longer so bad. With that cushion, even riskier loans could be made. Of course, among these riskier loans were actual people, who—as the lenders knew even if the borrowers did not—would not be able to pay back what they owed. Default was expected and planned for.

Yet despite this increase in defaults, there was an increase in repayments. Repayments would seem to indicate that debtors were actually able to borrow even more than they already had. But the repayments came from an unexpected source:

home equity loans. Investors, of course, didn't care where the money came from as long as it came. As long as home owners could continue to borrow against their houses, credit card-backed securities looked like good investments. With rising repayments, lenders believed that they had actually *underestimated* the risk of default, which further encouraged their loose lending.

This borrowing now increasingly took place through houses. Home equity loans began to be used in a very different way now that interest on money borrowed from a house was deductible, while credit card interest was not. By 1991, only mortgage interest was deductible.

In the 1990s, home equity loan use exploded as debtors shuffled their loans from cards to houses. Home equity loans were a seeming win-win. Home owners loved being able to tap "their" equity while still living in their houses, and banks loved to make home equity loans. Unlike their fixed-rate mortgages, few banks securitized their home equity loans. The yields on home equity loans—with their secured liens on houses and their higher interest rates—were too good.[38] Many of the home equity loans, unlike normal mortgages, were variable-rate, and even if they weren't, they were generally of a short enough duration to cause little interest rate risk to the bank. Borrowers and lenders both rode rising house prices to prosperity.

Borrowing against a house, on some level, required less financial reasoning than comparing two credit card offers. Comparing interest rates required math to calculate the costs and gains of switching. Home owners already "owned" the equity. It was the owners' to spend. Borrowing against a house was rooted as much in ideas of ownership as in such a financial calculation. The feeling of ownership allowed the choice to be easier, and nonnumeric, than the choice between two credit cards. Home equity loans were an easy sell.

Debt consolidation did not become the leading use of home equity loans until 1991, when the tax deduction on other forms of debt was fully eliminated. By the mid-1990s, 40 percent of home equity loans were for debt consolidation, nearly twice the percentage of the next most frequent use, home improvement. While 78 percent of consumers, in a 1996 survey, cited the tax saving of home equity loans as the reason they were better than other forms of debt, the use of home equity loans to consolidate debt did not happen overnight.[39] Indeed, the impetus for its necessity was the explosion of credit card debt made possible by securitization.

In the late 1990s, as housing prices continued to rise, lenders invented subprime mortgages. Demand for mortgage-backed securities had continued to rise, and with subprime mortgages investors could get an even higher return. Combining lenders who risked nothing with borrowers who believed there was no risk, mortgage capital, backed by securities, flooded the U.S. housing market. Subprime lending played out almost exactly the same as the Section 235 program had twenty-five years earlier. Hopeful home owners with little financial experience relied on the judgment of experts, who quickly packaged mortgages for resale.

In the aftermath of the collapse of the market for technology stocks in 2000, Alan Greenspan, the Fed chief who had presided over the economy since 1987, kept cutting the prime interest rate. President George W. Bush and Greenspan both feared a recession as the bubble in tech stocks burst. With a low cost of borrowing, businesses could keep growing and the economy could keep adding jobs and growth. The interest rate became so low as to be, after adjusting for inflation, negative. This low interest rate had effects that neither Alan nor George fully anticipated.

In the previous thirty years, as the global economy had finally moved past the destruction of World War II, the capitalists of the world had gotten rich on a level unseen since the Gilded Age. Not since the invention of the railroads had the bourgeoisie been so successful. Global trade, whether on the Internet or on container ships, had created vast wealth. This wealth, for both individuals and nations, needed to be invested. After the tech stock collapse at the turn of the millennium, fearful investors sought safety. But with U.S. interest rates so low, the traditionally safe investment, the U.S. Treasury bond, earned a meager return. The big global investors looked for an alternative to equities that offered both safety and a good return.

The mortgage-backed security, issued by government-sponsored enterprises such as Fannie Mae, presented an ideal alternative. With AAA ratings from Standard & Poor's and other credit-rating agencies, mortgage-backed securities appeared to be as safe as Treasury bonds but with a better return. Real estate prices had been going more or less up for a generation. What could go wrong? For most investors in mortgage-backed securities, the safety of the investment mattered most.

Yet, as we have all learned in the past few years, these securities were not nearly as safe as the credit-rating agencies made them out to be. Much of the discussion surrounding the current financial crisis has focused on it as a failure of capitalism. There is a pervasive sense that a few wrongdoers tricked us and, in doing so, undermined capitalism. The crisis, however, resulted not as much from hucksters as from the very success of capitalism. The question we need to answer is why the hucksters had so much money to misuse.

The money for all this investment came from the global success of capitalism over the past thirty years. Capitalism worked doing what it does best: creating profits for the owners of capital. The rising inequality of the U.S. economy, coupled with the saving economies of China and the Middle East, concentrated a vast store of savings at the top, desperate for investment. Investing in stocks was one option, but after the tech stock collapse, investors looked for a safer alternative that would still earn a decent return. The flood of capital into the mortgage-backed securities markets created a glut of money that needed to be put somewhere.

To invest this capital, mortgage companies needed to produce loans. The hard part was not getting money to lend—which had historically been the challenge—but finding borrowers who were willing to borrow. Lending standards, already historically lax, became almost comical. Buyers could get a mortgage with no income and no assets. Paperwork was scant. Mortgage companies pushed lending on more marginal borrowers, who, never having owned before and having watched housing prices rise as long as they could remember, took the first opportunity to join the ranks of American home owners. With incomes stagnant, the appreciation of a house's value seemed the only way to get rich. The seeming possibility of getting something for nothing also drew in the nonmarginal, who also saw the cheap money as their path to wealth. Even if you couldn't get a job, you could get leverage. By 2005, most borrowers intended to resell the property they bought at a profit. American housing became the province of subprime and speculative borrowers, not the stable market all the investors envisioned. For the mortgage companies, borrowers' defaults did not matter. The loss would be the problem not of the original lender but some investor in a distant country.

Or an insurer. Unlike the participation certificates of the 1920s, mortgage-backed securities, by the 1990s, had their risks carefully balanced by insurance policies—or so they thought. Such "credit enhancements" enabled even the riskiest of securities to acquire the vaunted AAA bond rating, making them safe bets for even the most conservative investors. For traditional insurance companies, the insurance policies seemed to be an easy source of revenue. The market was growing, unlike that for life insurance, and the rate of foreclosures was predictable, given a certain risk level. Reflecting the expected profits of this new kind of insurance, in 1998, American Insurance Group (AIG), a traditional insurance company dating back to 1919, made a $2.7 billion bid for a Miami insurer that specialized in securitizations. Stymied by the larger bid of its competitor Cendant, AIG began its own securitization insurance operation. Big insurance companies like AIG looked to securitization as a lucrative growth field, pouring money and talent into it. The insurance policies gave even risky mortgages the appearance of safety. As long as the insurance companies guaranteed the bonds, there was nothing to lose.

The credit-rating agencies occupied a bizarre position in this whole system. The major rating agencies—Standard & Poor's, Moody's, and Fitch—competed with one another for the business of rating their customers. Inevitably such an arrangement was compromised. If judges were paid more by defendants if they were acquitted, innocence would be found a shocking percentage of the time. All the credit-rating agencies had a strong incentive to help their clients get good ratings. Yet the ratings were treated as objective facts. Regulators used them to evaluate the investment decisions of pension fund managers. Private investors simply plugged them into their computer models. Everyone believed that the risks associated with AAA, AA, and BBB securities were accurate. The same AAA rating given to the United States could be given, through insurance and securitization, to nearly any group of home loans.

Having steadily risen since 1991, housing prices began to rise rapidly in the late 1990s. Bolstered by the low interest rates intended to stimulate the economy after the technology bubble collapse of 2000, Americans dived in headfirst. For most people, particularly of modest means, mortgages were the only kind of leverage they were able to get. Securitization provided endless capital, and investors required originators to produce more mortgages in which to invest. The traditional 20 percent down payment was no longer needed. Americans on the make could borrow large sums of money at a low cost and watch as house prices rose. Perhaps encouraged by a late-night infomercial, an "entrepreneur" would take out a $417,000 loan (the maximum for a conforming loan) to buy a house with only 5 percent down, or $20,850. If the price of that house rose 10 percent in a year—a number that happened in many markets and in every house flipper's head—the flipper would resell the house and would make $41,700, doubling their original money. With leverage, even small increases in asset prices could produce tremendous increases in returns. Watching those with houses get rich and brag about it, those without houses bought in, borrowing to the very limits of their budgets.

Nearly extinct since the Great Depression, interest-only

balloon mortgages reappeared amid this speculative frenzy. Whereas an amortized mortgage paid down the principal every month as a form of savings, in a balloon mortgage no principal was repaid. For a speculator, who expected to flip a house and cash out the increase in asset price, it was the ideal way to borrow. More expensive houses could be bought, and leverage could be maximized.

With a surging supply of mortgage capital, houses became almost ridiculously easy to acquire. A mortgage could be had without documentation, even if the borrower had a bad credit rating and no income. Lenders, at the same time, had none of their money on the line. With no restraint on the demand for housing, prices exploded. In short, the U.S. housing market became a speculative bubble. In that bubble, fueled by easy credit, how people borrowed mattered as much as how much they borrowed. The adjustable-rate mortgage, used by most home buyers by the peak of the housing bubble, made that speculation both possible and inevitable. Mortgage lenders happily accommodated any kind of budget, lending the money and then reselling the mortgage to be packaged as a security. Unlike the traditional thirty-year fixed mortgage, most new mortgages of the 2000s were adjustable—not because home owners wanted ARMs but because so much of the market was made up of speculators.

By the 2000s, as banks sought out new customers, the adjustable-rate mortgage was promoted again, but now in a climate of speculation rather than inflation. The introductory rates that had existed in the 1980s became more important than the "adjustment" feature. With introductory teaser rates, the interest rate on a loan would automatically increase after a year or two. If home buyers bought to the limit of their resources, they had only a few years to either resell the property or earn more money. The short period to resell the house or to earn more money made these teaser-rate ARMs more like the balloon mortgages of the 1920s than like fixed-rate mortgages. Only speculators and optimists could successfully carry out the scheme. But as housing prices rose, the lower interest rates of ARMs appealed to more Americans, who could not afford the houses that they wanted with the higher-priced fixed-rate mortgages. Adjustable-rate mortgages allowed home owners to borrow to the very limits of their income. The structure of the adjustable rate mortgage, intended to shield lenders from interest rate risk, only exposed them to another, worse possibility.

Who were the speculators? They were from a generation that had few other ways to make money. If asset prices were going up, incomes weren't. Though everybody could now get credit cards and mortgages, Americans' income inequality was rising, making fewer people able to pay back what they borrowed. The Internet economy of the 1990s accelerated the growing wealth and income inequality of the 1980s. A 1996 study by Standard & Poor's found that over the past ten years, 20 percent of workers had been laid off, and though 90 percent had found jobs, 40 percent of the new jobs paid less.[40] Every year good jobs were harder and harder to find, particularly for those without a college education. Buying and selling a house required very little education and, with the securitized mortgages, very little capital. The combination of the stagnating labor market and the go-go housing market was combustible.

For most people the madness of speculative bubbles is obvious only afterward. How to tell, in advance, if the rising price of an asset is a bubble? The easiest test is profits. Asset prices rise in a competitive market because the assets generate more money. If a company doubles its profits, it can double its dividend. A stockholder who receives twice the income from a stock can expect to see the stock double in value. The stock market weighs more factors than dividend yield, but as a rough yardstick, it still works—at least in the long run. Prices can't rise 10 percent forever without a 10 percent rise in profits. In a speculative bubble, prices rise without a rise in profits.

In the run-up to the crisis, careful observers could have noticed an inconsistency between housing prices and Americans' wages. Prices rose 15 percent a year, presumably from increased demand for housing. Yet Americans' incomes did not rise 15 percent a year. Average incomes, in fact, totally stagnated. Perhaps the increasing housing prices resulted from population pressures? Though the population did grow, it did not grow 15 percent a year. Such a large population shift could be possible locally, as factories opened or closed, as generations rediscovered city life or abandoned it, or some other factor, but in the housing boom of the 2000s, prices rose nearly everywhere, which demographics cannot explain. The rising housing prices did not result from either rising incomes or rising demographics but from speculation made possible by low interest rates, pure and simple.

Another observation could have been made at the microeconomic level. If you ever have had the pleasure of taking Economics 101, you have studied how supply and demand determine markets. Adam Smith first came up with them in *Wealth of Nations,* but you would have probably learned them from the Nobel Prize–winning economist Paul Samuelson in his economics textbook, aptly named *Economics,* which he first published in 1948 and which continued to be used—albeit through many editions—until the early twenty-first century. You would have learned that if prices go up, consumer demand will go down. This feedback between price and demand creates stable markets. In the coincidence of interest where the price offered by the buyer and the price asked by the seller intersects, the market is in equilibrium. In every economics classroom in the world, this equilibrium justifies the market economy. Markets where demand falls as price goes up are self-regulating. It is the opposite motions of price and demand that create reliable markets.

The trouble with speculation is that it flips the dynamic duo of Smith and Samuelson on their heads. Probably as you read the last paragraph, you wondered, "What if demand rose as price went up?" Such a question is straightforward since it reverses one part of the assumption. Yet in every version of *Economics* this thought experiment is soundly denounced. Economists call these fantasies Giffen goods, after the guy who first asked this question. A professor in Econ 101 will take about twenty seconds to dismiss the existence of Giffen goods. Impossible! Why would anyone want something more when the price goes up? Giffen goods undermine the self-regulation of the market. Rather than a negative relationship between demand and price, as in a normal market, there would be a positive relationship. As price went up, so would demand.

In such a world, the beautifully self-regulating market would rage out of control. The efficient market hypothesis would fail and prices would be meaningless, fueled not by real demand but by the rising price itself. Though this might not hold true for most things, it definitely describes speculative goods. Whether tulips in seventeenth-century Holland or housing in twenty-first century America, speculative goods are Giffen goods. And there is no equilibrium. The market cannot self-regulate.

In most speculative bubbles, the participants choose to be involved. Investors in Dutch tulips or tech stocks knew what they were getting into, and, in the end, only other tulip owners and tech stock investors got burned. Speculation in housing, however, affected not just a specialized niche but the two-thirds of Americans who owned homes. Though most home buyers in 2005 intentionally bet that housing prices would continue to rise, most of those who had bought homes in 2004 or 1994 or 1984 had not been speculating. For them, the speculation took hold of their most important asset and played havoc with their lives.

Until 2007, house prices and stock prices rose in concert. Debt flowed freely from mortgage-backed securities into homes, inflating prices, and then home equity loans turned the inflated prices into a way to borrow more on credit cards. Americans added up their debts and assets and still came out ahead. The debt mattered little because no matter how much it cost (which was little, with interest rates so low), the assets continued to rise in price. Investors with a cavernous appetite for AAA bonds bought as much debt as lenders could produce. As long as both housing prices and stock prices rose, as it seemed they would forever, everything would be fine.

Securitization may have transferred interest rate risk from lenders to investors, but it could not eliminate the greatest source of risk: wage instability. Since the beginning of the twentieth century, lending had relied on the steady incomes of industrial workers. As the postwar prosperity finally ended in the 1980s, older patterns of uncertainty reappeared. It was obvious to lenders that the greatest risk in a loan was a borrower's possible job loss. Professionals like doctors and lawyers had the lowest risk, while entrepreneurs had the highest risk, even if they earned the same money.[41] The important thing wasn't income but the stability of that income. Small-business owners might have lived very different lives from unskilled laborers, but according to mortgage insurers, they had the same risk. As Americans' working lives became more volatile, so too did their credit lives. Securitization could provide more capital, but it could not address the fundamental source of instability in the credit system.

So while individuals looked over their 401(k) statements approvingly and heard from the neighbors how house prices were going up, on the television and in the newspapers they kept hearing that other people did not save at all. The numbers that economists generated bore little relationship to the actual ways in which people saved, and though the people knew it, the media did not. When everyone is an investor, saving, it was thought, no longer mattered. As long as debt kept flowing, there would not be a problem.

In the fall of 2006, the impossible happened. Housing prices began to fall. As credit-rating agencies began to reassess the safety of the AAA mortgage-backed securities, insurance companies had to pony up greater quantities of collateral to guarantee the insurance policies on the bonds. The global credit market rested on a simple assumption: housing prices would always go up. Foreclosures would be randomly distributed, as the statistical models assumed. Yet as those models, and the companies that had created them, began to fail, a shudder ran through the corpus of global capitalism. The insurance giant AIG, which had hoped for so much profit in 1998, watched as its entire business—both traditional and new—went down, supported only by the U.S. government. The arcane operations of the credit markets spilled out into the larger economy, bringing about the greatest economic downturn since the Great Depression. The financial crisis began in subprime mortgages, but it quickly spread throughout the economy, as complex financial instruments betrayed both their inventors and their investors, just as they had in 1929. The global resale of debt had enabled borrowing on a scale unimaginable to the world of 1929, but the consequences were all too familiar.

CONCLUSION
TURNING THE MAGIC OF BORROWING INTO THE REALITY OF PROSPERITY

In 1821, a "Northern Farmer" wrote an impassioned defense of the borrower, calling for the end of imprisonment for debt: "Almost endless are the ways by which men become poor. Does it not often arise from causes which foresight cannot provide for, nor care prevent? . . . For all a man has is under the dominion of fortune."[1] Forces larger than ourselves are often of more consequence than our own actions. "The fair trader," Northern Farmer continued, "when he embarks his all on board a ship, knows not that he shall reach his destined port in safety. The sea rages, and in a moment his goods are gone. Is he a man of fortitude and integrity? Even if all this can be said of him, it gives him no power over elements, and to this providential event he is bound to submit with silence."[2] Today, we are not as much at the mercy of the waters as at the mercy of capital flows. The difference between them is that we can control capital. Though standing in silent submission might have made sense in the age of mercantilism, in our present age of securitization we must speak loudly and demand change in order to shape our fate. When we demand change, however, it must be considered in light of how things have actually operated in the past.

People have borrowed and lent to one another since the invention of money, but how Americans borrowed in the twentieth century was entirely novel. For most of history, personal debt was personal. It existed between two people who knew each other. With the beginnings of the resale of debt, from installment credit and mortgages in the 1920s, a new, impersonal relationship developed. Debt could be traded like any other commodity. Character, perhaps the most personal description imaginable, became abstracted into a credit score. Buying and selling debt became a specialist's task. The debt itself remained tied to the original purchase of cars, televisions, or houses. In the 1970s, this specialized network of resold debt was transformed again with securitization, which made debt look like any other form of security. A bond backed by credit card debt or mortgage debt could not be told apart from any other corporate bond. Consumer debt had become interchangeable. Easy to invest in, the supply of money for consumer credit reached unprecedented levels. The technical, proximate causes of the financial crisis are perhaps less important than the long-term shifts in the debt economy that made them possible. Easy access to credit is neither a good thing nor a bad thing; it depends on context. Credit is just one part of American capitalism. On the one hand, in the context of rising incomes and stable jobs, borrowing enabled postwar Americans to realize their material dreams—years before they could have saved up enough money to do so. Getting what you want now, without saving for it, should matter to all-too-mortal consumers. I would not want to wait until I was sixty years old to have my first dishwasher. One the other hand, encumbering oneself with debt when income is uncertain or stagnant can make borrowing less an opportunity than a shackle. As the volatility of American capitalism returned in the 1970s, consumers relied more on themselves than ever before. The return of economic inequality, all too familiar before World War II, had collided brutally with easy borrowing made possible through resellable debt. Hemmed in by low wages Americans looked for leverage in the only place that they could—through home mortgages. Even those who did not speculate enjoyed the rising home prices, cashing out all that excess home value through home equity loans and using the money to pay off their credit cards.

By the summer of 2009, pundits and policy makers claimed that the worst of the crisis was over. The National Bureau of Economic Research, which determines when recessions begin and end, announced that since GDP growth had returned, the crisis was over. The stock market had regained a lot of lost ground. Unemployment growth had slowed. Housing prices, in many markets, were actually increasing. Superficially, AIG and the rest of the securitization institutions were functioning again. The hundreds of billions of dollars shot into the economy to prop up key financial institutions appeared to have worked.

Yet today the underlying financial practices that enabled the crisis remain unfixed. Financial institutions and instruments are largely unchanged. Credit-rating agencies continue to operate unregulated, their AAA ratings as uncertain as they were before the crash. Mortgage lenders, though currently under scrutiny, have only to wait for the next opportunity to enable speculation. Adjustable-rate mortgages and teaser rates still lure people to budget themselves into bankruptcy. Securitization allows loans to occur without lenders putting any of their own capital at risk. But these financial practices are only the echo of the real problem in America.

The structural connection between economic inequality and the crisis remains ignored. The dangerous investment choices that precipitated the crisis are but a symptom of this underlying cause. Income stagnation continues, pushing Americans toward greater borrowing and less saving. Many of those who lost their jobs in the crisis remain unemployed but go uncounted since they have run out of benefits and haven't looked for work in the last two weeks (which is how the government measures unemployment). Even those who have found work have often had to accept lower wages. The media celebration of McDonald's National Hiring Day in early 2011 speaks to how far we have drifted from Ford's five-dollar day. Even for those with jobs, income interruptions remain as dangerous as ever, as unemployment times lengthen. Since health care insurance is tied to employment, illness and job loss can continue to be a double whammy. Compared to Europe, the limited welfare state has pushed Americans to borrow to bridge unemployment and pay for health care. Even for those with jobs, health care insurance remains expensive and, for the millions of uninsured or underinsured, remains a key cause of bankruptcy. Though other industrial nations allow their corporations to focus on profitability, we force our businesses to act as mini–welfare states, inefficiently tasking them with what should be a national concern.

Meanwhile, as those at the bottom hang on, profits continue to concentrate at the top. Without a good alternative, capital continues to be invested in consumer debt. It is more important to ask why there was so much money to invest in mortgage-backed securities than to ask about the particulars of how those investments went awry. Don't ask just why Americans borrowed; ask why our financial institutions lent! To avoid this calamity, we must not pretend that by sending some traders to prison we have rectified the economy. The crisis was caused not by a few individuals but by the structures in which those individuals acted. Mortgage bankers lent to people who could not pay back the money, but it didn't matter because investors, not bankers, would be left holding the bag. We must ask why these individuals made the choices they made and why those choices had such power over our lives. Changing the structure of lending, while difficult, is far easier than changing human nature.

The fragile recovery we now enjoy will wilt again as soon as interest rates rise. We are only in the eye of the storm. Though the Fed has promised to keep the prime interest rate near zero, in the long run the government must raise the interest rate, and when it does the true weakness of our economy will be revealed. At once, the adjustable-rate mortgages still extant will suddenly go up. Credit card rates, now adjustable as well, will rise. Minimum monthly payments will add to higher mortgage payments, pushing people beyond the limits of their fragile budgets. Americans will default at rates that will make the current crisis look like a foothill to the Rockies.

The solution to all these complex problems is surprisingly simple: investment. Investors, entrepreneurs, and corporations all lack productive places in which to put their money. Productivity and profitability are not aligned because financial instruments make it easier to invest in consumer debt than in business debt. Consumers borrow because it is cheap and easy to borrow, but lenders give them money because it is profitable. Investors, without new companies in which to invest, put money into mortgage-backed securities, inflating the housing market. For General Electric and Citigroup, it is more profitable to lend money on credit cards than to give loans to small businesses or even big businesses. Capital that in another time would have been put into new enterprises, creating jobs and raising incomes, instead goes into consumer credit. This has happened not because capitalism has failed but because it has been so successful. Global capitalism has been so profitable that there is now an overabundance of capital in the world and too few places in which to put it. As workers, Americans have seen that efficient capital operate with cheaper and fewer workers, cutting incomes. As consumers, Americans have access to cheap capital to borrow. Consumer credit is necessary for modern capitalism to function, but the excess of capital allowed to form at the very top is starting to inhibit the growth of the economy. High tax rates, like those we had during the postwar prosperity, put money in the hands of consumers and the government to spend. Since the Reagan administration, those tax rates have been falling. The justification of our low tax rates today is that the wealthy will invest their savings and grow the economy. Instead that wealth has been invested in speculation, destroying capital and hampering growth. If that capital were invested in businesses and not in consumer debt, the low tax rates could be justified. Consumer borrowing has crowded out business borrowing. The key question is, then, how can we enable good investment while keeping tax rates low?

As in the Great Depression, the government has the capacity and the responsibility to create new opportunities for investment, while not spending the money directly. The government can't replace capitalism, but it can guide it. Waiting and hoping that financiers will sort themselves out is the most dangerous form of delusion. New Deal regulation set limits on financial innovation—eliminating participation certificates and balloon mortgages—and with limited opportunity for financial profits, American capitalists turned to producing the best products and the services in the world. Finance was made to serve the real economy, not the other way around. The prosperity of the postwar period, built on debt, rested ultimately on strong regulations about how to use capital to fund that debt. Borrowing must play an important part in the economy, but it must be an ancillary part. When it is more profitable to build an electric car than to invest in a credit card, we will know that this crisis is over. Helping create new investment opportunities, as the federal government did with the formation of the aerospace and electronics industries, is the best way to divert capital away from speculators and into the hands of entrepreneurs. Though both are necessary, a carrot moves capital far better than a stick. Now as then, we must pull together and make capitalism work for us, as a nation. And today we have an opportunity to force finance to again support production.

Though the new Consumer Finance Protection Bureau is a good idea, we should be wary of regulation that says "no" rather than "yes." The history of U.S. finance shows that the carrot has always been more successful than the stick in aligning the interests of capital with those of society. The FHA, for instance, was successful because it channeled private capital into housing at a time when many people lived in hovels. Though we might debate the need for FHA loans today, they were most certainly needed in the 1930s. A similar logic must be employed today. Today we need jobs, not houses. We need to unleash our country's entrepreneurial spirit. Regulation intended to fix the financial crisis that looks only at the borrower and not at the lender misses the point. We must ask why investors prefer to put their money into consumer debt in the first place. The trouble with securitization wasn't the bonds, it was the mortgages. Creating a demand for mortgage-backed securities pushed brokers to scour the land for new home buyers. We need a way to push brokers to scour the land for business opportunities and then give them a way to measure the opportunities against one another. It became easier to lend mortgage money than make business loans. Securitization needs to be a mechanism that encourages money to be invested in productive businesses, not consumer debt. Houses produce no value. Securitization is potentially the most powerful financial tool invented in the twentieth century, and we have been using it to channel our capital into supersized shoes, not shoe factories. The solution to the crisis must address the intertwined problems of securitization, credit rating, and business investment. To save our economy, it must become easier for investors to lend to small business. Economic growth is small business growth.

We need to create two federal agencies. The first—let's call it the Bureau of Business Security—will evaluate businesses the same way that the FHA created standards for houses. The second will be an institution to coordinate the secondary market for the securitization of business loans—let's call that one Bobby Mac. Houses are all unique, as are businesses, but unlike for houses, we already have a common vocabulary—accounting—to describe firms. Every day Wall Street analysts evaluate the future risks and returns of businesses in the evaluation of stocks and bonds. The bureau would simply do the same. The bureau would create standards to evaluate a business as the FHA created standards to evaluate housing. Such standards would solve two problems. They would enable a more transparent evaluation of those companies' credit ratings, which were one of the core problems of the crisis. It would, more importantly, enable business investment to be carried out through securitization. What can be graded can be traded!

No doubt there would be objections to a federal program investigating all businesses. As with FHA loans, businesses could opt not to participate. Large firms with sufficient borrowing power, such as General Electric, would probably opt out. Businesses that refused to be investigated would simply not be able to securitize their debt through Bobby Mac. And there would be businesses, like houses, that would not be able to securitize their debt. Not all businesses will be able to be part of the system. But for most business owners, like most home owners, the capital will make it possible for their dreams to come true.

I suspect that the prospect of cheap borrowing would be quite a powerful carrot to make American business more transparent. On the stick side, potential investors would begin to demand that businesses provide the information. Securitization would be most important for all small and midsize companies, where the real growth potential in the economy resides. Many businesses fail, as many mortgages are foreclosed, but through risk management and federal standards, the bonds could handle that possibility. With good information, rating those companies would be more accurate and transparent. Unlike private credit-rating agencies, the bureau's future would not depend on giving businesses a good review. With a diversified portfolio of business investments, risks for investors would go down. Business investment wouldn't be the province of a few millionaires and their private equity; it could be done by average Joes with their pension funds. How much better would the world be if workers' pension funds were invested in activities that produced jobs instead of McMansions?

Regulation doesn't need to tell firms what to do, but it does need to provide the transparency for investors to act wisely and to help markets make technological transitions when there is a great deal of change. U.S. housing markets continue to require Fannie and Freddie and Ginnie to clear their secondary markets. Public institutions, such as Bobby Mac, would make private solutions possible. Private enterprise cannot create a secondary market for securitized business loans any more than it could create a secondary market for housing mortgages. Government cannot dictate the economy, but business cannot function without its structures. If we are to prevent this crisis from getting worse, we need to address its fundamental causes. A Bureau of Business Security would accomplish this goal, putting the United States on a path to growth and prosperity. A Bureau of Business Security would bootstrap us to a level of prosperity that is as incomprehensible today as the postwar prosperity was to the Depression.

Good debt and bad debt have nothing to do with the debt itself but what role that debt plays in our economy. Common sense often fails us when it comes to debt because we think of it in moral terms. Budgeting and borrowing with "good" forms of debt, such as mortgages and student loans, we judge ourselves—and others—for their "bad" use of credit cards. Seeing the ways in which debt has transformed us gives us a sense of how the meaning of debt depends on its historical context. And everyone involved in debt, whether of the personal, business, or government variety—which is to say every citizen of this country—is responsible for the conversation as to how we will structure debt within our society, how we can encourage it to serve as a beneficent genie in a bottle, which it undoubtedly has been, as opposed to an evil Pandora's box, which it just as surely has been as well. Debt, along with every other aspect of capitalism, is something that we have created and have the capacity to master.

NOTES

INTRODUCTION: EVERYTHING OLD IS NEW AGAIN

1 William H. Whyte, "Budgetism: Opiate of the Middle Class," *Fortune,* May 1956, 133.

CHAPTER ONE: WHEN PERSONAL DEBT WAS
REALLY BUSINESS DEBT (2000 B.C.–A.D. 1920)

1 Household Finance Corporation, *It's Your Credit Manage It Wisely* (Chicago: privately printed, 1970), 7.

2 Bruce Mann, *Republic of Debtors* (Cambridge: Harvard University Press, 2002), chapter 3.

3 William Cronon, *Nature's Metropolis* (New York: W.W. Norton, 1992), 319.

4 Fifth Annual Report of the Bureau of Labor and Industrial Statistics (Lansing, Mich.: 1888), 391.

5 Harold Woodman, *King Cotton and His Retainers* (Columbia: University of South Carolina Press, 1968), 282–286.

6 Ibid., 81.

7 Pete Daniel, *The Shadow of Slavery* (Chicago: University of Illinois Press, 1990).

8 Asian immigration had been severely restricted since the passage of the Chinese Exclusion Act. African immigration was nonexistent.

9 "Secretary Missing, $40,000 Gone, Too," *The New York Times,* March 16, 1928, 39.

10 Federal Trade Commission, *Report of the Federal Trade Commission on House Furnishings Industries,* vol. 1, January 17, 1923 (Washington, D.C.: GPO, 1923), 16.

11 Louise Conant, "The Borax House," *American Mercury,* June 1929, 169.

12 Legal Aid Society, *Fifty-fourth Annual Report of the President, Treasurer and Attorney of the Legal Aid Society for the Year 1929,* Annual Report 1929, 47. In balloon mortgages, buyers paid only the interest on the mortgage with the intent of paying off the principal in its entirety when the debt came due, which in practice happened infrequently.

13 "Loan Shark Tells Business Tricks; Foiled by Bureau," *Chicago Daily Tribune*, February 9, 1912, 1.

14 William Shepherd, "They Turn Your Promise into Cash," *Collier's*, February 19, 1927, 8.

15 Lendol Calder, *Financing the American Dream* (Princeton, N.J.: Princeton University Press, 1999), 120.

16 Ibid., 121.

17 Ibid., 130.

18 Archie Chadbourne, "Debt Is the Only Adventure a Poor Man Can Count On," *American Magazine* 104, December 1927, 45.

19 Calder, *Financing the American Dream*, 130.

20 Joseph Budnowitz, "Pawnbroking: A Treatise on the History, Regulation, Legal Decisions and a Comparison with Other Small Loan Agencies" (law thesis, Columbia University, 1931), folder "Levine: *The Law of Pawnbroking*, box 1, Russell Sage Foundation Papers, Manuscript Division, Library of Congress, Washington, D.C., 38 (hereafter RSF).

21 Reginald Smith, *The Facts About the Small Loan Business and the Scientific Rate of Fair Charges* (New York: Legal Reform Bureau to Eliminate the Loan Shark Evil, 1922), folder "Interest General," box 1, RSF.

22 "Small Loans Put at $2,600,000,000," *The New York Times*, April 27, 1930, 44.

23 Martha Olney, "Avoiding Default: The Role of Credit in the Consumption Collapse of 1930," *The Quarterly Journal of Economics*, February 1999, 322.

CHAPTER TWO: EVERYBODY PAID CASH
FOR THE MODEL T (1908–1929)

1 William Shepherd, "They Turn Your Promise into Cash," *Collier's*, February 19, 1927, 52.

2 David Hounshell, *From the American System to Mass Production, 1800–1932* (Baltimore: Johns Hopkins University Press, 1984), 218.

3 Quoted in Douglas Brinkley, *Wheels for the World: Henry Ford, His Company and a Century of Progress, 1903–2003* (New York: Penguin, 2004), 153.

4 Quoted in Allan Bogue, "The Land Mortgage Company in the Early Plains States," *Agricultural History*, January 1951, 24.

5 Henry Ford, *My Life and Work* (New York: Garden City Publishing, 1922), 40.

6 General Motors Corporation, Annual Report, 1922, 6.

7 Ford, *My Life and Work,* 103.

8 This argument is derived from Lawrence Glickman, *A Living Wage: American Workers and the Making of Consumer Society* (Ithaca, N.Y.: Cornell University Press, 1999).

9 Alfred Chandler, *Strategy and Structure: Chapters in the History of the Industrial Enterprise* (Cambridge: MIT Press, 1962), 114–130.

10 General Motors Corporation, Annual Report, 1924, 9.

11 General Motors Acceptance Corporation, Annual Report, 1927, 1.

12 General Motors Corporation, Annual Report, 1926, 9.

13 Ibid., 22.

14 Ibid., 15.

15 National Automobile Chamber of Commerce, "Automobile Manufacturing Conducted Almost Entirely on Its Own Capital," December 15, 1925, Historical Collections, Baker Library, Harvard Business School, Allston, Mass. (hereafter BAK), 2. Capital calculations by author.

16 Shepherd, "They Turn," 52.

17 Hounshell, *From the American System,* 276.

18 Ford Weekly Purchase Plan, Advertisement, *Los Angeles Times,* April 8, 1923.

19 "The Jewish Bloc in Mr. Ford's Presidential Path," *Literary Digest,* August 25, 1923, 49.

20 H. G. Andrews, "Henry Ford—Wall Street's Shock-Absorber," *The Nation,* January 24, 1923, 93.

21 "Henry Ford's Apology to the Jews," *Outlook,* July 20, 1927, 372.

22 General Motors Corporation, Annual Report, 1929, 20.

23 To add insult to injury, a series of court decisions banned the formal affiliation of Ford and Chrysler with any finance company. GM fought the decisions and managed to hold on to GMAC, as the lone car manufacturer with a captive finance company, until the 1950s. Paul Banner, "Competition, Credit Policies, and the Captive Finance Company," *The Quarterly Journal of Economics,* May 1958, 258.

24 J. George Frederick, "Dollar-Down Serfdom," *The Independent,* September 11, 1926, 299.

25 James Couzens, "Should We Stop Instalment Buying?," *Forum and Century,* May 1927, 655.

26 William Post, *Character, the Basic Rock Foundation of the Four Big C's in the Extension of Credit* ([Philadelphia]: 1920).

27 "Credit and Character," *Saturday Evening Post,* July 28, 1928, 1.

28 C. Reinold Noyes, "Financing Prosperity on Next Year's Income," *Yale Review,* January 1927, 227.

29 Ibid., 242.

CHAPTER THREE: FANNIE MAE CAN SAVE AMERICA (1924–1939)

1 Julius Gregory, "What Is Home Without a Mortgage?," *House & Garden,* December, 1931, 68.

2 Oliver McKee, "Helping Our Home Owners," *National Republic,* September 1932, 1.

3 W. C. Clark, "The Construction Industry: Outlook for 1930," *Review of Economics and Statistics,* February 1930, 23–29.

4 "Rising Residences," *Time,* November 25, 1935.

5 Ibid.

6 William Stoddard, "Investing in Homes," *The Outlook,* July 8, 1925, 374.

7 Herrick & Bennett advertisement, *Scribner's,* October 1918, 65.

8 "Issue of Mortgage Participating Certificates by Member Banks," June 15, 1946, "Mr Hammond to Federal Reserve Board," folder 430.1–2, Issue & Sale of Mortgage Participating Certificates by State Member Banks, box 2006: 430.1–2 1925–1946 to 430.1–17 1937, RG 82, National Archives, College Park, Md. (hereafter NARA).

9 "Issue of Mortgage Participating Certificates by Member Banks," June 15, 1946, "Norbett to Boothe, March 16, 1938," folder 430.1–2, Issue & Sale of Mortgage Participating Certificates by State Member Banks, box 2006: 430.1–2 1925–1946 to 430.1–17 1937, RG 82, NARA.

10 "Issue of Mortgage Participating Certificates by Member Banks," June 15, 1946, "Mr Hammond to Federal Reserve Board."

11 Ibid., 2.

12 Ibid., 7.

13 Farm Mortgage Bankers Association of America, *Special Bulletin,* no. 97, Science, Industry and Business Library, New York Public Library (hereafter *Special Bulletin*).

14 H. Thomas Johnson, "Postwar Optimism and Rural Financial Crisis of the 1920s," *Explorations in Economic History,* Winter 1973–74, 173–192.

15 Lee Alston, "Farm Foreclosures in the United States During the Interwar Period," *Journal of Economic History,* December 1983, 891.

16 Ibid., 888.

17 Ibid., 894.

18 *Special Bulletin*, no. 99, 2.

19 *Special Bulletin*, no. 101, 2.

20 *Special Bulletin*, no. 102.

21 "Denies Inflation in Building Here," *The New York Times*, December 22, 1925.

22 *Special Bulletin*, no. 105, 2.

23 Ibid.

24 Nugent Dodds, "The Mortgage Racket," *Collier's*, September 5, 1931, 16.

25 "Getting Away from the Short-Term Mortgage," *Literary Digest*, September 16, 1933, 37.

26 "Sins of the Mortgage Bonds Are Visited on the Building Field," *BusinessWeek*, October 19, 1930, 11.

27 Hammond, Division of Bank Operations to Federal Reserve Board, "Mortgages, etc. Sold by Member Banks," folder 430.1–2, Issue & Sale of Mortgage Participating Certificates by State Member Banks, box 2006: 430.1–2 1925–1946 to 430.1–17 1937, RG 82, NARA, 2.

28 Only 16 percent of banks offered mortgage bonds, but in the collapsing sample 30 percent offered such bonds; thus they had twice the rate.

29 Hammond, Division of Bank Operations to Federal Reserve Board, "Mortgages, etc. Sold by Member Banks," 3.

30 Herbert Hoover, "Address to the White House Conference on Home Building and Home Ownership," December 2, 1931, in John T. Woolley and Gerhard Peters, The American Presidency Project [online]. Santa Barbara, Calif. http://www.presidency.ucsb.edu/ws/?pid=22927.

31 Eleanor Roosevelt, "I Answer Two Questions," *Women's Home Companion*, December, 1933, 24.

32 Josephine Lawrence, *If I Have Four Apples* (New York: Frederick Stokes, 1935), 75; now forgotten, *If I Have Four Apples* was a *New York Times* best-selling novel for most of 1936 and a Book-of-the-Month Club selection. *The New York Times*, February 2, 1936, December 29, 1935.

33 Lawrence, *If I Have Four Apples*, 73.

34 Ibid., 17.

35 Ibid., 44.

36 See Michael Bernstein, *The Great Depression: Delayed Recovery and Economic Change in America, 1929–1939* (Cambridge, England: Cambridge University Press, 1989), for what I think is the best explanation of the

crash and the recovery. Also see "Reviews Theories on Slump Remedies," *The New York Times*, September 4, 1932.

37 "Economic Abuses Blamed for Crisis," *The New York Times*, December 4, 1932.

38 Ibid.

39 "Text of the Address by Ogden. L. Mills," *The New York Times*, January 26, 1932.

40 Max Nahm, "Debt and Depression," *Credit and Financial Management*, September 1935, 12.

41 Rolf Nugent, "Installment Selling Proves Itself as Good Merchandising," *Printers' Ink*, May 1932, folder "1927–1934 General," box 166, RSF.

42 "Installment Credit Held Successful," *The New York Times*, August 1, 1930.

43 "Defends Time Payment Sales," *The Wall Street Journal*, May 1, 1931.

44 Milan Ayres, "Rapid Amortization Produces Stable Installment Credits," *Bankers Monthly*, January 1932, folder "1927–1934 General," box 166, RSF.

45 "Dr. Klein Defends Installment Sales," *The New York Times*, May 18, 1931.

46 *Economic Report of the President 1969* (Washington, D.C.: GPO, 1969), 228; Federal Reserve, *Twenty-fifth Annual Report of the Board of Governors of the Federal Reserve System Covering Operations for the Year 1938* (Washington, D.C.: GPO, 1939), 23.

47 Lawrence, *If I Have Four Apples*, 104.

48 Ibid., 4.

49 "Industry: Big Push," *Time*, August 28, 1933.

50 FDR to James Moffett, folder Correspondence Between State Governors and Pres. Franklin D. Roosevelt Concerning FHA Legislation 1934–1935, box 1 A1, entry 11, RG 3, Records of the Federal Housing Administration, NARA.

51 "Housing: Trouble; No Trouble," *Time*, December 3, 1934.

52 "Milestones, Feb. 8, 1937," *Time*, February 8, 1937.

53 "Housing Trouble; No Trouble."

54 "Business: Fancy Mortgages," *Time*, September 30, 1935.

55 "Sees 'Rent Dole' in Public Housing," *The New York Times*, October 28, 1934.

56 Walter Schmidt, "Complete Recovery of Building Industry," *Architectural Record*, November 1934, 317.

57 "The Presidency: Big Kitty," *Time*, April 22, 1935.

58 Federal Housing Administration, *First Annual Report* (Washington, D.C.: GPO, 1935), 18.

59 See Thomas Sugrue, *The Origins of the Urban Crisis* (Princeton, N.J.: Princeton University Press, 1996) for more on the history of racial segregation and mortgages.

60 "People, May 2, 1938," *Time*, May 2, 1938.

CHAPTER FOUR: HOW I LEARNED TO STOP
WORRYING AND LOVE THE DEBT (1945–1960)

1 Lynn Spigel, *Welcome to the Dreamhouse* (Durham: Duke University Press, 2001), 49–50.

2 John Gribbon, "A New Approach to Credit," *Credit Management Year Book, 1961–1962* (New York: National Retail Dry Goods Association, 1961), 10.

3 The correct Latin is actually *in loco mariti.*

4 "Prize Answers to Question Whether Husbands or Wives Are More Extravagant," *The Washington Post*, February 14, 1915, E3.

5 "What If You Don't Pay Your Bills?" *Changing Times*, November 1953, 20.

6 "Beating the High Price of Coffee," *Changing Times*, July 1954, 15.

7 Frederick Walter, *The Retail Charge Account* (New York: Ronald Press, 1922), 41.

8 Bloomingdale's advertisement, *The New York Times*, November 28, 1947, 18.

9 Bloomingdale's advertisement, *The New York Times*, December 2, 1946, 7.

10 Robert Wallace, "Please Remit," *Life*, December 21, 1953, 42.

11 "Christmas at Macy's," *Life*, December 13, 1948, 91.

12 A&S advertisement, *The New York Times*, November 15, 1954, 9.

13 Wallace, "Please Remit," 51.

14 "Diner Club Stunt Ups Eateries' Take," *Billboard*, August 5, 1950, 40.

CHAPTER FIVE: DISCOUNTED GOODS AND
DISTRIBUTED CREDIT (1959–1970)

1 Laura Rowley, *On Target* (Hoboken, N.J.: John Wiley & Sons, 2003), 117.

2 Carl Ryant, "The South and the Movement Against Chain Stores," *Journal of Southern History*, May 1973, 207–222.

3 "Retail Trade: Blow Against Price-Fixing," *Time,* June 4, 1951.

4 Solomon Sherman, "Whither Fair Trade Laws? An Appraisal of the United States Supreme Court Position in the Light of *Lilly v. Schwegmann,*" *American University Law Review,* December 1953, 22–26.

5 Quoted in David Rachman, "What Lies Ahead for the Discounters?," Discount Operators National Show, Modern Retailer's Seminar Proceedings, 1961; Malcolm McNair, "The American Department Store, 1920–1960: A Performance Analysis Based on the Harvard Reports," *Bureau of Business Research Bulletin* no. 166, Harvard University (1963): BAK, 25.

6 "Are Fair Trade Laws Obsolete?" *Kiplinger's Personal Finance,* June 1974, 36.

7 Gerald Ford, "Statement on the Consumer Goods Pricing Act of 1975," December 12, 1975, American Presidency Project, www.presidency.ucsb.edu/ws/index.php?pid=5432.

8 Perry Meyers, *Profile of a New Market Place: A Pilot Study of Discount Store Customers, August 1961,* appendix, "Most Frequently Mentioned Advantages and Disadvantages of Discount Stores."

9 Rachman, "What Lies Ahead for the Discounters?," 40.

10 Meyers, *Profile,* i–iii.

11 Ibid., iii.

12 Brecker, Discount Operators National Show, Modern Retailer's Seminar Proceedings, 1961, 130.

13 Ibid., 161.

14 "The GEM Story: Part One," *Discount Merchandiser,* January 1962, 15.

15 "Target's New Thrust and What It Takes," *Discount Merchandiser,* April 1969, 59.

16 Meyers, *Profile,* iv.

17 "Life Study," *Discount Merchandiser,* June 1962, 64.

18 Meyers, *Profile,* appendix.

19 Ibid., vi.

20 "The True Look of the Discount Industry: 1961," *Discount Merchandiser,* July 1962, 27.

21 "Miracle at Kresge's," *Discount Merchandiser,* December 1964, 39.

22 "Sales of the Top 52 Companies," *Discount Merchandiser,* January 1968, 28-TL. Target was ranked 21st, Schwegmann Bros. 35th, Caldor 37th, and Wal-Mart was still nowhere to be found.

23 Goodman, Discount Operators National Show, Modern Retailer's Seminar Proceedings, 1961, 135.

24 Only 5 percent of stores were in shopping centers in 1967. "The $100 Million Club," *Discount Merchandiser*, January 1968, 36-TL.

25 Meyers, *Profile*, 10. Percentages reconstructed from data in table 2.

26 The Gap, 10-K, 1977, F-2. Accounts receivable made up only 2 percent of current assets.

27 Ibid., 2.

28 Ibid., 3.

29 Ibid., 18.

30 The Gap, Annual Report, 1977, 4.

31 Louis Nevaer, *Into—and Out of—The Gap: A Cautionary Account of an American Retailer* (Westport, Conn.: Quorum Books, 2001), 19.

32 Ibid., 21.

33 Ibid., 37.

34 "Caldor: Sales Are Good Close to Home," *Discount Merchandiser*, October 1963, 36.

35 "109 Leading Discounters," *Discount Merchandiser*, July 1963, 30–31.

36 "Credit Is Nice but It Can Cost You," *Discount Merchandiser*, July 1965, 44–45.

37 Bernard Korn, "All About Credit Plans," *Discount Merchandiser*, May 1962, 58.

38 "Not Everyone's Pushing Own Cards," *Chain Store Age Executive*, January 1977, 26.

39 Except grocery stores. "Share of Major Retail Sales by Type of Store," *Discount Merchandiser*, June 1966, 63.

40 "Why Big Stores Are Taking Outside Credit Cards," *BusinessWeek*, September 3, 1979, 134.

41 SRAC, Annual Report, 1967.

42 "Take Over the Country," *BusinessWeek*, August 4, 1975, 53.

43 "Links in a Chain," *The Wall Street Journal*, March 8, 1977, 1.

44 Ibid., 1. Kmart also leased its properties, rather than buy them outright, since its scarce capital was better put into merchandise than land.

45 "S.S. Kresge's Chairman Talks on Discounting," *Discount Merchandiser*, January 1968, 107.

CHAPTER SIX: BRINGING GOOD THINGS TO LIFE (1970–1985)

1 "Bank in the Billfold," *The Wall Street Journal*, December 1, 1965, 1.

2 Joseph Miraglia, "My $10,000 Credit Card Binge," *Life*, October 26, 1959, 53.

3 "High Finance: Fun on the Card," *Time,* October 19, 1959.

4 Joseph Plummer, "Life Style Patterns and Commercial Bank Credit Card Usage," *Journal of Marketing,* April 1971, 37.

5 Subcommittee on Financial Institutions, Committee on Banking and Currency, Senate, *Bank Credit-Card and Check-Credit Plans,* 90th Cong., 2nd Sess., October 9–10, 1968, 277.

6 "Bank in the Billfold."

7 *Bank Credit-Card and Check-Credit Plans,* 273.

8 Ibid., 266.

9 Matthews and Slocum, 74.

10 Calculation by author based on *Bank Credit-Card and Check-Credit Plans,* quoted in Weistart, "Consumer Protection," footnote 28.

11 "Bank in the Billfold."

12 Ibid.

13 Ibid.

14 *Bank Credit-Card and Check-Credit Plans,* 325.

15 Ibid., 66.

16 "Bank of America Plans Nationwide Licensing of Its Credit Cards," *The Wall Street Journal,* May 25, 1966, 7.

17 Ibid.

18 John Weistart, "Consumer Protection in the Credit Card Industry: Federal Legislative Controls," *Michigan Law Review,* August 1972, 1479.

19 "Chicago's Credit Card Crisis," *BusinessWeek,* July 15, 1967, 35.

20 Harold Taylor, "The Chicago Bank Credit Card Fiasco," *Banking,* Winter 1968, 52.

21 "Chicago's Credit Card Crisis."

22 Taylor, "The Chicago Bank Credit Card Fiasco," 50.

23 *Bank Credit-Card and Check-Credit Plans,* 64.

24 Ibid., 19.

25 *Bank Credit-Card and Check-Credit Plans,* 290.

26 Paul O'Neil, "A Little Gift from Your Friendly Banker," *Life,* March 27, 1970.

27 "How a Louisville Bank, Hardly a Giant, Has Become Huge in Credit Card Field," *The Wall Street Journal,* September 6, 1972, 5.

28 Taylor, "The Chicago Bank Credit Card Fiasco," 50.

29 "Do You Really Benefit from Bank Credit-Card Plans?," *Better Homes and Gardens,* November, 1967, 6.

30 "Buy Now, Pay Never," *The Wall Street Journal,* November 18, 1970, 1.

31 Irwin Ross, "The Credit Card's Painful Coming-of-Age," *Fortune,* October 1971, 111.

32 "Debate over Magnetic Tape Credit Card Fueled by Contest on How to Defraud It," *The Wall Street Journal,* April 13, 1973, 7.

33 *Bank Credit-Card and Check-Credit Plans,* 31.

34 Ibid., 44.

35 Ibid., 64.

36 Daniel Cowans, "Present Bankruptcy Act Defective," quoted in *Bank Credit-Card and Check-Credit Plans,* 53.

37 *Bank Credit-Card and Check-Credit Plans,* 65.

38 H. Lee Matthews and John Slocum, "Social Class and Commercial Bank Credit Card Usage," *Journal of Marketing,* January 1969, 73.

39 Ibid., 76.

40 "Californians Charging Away," *The Wall Street Journal,* March 15, 1968, 32.

41 Ibid.

42 "Banks Trust Joins BankAmericard Plan, Will Issue Cards in '69," *The Wall Street Journal,* November 4, 1968.

43 *Bank Credit-Card and Check-Credit Plans,* 284.

44 Ibid., 260.

45 The Federal Reserve made a similar argument in its 1968 study of the nascent credit card industry. See *Bank Credit-Card and Check-Credit Plans,* reprinted in House Subcommittee on Special Small Business Problems, *The Impact of Credit Cards on Small Business,* June 8–10, 1970, 247–350.

46 *Bank Credit-Card and Check-Credit Plans,* 277.

47 Ibid., 12.

48 Ibid., 295.

49 Ibid., 284–285.

50 "Can Stores Trump Bank Credit Cards?," *BusinessWeek,* January 30, 1971, 63.

51 "Californians Charging Away."

52 "Bank in the Billfold," 1.

53 *Bank Credit-Card and Check-Credit Plans,* 15.

54 Ibid., 24.

55 House Subcommittee on Special Small Business Problems, *The Impact of Credit Cards on Small Business,* 1.

56 Patrick Kildoyle, "Bank Credit Card and Check Credit Plans in the Second District," *Federal Reserve Monthly Review,* January 1969, 12.

57 O'Neil, "A Little Gift."

58 Letters to the Editor, *Life,* April 17, 1970, 28A.

59 "Can Stores Trump Bank Credit Cards?," 121.

60 "Atlanta's First National Sees Depressed 1st Half," *The Wall Street Journal,* June 1, 1970, 8.

61 "Citicorp Posts 19.4% Rise in Net for 2nd Quarter," *The Wall Street Journal,* July 13, 1971, 5.

62 "Clash over Credit," *The Wall Street Journal,* March 4, 1971, 1.

63 "Minneapolis Bank to Give Its Card-Holders a Charge," *The Wall Street Journal,* February 23, 1973, 18.

64 "Chain, Bank Americard in Minnesota Stop Revolving Credit, Fighting Usury Ruling," *The Wall Street Journal,* April 30, 1971, 4.

65 Ibid.

66 Ross, "The Credit Card's Painful Coming-of-Age."

67 Thomas Williams, "Asking the Right Questions About Bank Cards— You Have Done a Great Job . . . Just Don't Give It Away," *Banking,* September 1978, 84.

68 "Can Stores Trump Bank Credit Cards?"

69 "Why Big Stores Are Taking Outside Credit Cards." This point was made by Interbank (Master Charge)'s Kneeland Moore, marketing VP.

70 "More Stores Using Bank Cards," *Chain Store Age Executive with Shopping Center Age,* January 1977, 25.

71 "Bank Card Holdouts Fading Under Pressure," *Chain Store Age Executive with Shopping Center Age,* February 1979, 36.

72 "Why Big Stores Are Taking Outside Credit Cards," 132.

73 "Bank Card Holdouts Fading Under Pressure," 41.

74 Ibid., 33.

75 "Why Big Stores Are Taking Outside Credit Cards," 134.

76 "The Big Push for Credit," *Chain Store Age Executive with Shopping Center Age,* January 1977, 23.

77 "More Stores Using Bank Cards," 25.

78 "Bank Card Holdouts Fading Under Pressure," 36.

79 "Department Stores Begin Adopting Bank Cards," *Banking,* August 1976, 62.

80 "Fear of Buying," *The Wall Street Journal,* December 16, 1980.

81 Ibid.

82 "When Banks Start Carrying Two Cards," *BusinessWeek,* November 22, 1976, 64.

83 "Bank Americard to Get a New Name: Visa," *The New York Times*, September 11, 1976, 41.

84 "Bank Card Holdouts Fading Under Pressure," *Chain Store Age Executive*, February 1979, 41.

85 "Tough Future for Small Card Plans," 136.

86 "Variable-Rate Loans Rise," *ABA Banking Journal*, October 1984, 154.

87 "More Stores Using Bank Cards," 26.

88 "The Age of Plastic's First Card Shark," *New York Magazine*, January 14, 1991, 32.

CHAPTER SEVEN: IF ONLY THE GNOMES HAD KNOWN (1968–1986)

1 Thomas Sugrue, *The Origins of the Urban Crisis* (Princeton, N.J.: Princeton University Press, 1996).

2 Senate Committee on Banking and Currency, *Financial Institutions and the Urban Crisis*, 90th Cong., 2nd Sess., September 20 and October 1–4, 1969, 177.

3 Ibid., 20.

4 Department of Housing and Urban Development, *Homeownership for Lower Income Families (Section 235): A HUD Handbook, October 1968* (Washington, D.C.: GPO, 1968), foreword.

5 Everett Spelman, "Federalization & Housing: At Point of No Return?," *Mortgage Banker*, June 1971, 57.

6 Robert Gray, "Good Counseling: The Answer in Successful 235 Housing," *Mortgage Banker*, August 1971, 14.

7 Ibid.

8 Spelman, "Federalization & Housing," 54; Eugene Cowen, "The Nixon Program for Housing," *Mortgage Banker*, July 1971, 10.

9 Spelman, "Federalization & Housing," 56.

10 Philip Jackson, "The Commitment Is Massive, but So Is the Problem," *Mortgage Banker*, June 1972, 6.

11 To qualify, a family could earn no more than 135 percent of the local public housing income limit, which was based on local economic conditions and family size. A family of four could earn up to $5,805 in Red Bay, Alabama, $6,615 in Paterson, New Jersey, and $7,695 in Boston, Massachusetts, for example. Department of Housing and Urban Development, *Regular Income Limits for Sections 235 and 236 Housing (Based on 135 Percent of Public Housing Admission Limits)* (Washington, D.C.: GPO, 1969).

12 Department of Housing and Urban Development, *1970 HUD Statistical Yearbook* (Washington, D.C.: GPO, 1970), 234.

13 Philip Brownstein, "The 1968 Housing Bill," *Mortgage Banker,* May 1968, 20.

14 Ibid., 21.

15 House Committee on Banking and Currency, *Investigation and Hearing of Abuses in Federal Low- and Moderate-Income Housing Programs,* 91st Cong., 2nd Sess., December 1970 (hereafter *Investigation and Hearing*), 5.

16 Department of Housing and Urban Development, *Guide for the Recording of Single Family Homes Sales for Use as Appraisal Data* (Washington, D.C.: GPO, 1968), foreword, 1–3.

17 *Investigation and Hearing,* 108.

18 Ibid., 113.

19 Ibid., 170.

20 Ibid., 108.

21 *Investigation and Hearing,* 8.

22 Ibid., 108.

23 House Committee on Banking and Currency, *Interim Report on HUD Investigation of Low- and Moderate-Income Housing Programs,* 92nd Cong., 1st Sess., March 31, 1971 (hereafter *Interim Report*), 113; "Jersey Screened for F.H.A. Abuses," *The New York Times,* January 8, 1971, 29.

24 *Interim Report,* 107.

25 Ibid., 6.

26 *Interim Report,* 103; *Investigation and Hearing,* 103.

27 *Interim Report,* 48.

28 Ibid., 49.

29 *Investigation and Hearing,* 133.

30 Ibid., 188.

31 The staff report found that "the construction is of such poor quality and the cost so questionable that the projects can best be described as 'instant slums.' " *Interim Report,* 105.

32 Gray, "Good Counseling," 6, 12.

33 *Interim Report,* 105.

34 *Investigation and Hearing,,* 133.

35 *Investigation and Hearing,* 31. Twenty-seven of fifty-seven home owners abandoned their houses.

36 Ibid., 34.

37 United States Commission on Civil Rights, *Home Ownership for Lower Income Families: A Report on the Racial and Ethnic Impact of the*

Section 235 Program (Washington, D.C.: GPO, 1971) (hereafter *Home Ownership*), 46.

38 Ibid., 45.

39 Ibid.

40 Ibid., 8.

41 Ibid.

42 Ibid., 69.

43 Department of Housing and Urban Development, Office of Audit, "Audit Review of Section 235 Single Family Housing," December 10, 1971 (Washington, D.C.: GPO, 1971), Vertical Files collection, Loeb Library, Harvard University, 4–5, 10.

44 Ibid., 18. The audit surveyed 609 houses, of which 260 were overvalued.

45 *Home Ownership*, 59.

46 Ibid.

47 Ibid.

48 John Sparkman, "Outlook for Housing Legislation in 1971," *Mortgage Banker*, July 1971, 22.

49 John Monagan, "Picture of Failure," *Mortgage Banker*, July 1972, 18.

50 John Wetmore, "FHA Operation Now Vital to Secondary Mortgage Market," *Mortgage Banker*, December 1973, 61.

51 Ibid.

52 *Investigation and Hearing*, 188.

53 The report was widely discussed, making, for instance, the front page of *The New York Times* ("U.S. Report Finds Fraud in Housing," January 6, 1971, 1).

54 *Interim Report*, 2; "Romney, in Shift, Freezes Disputed Home Aid to Poor," *The New York Times*, January 15, 1971, 1.

55 Spelman, "Federalization & Housing," 57.

56 *Investigation and Hearing*, 237.

57 Ibid., 239.

58 "The Feuding over Who Runs Fannie Mae," *BusinessWeek*, September 12, 1977, 74.

59 "Does Fannie Mae Play Conflicting Roles?," *BusinessWeek*, December 13, 1976, 34.

60 Kenneth Thygerson, "Housing and Freddie Mac," *American Banker*, February 25, 1983, 13.

61 Eric Berg, "Trading Home Loans Like Bonds Draws Billions," *The New York Times*, January 22, 1984, F1.

62 "Mortgage Pools Have Splashy Yields," *Fortune,* October 23, 1978, 139.

63 "The Private Sector Apes Ginnie Mae," *BusinessWeek,* July 25, 1977, 110.

64 "Mortgage Pools Have Splashy Yields," 140.

65 "The Private Sector Apes Ginnie Mae," 112.

66 "How to Get a Piece of the Action," *BusinessWeek,* November 10, 1980, 148.

67 Title V, State Usury Laws, Part A, Mortgage Usury Laws, Depository Institutions Deregulation and Monetary Control Act of 1980.

68 "The Garn–St Germain Act of 1982 and Mortgage Lending; Two Provisions Affecting Adjustable Rates and Due-on-Sale Enforcement Will Bear Watching," *American Banker,* May 16, 1983, 21.

69 "Today's Mortgage Market Has Primary Flexibility and Secondary Depth," *ABA Banking Journal,* April 1983, 118.

70 Rosemary Rinder, "How Real Is ARM 'Repayment Shock'?" *ABA Banking Journal,* April 1983, 47.

71 Eric Berg, "Fixed-Rate Mortgages Held Threat to Lenders," *The New York Times,* March 10, 1986.

72 "How the Thrifts Can Unload Old Mortgages," *BusinessWeek,* January 18, 1982, 29.

73 "Saving Fannie," *Forbes,* October 26, 1981, 54.

74 Ibid.

75 "The Feuding over Who Runs Fannie Mae," *BusinessWeek,* September 12, 1977, 15.

76 "Freddie Mac and Fannie Mae Changing Their Role," *National Mortgage News,* September 22, 1986, 22A.

77 "Securitising the American Dream," *The Economist,* June 14, 1986, 78.

78 "Freddie Mac Announces Sale of Mortgages," *Business Wire,* November 15, 1985.

79 "Rise of National Mortgage Market," *The New York Times,* January 22, 1984.

80 "Consultants Say Management of Risk Is Key to Mortgage Industry," *National Mortgage News,* August 12, 1985, 15.

81 Berg, "Fixed-Rate Mortgages Held Threat to Lenders."

82 Sanford Rose, "Random Thoughts," *American Banker,* November 8, 1988, 1.

83 "Secondary Mortgage Market Takes the Lead: But Some Doubt Its Potential to End the Housing Credit Gap," *American Banker,* August 24, 1983, 1.

84 "The Secondary Mortgage Market: Having It All Is Key to Success," *American Banker,* December 14, 1983, 4.

85 "Securitising the American Dream," 78.

86 "The Secondary Mortgage Market: Having It All Is Key to Success."

87 "How the Thrifts Can Unload Old Mortgages," 29.

88 "S&Ls Have a New Way to Raise Money," *BusinessWeek,* September 8, 1975, 58.

89 "How the Thrifts Can Unload Old Mortgages," 29.

90 Berg, "Fixed-Rate Mortgages Held Threat to Lenders."

CHAPTER EIGHT: THE HOUSE OF CREDIT CARDS (1986–2008)

1 William Rothschild, *The Secret to GE's Success* (New York: McGraw-Hill, 2007), 116.

2 Jeffrey Birnbaum and Alan Murray, *Showdown at Gucci Gulch* (New York: Random House, 1987), chapter 1.

3 Ibid., 57.

4 Jane Nelson, "Identity Crisis at Fannie Mae?," *U.S. Banker,* July 1985, 16.

5 "President Signs Measure Boosting Private Secondary Mortgage Market," *Bond Buyer,* October 8, 1984.

6 "Taxing Housing," *United States Banker,* April, 1986, 4.

7 "Popularity and Paper Crunch Hobble Ginnie Mae," *The New York Times,* April 14, 1986.

8 Peter Yoo, "Charging Up a Mountain of Debt: Accounting for the Growth of Credit Card Debt," *Federal Reserve Bank of St. Louis Review,* March–April 1997, 4.

9 A. Charlene Sullivan, "Do State Rate Caps Make Sense?" *Credit Card Management,* March 1992, 21.

10 "City National Makes Electronic Banking Work," *BusinessWeek,* February 27, 1978, 76.

11 Author interview with Mark Stickle, April 9, 2009.

12 "The Grapevine," *Asset-Backed Alert,* June 26, 2000; "Product Focus: Bowie Bonds," *Operations Management,* March 24, 1997. Owing to his greatness, David Bowie's bonds carried a AAA rating.

13 "Securitising the American Dream," *The Economist,* June 14, 1986, 78.

14 "Trend Toward Selling Off Assets as Securities Seen Growing," Associated Press, March 22, 1986.

15 Ibid.

16 "Success of MBS Issues Could Lead to Many Asset Packages," *National Mortgage News,* February 10, 1986, 13.

17 Ibid.

18 Linda Punch, "The Legacy of Card Bonds." *Credit Card Management,* May 1998, 36.

19 Kevin Higgins "The Comeback in Card Bonds," *Credit Card Management,* March 1995, 61.

20 Linda Punch, "The Legacy of Card Bonds."

21 "With Its AFL-CIO Card Gone, Bank of New York Looks for a Niche," *Credit Card News,* July 1, 1996.

22 "The Union Plus Card Gets Promoted to Gold Status," *Credit Card News,* September 15, 1997; "A Desire to Shed Debt," *Credit Card News,* February 1, 1997; "With Its AFL-CIO Card Gone."

23 "The Union Plus Card Gets Promoted to Gold Status" and "Household's Labors Bears Fruit at Rival's Expense," *Credit Card News,* March 1, 1996.

24 John Stewart, "Chicago Credit Card Issuers Enter Worldwide Bond Market," *Crain's,* November 19, 1990, 40.

25 Ibid.

26 Ibid.

27 Ibid.

28 David Rosenbaum, "High Credit Card Rates: A Luxurious Necessity?," *The New York Times,* November 24, 1991.

29 Peter Lucas, "Card Marketers Know the Score," *Credit Card Management,* September 1992, 76.

30 John Stewart, "Goodbye, Fat City," *Credit Card Management,* March 1992, 70.

31 Kevin Higgins, "The Seller's Market for Bad Debt," *Credit Card Management,* January 1993, 20.

32 Linda Punch, "A Sobering Year," *Credit Card Management,* June 1992, 52.

33 "A New Twist on Card Bonds," *Credit Card Management,* September 1996, 38.

34 Jane Adler, "The Boom in Bad-Debt Bonds," *Credit Card Management,* February 1998, 73.

35 Ibid.

36 "A New Use for Bad Debt: Backing Up Card Securities," *Credit Card News,* July 1, 1996.

37 Adler, "The Boom in Bad-Debt Bonds."

38 "Who's Afraid of the Secondary Market?," *ABA Banking Journal,* August 1984, 50.

39 Linda Punch, "The Home-Equity Threat," *Credit Card Management,* September 1, 1998, 112.

40 "Some Bad News on Credit Quality from Standard & Poor's," *Credit Card News,* November 15, 1996.

41 "Evaluating the Risk of a Mortgage Borrower: Conventional Rules Not Always Appropriate," *American Banker,* October 15, 1984.

CONCLUSION: TURNING THE MAGIC OF BORROWING
INTO THE REALITY OF PROSPERITY

1 "On Imprisonment for Debt, by a Northern Farmer," *The Debtor's Journal,* February 24, 1921, 90.

2 Ibid.

ACKNOWLEDGMENTS

Writing a book is always a group effort, even if only one person's name ends up on the jacket. This book would not have happened without the dogged encouragement of my friend Matthew Pearl, who pushed me to think about a broader audience for my research. Eric Lupfer is the greatest agent a young historian could have, and I am fortunate to have met him so early in my career. Jeff Alexander, my editor, pushed me to ask the largest possible questions in the clearest possible way. Countless friends and family members discussed the book along the way. A special few endured the rough drafts and gave me close reads: Rachel Hyman, Patty Kuzbida, Greg Kuzbida, Kelley Kreitz, Brian Pellinen, Bill Rankin, Raphaelle Steinzig, Tara Smith, Weston Smith, and Ginger Myhaver. *Borrow* is as much their book as mine.

In all things, Katherine Howe is a wonder to behold. Her generosity of mind is evident in this book's language, and her generosity of heart in her support from the book's conception through its completion.

I dedicate this book to my mother, Patty Kuzbida, whose steadfast encouragement made this, and everything else in my life, possible. She has been a true role model for creativity, curiosity, and commitment—everything a mother should be.

INDEX

Page numbers in *italics* refer to illustrations.

ILLUSTRATION CREDITS